THE ESSENTIAL HENRY LONGHURST

Drink up, Gentlemen   *12 June 1958*

I do not know what would happen to British golf if clubs in this country were to go dry, but I do know what would happen to the clubs themselves. They would go bust! Every one of them.

I am myself, as many readers will be aware, a virtual teetotaller, but I always lift my hat to those who lift the elbow, since without them the rest of us would have to pay about double our present subscription in order to keep the club going.

Perhaps there is more cant and hypocrisy talked about drink than any subject other than sex. The truth is, that those who drink – and smoke – pretty well keep the country going, never mind the golf club . . .

CHRIS PLUMRIDGE is a freelance golf writer and columnist who has contributed to many newspapers and magazines throughout the world. For the past ten years he has provided the regular column for *Golf Illustrated* and reckons he is now well into his second 500,000 words for the magazine. He is the author of four books on golf and has contributed to and edited many other books on the game. A single figure handicap golfer for 25 years, he lives with his wife and two daughters in a small Buckinghamshire village which is ideally located a few minutes away from his home course of Beaconsfield.

THE ESSENTIAL
HENRY LONGHURST

The best of his writing in
Golf Illustrated

Edited by
CHRIS PLUMRIDGE

Foreword by
Harry Carpenter

PAN BOOKS
London, Sydney and Auckland

First published 1988 by William Collins Sons & Co Ltd
This edition published 1990 by Pan Books Ltd,
Cavaye Place, London SW10 9PG
9 8 7 6 5 4 3 2 1
© Golf Illustrated 1990
ISBN 0 330 31178 6

Printed in England by Clays Ltd, St Ives plc

Contents

Foreword

I can see him now, hunched over his TV monitor in the BBC commentary box, wearing that crumpled tweed jacket, the checked shirt, the Royal St George's green-and-gold striped tie, with the headphones jammed on his ears *over* the battered flat cap. Henry Longhurst, of course. On his screen he sees Arnold Palmer addressing the ball for a drive and accidentally dislodging it from the tee-peg (or peg-tee, as Henry would have said). As the ball topples, Henry rumbles quietly: 'Now, all across the nation, people are muttering, one!'

That was the gift he had, of putting our thoughts across in a way we wished we could copy. His art was simplicity, which comes from long experience of the subject and an instinctive understanding of the viewer's need. It never occurred to Henry that there should be anything other than restful periods of silence in his TV golf commentaries.

'Golf is a slow game,' he would say. 'You hit the ball and then there's a wait while you walk after it, before you hit it again. You don't need to talk nineteen to the dozen. The viewer only gets annoyed.'

When he did speak, the words were so often memorable. Was it Tony Jacklin who had that putt of just an inch or two to clinch the Open and when it was tapped in, Henry accompanied it with: 'Surely the shortest putt that ever won an Open'?

We tend to forget that despite his long and distinguished career on and off the golf course, Henry's years of fame as a television commentator were really quite short. Yet in that time he made friends and found admirers around the world.

His name is a legend in the United States, where the art of silent commentary had never before been practised. American colleagues of that time still talk of him in awe and his name is preserved in the list of 'tec reqs' (technical requirements) for American outside broadcasts. Henry had no head for heights, other than in a plane, and found it impossible to hoist himself up a vertical ladder. The Americans built him a staircase to his perch overlooking the 16th at Augusta. To this day a wooden staircase at any outside broadcast in America is known as a 'Longhurst Ladder'.

It pleases me immensely that the 'C' in H.C. Longhurst stood for Carpenter and it was a privilege to have worked alongside him. Now the readers of these pages can enjoy the wit and wisdom of the finest of all golfing chroniclers.

For a few happy years Peter Alliss and I would journey each Christmastime to Henry's home between the windmills on the South Downs, where we would look back over the year's golf in front of the TV cameras. As anchorman, it was my pleasant duty to thank Henry for his hospitality and ask if we might return for more of the same the following year. To which Henry invariably replied: 'Yes, if I should be spared'.

He was not spared long enough and we miss him.

Harry Carpenter
April 1988

Introduction

The first edition of *Golf Illustrated* was published in 1890 which makes it, by a considerable distance, the world's oldest golf magazine. In nearly a century of covering golf many famous names have graced its pages but none, I suspect, with quite the same appeal as Henry Longhurst.

For a period of fifteen years (1954–69) Henry contributed a regular column to the magazine and brought to it the same wit, zest and style which so endeared him to readers of the *Sunday Times*. The editor of *Golf Illustrated* at that time was Tom Scott and when he 'landed' Henry as a contributor in 1954, the two of them worked out a formula whereby the editor would pose a question pertaining to a particular aspect of the game and Henry would answer it. It was a simple device but how well it worked for it allowed Henry to expound on practically everything connected with golf and therefore, life itself, for as Henry was fond of saying: 'The more I think about golf, the more I think it's like life'. Henry's *Golf Illustrated* column also allowed him to ride some of his favourite hobby-horses, to test out any new theories on the swing and to act as a kind of consultant *in absentia* on the administration of the game at all levels. Observant readers will note that the longest chapter in this book is the one entitled 'Committee Man'. This is so called not because of Henry's unflagging service on various committees—I doubt if he ever served on more than one committee in his life—but because he had an unfailing instinct for knowing what was good for golf and golfers, particularly at club level. It also gave him the opportunity to air his views without actually having to serve on a committee!

Many of these views on golf, and on life, were somewhat reactionary and he made no bones about his politics on certain issues, but he moved freely among dukes and dustmen while admitting a degree of snobbishness in preferring dukes because they were usually more interesting.

He had a few pet subjects which invariably received the rough edge of his pen, namely, slow play, 'cabin trunk' golf bags, trollies or 'perambulators' as he called them, the fourteen-club set, the cost of golf equipment and he united all in his implacable hatred of what he termed 'The Common Enemy'—the Inland Revenue. What he would think of the present day scenario hardly bears thinking about! Slow play has spread like a disease across the world, huge golf bags carrying the full complement of fourteen clubs are now mounted on electrified trollies (Henry actually predicted the arrival of these and was in favour of them), the cost of equipment has risen astronomically and we all still struggle under the yoke of the 'Common Enemy'. Incidentally, throughout this book all references to prices have been left as they were at the time of writing so that you, the reader, can gasp in awe and wonderment at the price of a new golf ball in 1956 (4/3d for the small one and 4/6d for the large one) and no attempt has been made to convert prices to decimalized coinage. Henry himself was always particularly scathing about what he called 'the new pee'.

Henry always had the greatest admiration for the professional golfer and was loathe to criticise their performance in tournaments. He understood the pressures a man had to face needing 'level fours' over the last five holes to win a championship or tournament. It was an understanding gained from a playing career which saw him captain Cambridge, win the 1936 German Amateur championship and remain a scratch golfer for some twenty-five years. Having 'been there' as it were, gave his comments an authenticity which is rarely afforded to those who write about golf for what is laughingly called a living.

In terms of golf journalism, Henry's contribution was incalculable. For forty-seven years Bernard Darwin had written for *The Times* under the heading 'Our Golf Correspondent' since it was the policy of that paper to maintain anonymity. Henry brought golf writing out of that closet and gave it status and credibility, and all of us who have followed in his considerable wake should offer him a silent prayer of thanks. Certainly my own introduction to writing about golf was influenced by Henry and my first encounter with him occurred when I was a pupil at St Bede's Preparatory School in Eastbourne back in the early 1950s. Unlike St Cyprians, Henry's prep school, St Bede's had no tantalizing views across the links of

Royal Eastbourne but nevertheless, in my case, the golf bug had bitten deep. Henry's son, Oliver, later so tragically killed in a car accident, was also a pupil at St Bede's and I remember my father pointing out to me at a parents' day 'the famous golf correspondent, Mr Henry Longhurst' before effecting an introduction. From a distance of some thirty-five years the details of that meeting are somewhat hazy but I do remember that it prompted me to start taking *Golf Illustrated* to find out what Mr Longhurst had to say. Later I came to know Henry on a professional basis and although I was a relative newcomer to the business, he was always unfailingly courteous, kind and helpful.

Editing this book has been a joy, an unashamed wallow in the talent of a man who took golf as a text and turned it into a philosophy for life. The pleasures of golf come in many forms but reading Henry Longhurst is an essential pleasure that each successive generation of golfers should experience as regularly as possible.

Chris Plumridge
April 1988

CHAPTER ONE

Theory and Practice

5 May 1954

The Perversity of Putting

Putting is a form of self-torture by which I have been fascinated throughout my golfing life. Long, long ago—and if you don't believe it, I am not arguing the point—I had a period when for two or three years I could putt as well as anyone in England, though I was no great shakes at the rest of the game. Then I learnt to play golf quite reasonably well and the putting sank first to moderate and then to the lowest depths of the 'jitters'. Finally, the rest of the game departed and the putting returned. A perverse life, indeed!

The day on which the putting returned, though I did not know it at the time, was when somebody thrust into my hand during the Ryder Cup match at Pinehurst three years ago, a brass-headed putter. It was a gift, he said, and certainly I would not have had it for anything else. It is a foul-looking object, with an upturned projection behind the shaft, bearing no resemblance to a traditional golf club, and for some time I was too ashamed to be seen with it in public. I christened it the Farouk putter, as being the sort of instrument that that monarch *would* have, and in many quarters the name has stuck.

If I were advising some young player who wished to learn to putt well enough to make a name for himself in golf, I should tell him that first of all he must somehow school himself to *take the emotion out of putting*. To hole a four-foot putt, or for that matter, a ten-foot putt, is a very simple matter indeed—physically. You can do it with any manner of putter, any manner of stance, and any manner of grip. The reasons why you miss come from the mind, not the body.

When you have the jitters, or the 'yips' as the Americans call them, emotion has taken charge. The blood pumps feverishly down through the elbows and you don't know whether to make the stroke 'on the jerk', or between the jerks, or get up and start all over again. I hardly like to write about it.

The finest mental conception of putting that I know is to compare it with the act of firing a rifle. To hit the bull's eye all that you can do must be done at 'this end'. You can only point the thing in the right direction, hold it still, and fire. When you have got one last shot for a 'possible', there is *still* nothing more that you can do than point it in the right direction, hold it still, and fire. So it is with putting. There is nothing in the world that you can do to hole a putt more than to aim the putter in the right direction, hold it on its line, and fire.

After years in the wilderness with long and short putters and every kind of stance, the Farouk putter brought home to me the old forgotten principles of putting. It gives you something to think about while you are putting and keeps your mind off thoughts like 'this for a three', or 'this not to take three putts', and such like.

Firstly, it has an exact hitting-point, like the 'spring' in a cricket bat, and this hitting-point is not in the centre of the face but the point at which the shaft joins the head, which is nearer towards the heel—at the bottom of the stalk, as it were. You, therefore, have to set it behind the ball with much more care than other putters, and this takes your mind off what you shouldn't be thinking about.

Then again, owing to the long projection towards the heel, it seems to me at any rate that you can see, in a way that does not apply to traditional putters, *exactly where it is pointing*—to within half an inch, say, on a 12-foot putt—and this fills your mind with the thought that your sole object in the world at this moment is to move it to and fro in that direction. And with any luck, if you don't dither about too long, you will find you have done it—before the awful thoughts creep in to put you off.

Having directed my imaginary young friend to the rifle-firing principle, to which all of the above conforms, I should then direct him to one or two precepts I have learnt from the greatest holer-out in the world today, Bobby Locke. One is very simple, and you will say that you knew it all along, but you didn't, you know. It is that never again in all your life, on whatever greens you may play in any part of the world, will you have anything but a dead straight putt.

Go back to rifle shooting. You may have to lay off for the wind, but so far as you are concerned you are firing a straight shot. So with putting. There may be a borrow and the ball may travel a banana-shaped course. But you don't hit it banana-shaped. You hit it dead straight—somewhere. The fact that the point at which you hit it dead straight is to the right or left of the hole is irrelevant. Simple maybe, but you will be surprised how it 'unclouds' the mind. Just think of it. You will never have a curly four-footer again!

Of course, Locke has other principles. He reckons to hit the ball clean. No nonsense about top spin and so forth—just hitting the ball and only the ball. No smudging the grass. That is why he judges a putt by the noise it makes. Listen to his, next time you see him. They all go 'ping', even the four-footers being audible at the edge of the green.

He has a 'drill' too, which never varies. Two practice swings, a pace forward, one look at the hole, and away she goes—for better or for worse. He even stuck to it when he had a four-footer to tie for his first Open, and there aren't many of us who would not have taken just one extra look then!

Of course, the main secret of putting for the handicap player is to use the American ball, which you really *can* hit clean. It gives you such an advantage that it is almost a shame to take the money. If you don't believe it, put a big and a small one down side by side and see which you would rather back yourself with!

18 August 1955

Playing Badly Well

According to American standards there may be perhaps a couple of amateurs in this country who might be labelled first class. According to our own standards one might include the two or three hundred who, aided in some cases by a charitable shortening of their handicaps by their home club committees, find themselves qualified to play in the championship. The other half-million or whatever it is are in some degree or other inferior. Some are quite moderate, the vast majority are cheerfully and incorrigibly bad. Among the latter, alas, is now numbered your correspondent. To all of us the art of playing badly well becomes more important as the years go on.

It is the art of making the best of a bad job. As an enthusiastic undergraduate, playing really quite well in those days, I was constantly being beaten by people who palpably did not play golf as well as I did. They simply played less well better than I played well, if you see what I mean. It is really a question of making up by guile, craft and common sense what you now lack, or never had, in the way of playing ability—a question of applying to your golf approximately the same amount of intelligence that you apply to your business. In a recent readable book called *The Natural Way to Better Golf*, Jack Burke Jnr calls it 'percentage golf', a good term I think, which he defines as 'not so much the science of playing the game with the shots of which you are capable of playing but without the shots of which you are incapable'.

That is perhaps a rather negative approach. Let us instead find some positive examples. For instance it is my impression that nearly everyone is short nearly all the time. If in your factory you found that the machinery was delivering short measure nine times out of ten, you would adjust the machinery. This is one of the first processes in the art of becoming a better bad golfer. Let us say that a perfect shot with your 5-iron will just reach the flag. What club should you take? My answer is a No. 3. The reasoning is thus: If a perfect five will just reach the flag, a perfect four will just reach the back of the green. How may perfect shots do you hit? One in ten? Very well then. Nine times out of ten your 3-iron will at the very best reach the back of the green. More likely it will be just right. The tenth time it will go over the back, amid loud cries of admiration which will put you on your mettle for the little chip back. On percentage you will be not less than 75 per cent up on the man who takes a No. 5.

To the average golfer there is no more difficult orthodox shot than the iron from a close lie on the fairway. The closest lie you can get is on the tee. The good bad player therefore never in any circumstances fails to tee up his ball on the short holes. If there is an easier shot in golf than a 5-iron off a reasonably high tee, I have yet to discover it. I am glad to find that Burke's 'percentage golfer' also tees up on the short holes.

A golfer with the phenomenal accuracy of Henry Cotton in his great days is faced with the difficulty of getting long putts dead at the par-five holes, which he has reached with two wooden club shots, and of holing the four- and five-yarders for a three at the par-four holes. The average player is not on the green in the right number. He is somewhere round about it. His problem is to try to get down in two more but above all to make sure that he does not take four more. No physical strength is required in this process. Without posing as a teacher of golf, my observation leads me to treat with suspicion any club with a rounded sole and always to take one with a straight sole if it is humanly possible. The fluffed niblick off perfectly flat open ground was always good for two or three holes start against Oxford or Cambridge in the old days and I fear I did club golfers a disservice in christening it the 'undergraduate shot' and by thus publicising it removed it from their repertoire. At any rate they don't seem to play it nowadays and the more's the pity. On the other hand many a crafty bad player has reduced pitching to a fine art by standing in front of the ball and giving it a whole-hearted downward jab with his niblick, a splendidly safe shot once you have got it into your system and one with which I should be the last to interfere.

Many bad players are still mortally afraid of bunker shots, when with the modern tool (which ought, of course, to be banned) the recovery shot simply 'splashed' out of the sand by hitting a couple of inches behind, really is the simplest in the game today. With this shot, *and no other*, the crafty bad player gets out somewhere on the green, certainly in nine cases out of ten and sometimes by a pure chance quite near the hole. The fatal thing in bunker play is to get too good a lie and fancy that you can 'nick it out clean'. You might do—but the percentage golfer never tries.

Of course there are bunkers in other places than round the green and here again the percentage golfer scores. Having got in, he *gets out*. The test is simple. Can you possibly get on the green from that bunker? No. If you get out now, can you get on quite easily with the next? Yes. Well, what are you doing with that 6-iron then? Put the damn thing away and use your head instead.

Some of the best putters in the land are seventy and over, so there is hope in this department for all of us all the time. There is no reason why we should not to the end of our days be as good a putter as the average club professional, who probably plays less than we do anyway. If you get the 'twitch', of course, that is a matter for the trick cyclist, or the hypnotist. I know, for I have had it, and for all I know may have it now.

After which, as Frankie Howerd says, the *best* of luck to you. As you get worse, you may get better.

22 March 1956

The Secret of Golf

Of course there is a secret of golf! Otherwise what hope would there be for any of us going on? I found it only the other day. So apparently did Ben Hogan, the only difference being that he reputedly received ten thousand dollars for revealing his. So far as I could discover, it amounted to little more than gripping the club as Harry Vardon did. Henry Cotton who has held the club in this orthodox way all his life, appeared to have broken down the secret a little further and to be dealing with the feeling in the individual fingers—though, as a correspondent reasonably asked on reading it, 'What happens if my fingers don't feel like Cotton's?'

We all know really that there is no single secret of golf, but is there a soul amongst us who has not at some time discovered one that works for him or herself at that moment? We do it with driving, with iron play, with the short game, and with putting. With putting, I suppose, three times for all the rest put together. The only trouble—and it really is rather an extraordinary thing, when you come to think of it—no sooner do we discover these secrets, which positively 'make' our golfing lives for a while and are passed on with such altruistic if tedious enthusiasm in the bar, then we forget them. Or we let them lapse and then are frightened to return to them in case they do not work any more.

This certainly is the case with the most profound and efficacious 'secret of golf' that I ever discovered. It must have been six years ago but I could walk to within a yard or two of the spot where I discovered it. This would be a point well down the 14th fairway on the Old course at Walton Heath, a little on the right. For those who do not know Walton, this is a pretty long hole, but it slopes downward and the prevailing wind is behind, so that there are times when a moderately competent performer can get on in two. This was one of them.

On that day the second shot was clearly going to be a brassie but, equally clearly, if I hit it I could reach the green. I walked to my ball to find it lying in an enormous divot mark. As I was playing with W. Emsley Carr, by whom I do not care to be beaten, it was no time to carry on alarmingly, calling upon the Almighty to witness, etc., but to decide what was the best thing to do and get on with it. I thought that a 3-iron would best meet the case. It would squeeze it out of the divot mark and with luck, though it would not fly high, the wind and the slope would help it along sufficiently to leave me with a longish pitch to the green. The one obviously useless thing was to 'have a go at it', either with a 3-iron or anything else.

With this in mind, and wishing to emphasise that on account of monstrous misfortune I was having to play a strategic stroke and was certainly not flattering myself that I could get up with an iron, I stepped up to the ball in a deliberately casual and relaxed fashion and very quietly 'played short'. The ball flew off as though fired from a rifle. I can see it now. It described precisely the trajectory I should have hoped to see with the brassie from a proper lie and finished on the centre of the green. I stood rooted to the spot, with feelings akin to those of St Paul after the episode on the road to Tarsus. Not only had I never played an iron shot like this before: I had never contemplated that the miscellany of muscle, bone, brain and plain avoirdupois that make up my person could ever combine to play such a one—from a fairway, never mind from a divot mark.

I wandered down the fairway as one in a dream. Perhaps at long last this was it. The final revelation. The Secret of Golf.

If by playing short with a 3-iron out of a divot mark you got the length of a brassie shot, how far would you not go if you played short with a driver? I simply couldn't wait. I teed up at the next hole, with a nasty crosswind from the left, solemnly pretending that my ball was lying in a divot mark and that the best I could hope for was to knock it gently as far as the edge of the fairway. It flew farther and straighter than I had ever hit one before. The spell continued. I wondered what my record would have been if I had known this twenty years before. The English championship once or twice: that went without saying. The Amateur probably once, the Walker Cup several times.

I forget how long it lasted. Certainly through one Halford Hewitt week-end because I remember the comments of three friends with whom I played in a practice round when they found themselves casually outdriven by 15 yards. It lasted through the competition that year but thereafter it fades into the memory. All I know is that for that blessed spell I hit the ball not less than 25 yards farther than I had ever hit it before or have ever hit it since.

The unintelligence of golfers, as such, is a subject which never ceases to intrigue me and on which I have often commented. Competent captains of industry will do things on the golf course of a stupidity which in their business would land them in bankruptcy within the year. Being an observer, rather than a player, I have hitherto looked down upon them with smiling indulgence and a pronounced air of superiority. Now I come down to earth. I am even as other men are. I discover, if not the secret of golf, at least the secret of *my* golf. It fades away, and only after six years do I so much as remember that it existed. I can't wait to try it again. I will start playing short again the very next time I play.

And no doubt this time get shorter and shorter and shorter!

4 May 1967

Less Levoduction and Levorotation

I am reminded of the great chess player who played twenty-five matches simultaneously, blindfolded—and lost them all. I am reminded of this because in emerging from hibernation and getting down to some elementary practice in order to try to break 100 in the spring meeting at St Andrews, I have just hit 68 shots with a 9-iron, and missed them all. I am therefore particularly well placed to criticise golfing teachers. For all that, I propose to do so and I go into battle by cheerfully declaring that the latest 'fashionable' teacher in America, Paul Bertholey, is by any standard talking rubbish. I make this assertion, without offence and with the utmost goodwill, on two counts.

The first is that I cannot understand the jargon in which he writes and, whether in fact he is right or wrong, it makes no difference if I personally cannot understand what he means. Read Churchill, or indeed read Field Marshal Montgomery. In neither of them will you find a single line that you or I cannot readily understand. This is the first and acid test of all writing. Breaking down the sources of power in the golf swing, Bertholey says that the principal one is 'a rhythmic blending of levoduction and levorotation of the mass of the lower body'. After considering the sources of power, we are now to turn to the 'multiplant or gearing factor'. Then we are to 'let our neuro-muscle structure act in opposition to all our instinctive inclinations' and finally 'contain the power of our swing by muscle anatogism'. This to me is meaningless jargon and therefore by my own definition rubbish, even if what Betholey means to convey is sensible and true.

Secondly, I think it is rubbish to suggest that a human being can consciously direct his various muscles in the course of a vigorous movement like a golf swing. I think that teachers of this kind tend to study instantaneous photographs (perhaps one of the biggest curses in all golf teaching) and then, having found out what the eye is not quick enough to see and the senses not quick enough to detect, work backwards from that and declare that this is what we ought to try consciously to do. The classic example is the revelation by the high speed camera that Bobby Jones in his prime was on both toes at the moment of impact. Nobody knew this before, least of all the great man himself. It would be rubbish, to my mind, to teach people to rise on both toes as they hit the ball, just because the fast camera showed Bobby Jones to do so.

Ben Hogan's much praised and beautifully produced golf book was illustrated by a brilliant anatomical artist, Anthony Ravielli, and one of the more notable illustrations showed a golfer naked both of clothes and of flesh and dressed, so to speak, only in his muscles. One of the better golfing jokes was to me the fact that Stephen Potter in his original and immortal *Gamesmanship* book had on the back of the jacket an almost identical drawing, designed to be shown to one's opponent in order to put him off!

One of the most destructive faults in golf is 'thinking on the stroke'. You must do your thinking before the stroke, and then go and make it. You can also think after the stroke—but never during it. In the course of hitting my 68 9-irons without catching a single one anywhere except on the toe, I was thinking all the time. A bit of Jacobs here, a bit of Cox there; bits of my own memories of better days; occasional memories of Leonard Crawley, who for my money is the best teacher of them all—but I have to have him standing over me or it doesn't last.

I remember, when enlarging once before on this theme of being unable to consciously direct one's muscles, seeing whether I could detect the first movement of starting walking forward from a stationary position with the feet together. I forget my conclusion then, but I have just this moment tried it again. I invite the reader to do so. It hardly takes a moment, and really is quite enlightening. I assume that you start in proper military fashion with the left foot. You are now going to write a treatise telling the learner which muscles he must use in order to start forward. Well, what do you do first? I thought for a moment that you lifted the left heel. But of course before you do this you have got to shift the weight to the right foot—or haven't you? So far as teaching somebody to walk is concerned, this sort of thing is rubbish. The only thing you can do is to say 'Take a pace forward with the left foot' and let nature take its course. If they fall over, they had better try again.

Bertholey thinks that 'a rhythmic blending of levoduction and levorotation' (which simply means pushing forward to the left and rotating to the left) accounts for 50 per cent of the power of the swing, and 'torsion' (I am not sure of the distinction between this and levorotation) for another 35 per cent. This leaves only the remaining 15 per cent for arm action and hands. Cotton on the other hand, by no means inferior as a striker of the ball, to my mind, to Hogan, rates the arms and hands at 85 per cent. Harry Vardon in a memorable and completely lucid phrase called the hands 'the chief point of concentration in successful golf'.

Casting my mind back to the stout figure on the practice ground this afternoon heaving and lurching at the ball with the 9-iron, I do not need much convincing that we could do with a lot more from the arms and hands and a damned sight less of the levoduction and levorotation.

10 July 1958

Thoughts on Slicing

Have I any thoughts on slicing? Have I any experience? Only about thirty-five years of it—except for a welcome break during the war, and even then the only reason why I did not slice was that I did not play.

The St Andrews golfer grows up with a hook. He has to, or he will run out of ammunition. On the Old Course you can hook to your heart's content from every tee except two. Having done so, you will very often find your second shot pretty well unplayable, but that is another matter. A slice from the tee is lethal from the start: lost ball or out of bounds.

It was my own fortune to be brought up on a course, known then as Bedford and now as Bedfordshire, with precisely the opposite characteristics. Not only did the lies in winter lend themselves to a cutting-up motion but there were no fewer than eight holes where a hook spelt disaster—and none where a slice did you any great harm. Hazards on the left included the Great Ouse, the Midland Railway, the allotments, one meadow, two cornfields, and Mr Somebody's garden.

This sort of thing eats into a young man's golfing soul. At the crucial moment as the club is about to come into the ball, the small voice whispers: 'Look out! the railway' and so quick is the transmission of human thought that the left shoulder has time to twist out of the way and the left hand to move ahead, at the same time opening the face of the club to make doubly sure. The ball flashes off the heel over the low-cut hedge towards the Biddenham signal box, straightens out to proceed for a while above the rails and curves gently back to pitch in the middle of the fairway, where for good measure it screws sharply to the right and slightly backwards. And the second shot does the same.

When you have done this throughout the whole of your formative years, and not without a certain degree of modest success at that, it becomes part of your make-up, like having one leg shorter than the other, and you learn to live with it rather than do anything to change it. Indeed, I can say with a sort of inverted pride that in certain quite distinguished golfing circles I can claim to have put a new word into the golfing language and that to describe a shot as having a bit of 'Bedfordshire' on it is to be at once understood.

Now all is changing. When the television was over at Wentworth and we were left with a deserted course, out by the 7th, I ventured upon a lesson with my fellow contributor, Bill Cox, who seemed convinced that you can, after all, teach an old dog new tricks. And new, indeed they were. I now show four knuckles of the left hand—that being all there are to show—while the right hand appears to have vanished under the shaft. I stand facing out to the right to such a degree that the thought enters my head that, if I don't unwind this lot pretty soon, my drive will hit the tee box.

Sometimes, miraculously as it still seems, they go straight and, what is more, far—but more often the Old Adam is too strong. 'Look out! the fairway' the small voice yells and the disintegration is terrible to see—as though you had suddenly loosened every screw in a windmill going full tilt in a high wind. Often, however, the result is a savage hook and this, to me, is a source of much gratification. With a hook you feel at least that you put it there. With a slice it went there because you could not stop it. At the 4th hole at Cooden the other day from the right of the fairway I hooked one that whizzed across the fairway, over the semi-rough and the thick rough, across the dyke and the distant boundary, clean off the course by 30 yards.

'I've been here thirty years and never seen anyone put one there,' said my opponent's caddie. I could have shaken him by the hand!

16 April 1959

'Under and Through' not 'Over and Round'

Like thousands of golfers my own natural tendency is to swing 'over and round' instead of 'under and through'. If you keep the face shut, this produces a pull and sometimes a violent hook. More likely you open the face at the last moment to counteract what you can feel going on and this produces a pathetically feeble 'smeary' kind of slice.

My own six-day experience—on six beautiful courses in the West of England—produced results and conclusions which may be of interest to other handicap golfers. Before the opening tee shot, at Burnham, I happened to remember an old tip, retailed to me again the other day by Mr Jack Perkins, who continues to play so well at Moor Park, that if you are on the wrong side of forty you must keep your left heel on the ground from start to finish.

Try it. It is not so easy as it sounds—but it works. It keeps you anchored. At any rate the first drive went off like a bullet and proved, what I was beginning to doubt, that the thing *could* be done. It worked, when I remembered, with every club in the bag.

When you hit a good one, of course, you hit at the next one a good bit harder, just for good measure now that you have 'got it'. This results, in my own case, in the right foot flying off the ground, the player finishing facing square to the hole and the ball in a bush, half left, at a range of about 40 yards. You then go back to the beginning and start again.

This really ludicrous shot inclined me to the belief that you should keep your left heel on the ground all the time and your right heel on the ground until you have actually struck the ball. Then, if you keep your head still as well, some really encouraging results are liable to ensue.

I have always believed that 'over and round' golfers—which means most handicap golfers, for this is only our old friend the 'beginner's loop' under a new name—stand, without knowing it, facing to the right of the hole. The result is that, in order to hit it *at* the hole, they have to haul the club, or themselves, or both, round towards the left—with one of the two effects previously described. I know this is very often true in my own case. Very obvious, but surprisingly hard to cure.

One's next commonest faults is, of course, 'hitting from the top'— especially in the early morning. No sooner is the club up than a furious snake-killing heave sends it flying down again dissipating its energy at the top of the swing instead of at the ball. Apart from swinging so slowly as to be almost unbelievable, the only suggestion I can offer is to try to time one's self to hit after the ball has actually gone. As one is always too soon, this often works out just about right.

For anyone who could once play reasonably well the really annoying thing is to find that with every club in the bag one can still hit the occasional absolutely painless and, within one's own limitations, absolutely perfect shot. If this time, why not next? I suspect the answer to be that one is not standing right, for sometimes everything seems to be in the right place and you know that a good shot is coming. Furthermore it always does.

Of one thing I am quite sure, that a good score comes only from constant concentration, and this, as one's interests in life widen and one's determination at golf recedes, is difficult indeed. You are either, say, admiring the daffodils at Mortonhampstead or concentrating on getting down in two more from just off the green. In the old days I could switch my mind from one to the other. Now it is half on the daffodils and half on the chip. For this I have no solution, for I am not prepared to give up the daffodils of this life.

9 July 1959

Copying the Best

Golf, of course, is *the* game for watching good players and profiting personally from it. One might observe cynically but with much truth that the spectators of most games today do not play the games themselves, so they have nothing to learn anyway. Though the television is undoubtedly bringing to professional tournaments a great number of people who have never played golf but have seen for the first time what a free and easy atmosphere seems to prevail and, as so many have declared to research-enquirers, 'what a lovely place it seemed to be', it must still be true that the vast majority in an average golf 'gallery' do, in fact, play themselves.

They therefore have something personal to learn and an opportunity unparalleled in any game except perhaps snooker of getting really close to the experts in order to learn it. Whether they are capable of doing so depends largely on the individual. Years ago I remember quoting Henry Cotton on this very subject: 'It may be claimed that the majority of those who endeavour to learn by imitation are not mentally equipped to assimilate what they see, and consequently they do not imitate at all.' True, no doubt, of many but certainly not of all.

Those who were interrupted by the war at what they were pleased to call their peak may agree with me that it seemed easier before the war to look at a good player and influence one's self for the better than it ever has been since. That at least is my own experience. To play with Cotton in those days led to a direct and immediate improvement in one's game. He was, if I may use the past tense—I hope unjustly—essentially a simple player. Though his swing is shorter and, I dare to suggest, faster today, you can still see that his tidy mind permits none of the unnecessary frills, mannerisms or eccentricities which might appeal to the less discerning imitator.

Cotton always seemed to me to have refined or 'cleaned up' the golf swing, as a writer tries to clean up or refine a sentence. Enough words to say what you mean to say; the right words to convey only what you mean; no long words where short ones will do; and a full stop at the end. His golf, in fact, was rather like Sir Winston Churchill's English. You could not match it but could not fail to be the better for trying.

Of course, for the purpose of imitation, you have to be sensible enough to pick the right man. He must, I think, bear some sort of resemblance to yourself in size and physique. I used, for instance, to be able to 'see' myself playing like Cotton (loud and prolonged laughter!) whereas I could hardly see my present more portly shape playing like, say, Bernard Hunt or Harold Henning.

Nor, again, do I see the middle-aged golfer learning a lot from Harry Weetman, who is immensely strong and, like P. G. Wodehouse's immortal character, 'never spares himself in his efforts to do the ball a violent injury'. Again, I remember half the Cambridge team of which I had the honour to be captain being temporarily ruined by trying to copy Abe Mitchell. Our wrists beside his were like match sticks.

Other players, like Harry Bradshaw and Bobby Locke, are in certain respects a law unto themselves. One is talking, of course, of copyable methods, not of results—though I have sworn to myself, after playing with him once again this year, that I will forthwith and forever make up my mind to find some form of 'drill', like Locke, that suits my own speed of play and concentration and stick to it.

I know I have mentioned it before but cannot forbear to do so again. It really is ridiculous that for a standardized stroke like a drive or a putt we do not all decide on the set of movements that suits us best—how many shuffles of the feet, how many waggles, how many looks at the hole and so on—and then set the machinery, such as it is, in motion in the same way every time. We may not be able to swing like the masters but this at least is one thing that we *can* do!

For myself I have always felt that the greatest benefit to be derived from watching professionals is general rather than specific—and, strangely enough, it does not apply to the best of amateurs, even when they are engaged in beating the professionals. I refer to the sense of rhythm and being-in-balance that nearly all professionals seem to convey—even when they are in the act of driving out of bounds!

Is there any real reason why we should not do the same? I don't say that many of us can hope to convey an impression of grace and beauty with our swings, but at least we could finish on both feet and with both hands on the club. We need not find ourselves facing the hole, hauling the club up and down with a sort of bell-ringing act.

On the whole professionals seem to me to set about things in a more business-like sort of way than even the best of amateurs—and in being business-like they don't seem to make such a 'business' of it. This, I am sure, is due to the cardinal—and highly understandable—failing of almost all amateurs, namely 'thinking on the shot'. After all, golf does not come naturally to us. We *have* to think about it. But the answer is to do the thinking first and then, for better or for worse, go up and hit the shot. After which one can immediately set about thinking again—not, as one might, about the next shot but what went wrong with the last.

19 January 1961

Getting Set up Right

It took more than thirty years of golf for me to discover, too late, what is palpably the 'correct' way to play. It came from Peter Thomson and was revealed in the *Sunday Times* of 24 July 1960. Let me try to summarize it, so that you can experiment with it. It began when we were playing together and he said: 'Well, for a start you are *set up all wrong*.'

Getting set up right is the whole basis of Thomson's play—and he did after all win four Opens in five years. The basis in turn of getting set up right is to address the ball in as nearly as possible the position in which you hope to be when you hit it. You obviously cannot hope to hit it properly unless your left arm and the club are in a straight line. You cannot hit it with a kink in the left wrist. Just try it and see.

Take hold of your driver, with the ball opposite the middle of your left foot, and address it with the left arm alone, so that you could make a one-armed shot. (Incidentally this settles the correct grip with your left hand. No need to worry about the old business of 'How many knuckles do you show?' Don't look. Nature has told you already.)

In this position your right arm is not long enough. It won't reach. How do you get it on to the club? There are two ways and, as in life itself, the easy one is the wrong one. The easy way is to reach *over* with the right arm, at the same time kinking the left wrist back to meet it and, almost certainly, shuffling forward a bit so that the ball has gone back behind the level of the left foot. Quite comfortable. The set-up is now ruined. You cannot *hit* the ball in that position.

Let us start again. The other way of putting the right hand on the club is to reach *under*, with a sharp tilt of the left shoulder up and the right shoulder down, keeping the left arm and club in the original straight line. If it is uncomfortable, it only shows how wrong you were before, *but*—ask your friends and they will at once say you 'look like a golfer', and you will say the same to them.

Thomson in one line settles what takes a whole chapter in most books. How do you grip with the right hand? Well, you just *put it on*. You will find that you are automatically in the classic position with the two V's pointing to your right shoulder. What about your feet? Well, you lay down a club pointing to the hole and put them against it. That finishes that. Incidentally, try laying a club against your chest. In the comfortable position you will find it pointing miles to the left of the green. When set up right, it will point at the flag.

How do you start the club back? (Always worth a chapter, plus film-strip illustrations!) Well, says Thomson, '*You draw it straight back*.' Draw it straight back till it disappears from the corner of your eye and let nature take its course. The only proviso is: 'Don't sway back with it yourself. Keep your weight on both feet.'

Here is an interesting, and perhaps surprising, thing—which I found of remarkable benefit when I last played with any seriousness, in the sunshine of America. Thomson's answer to 'How hard do you hold on to the club?' He holds it as you hold an axe; that is, only just tightly enough to raise its weight. Instinct ensures that you grip at the moment of impact. He does not reckon to *hit* with the club, but merely to *accelerate* it, as you do an axe. Try this one too. It is quite remarkable when you get the hang of it.

One last point, especially with the driver. Your head must be *behind* the ball when you hit it, in other words a plumb line from your nose at the moment of impact should strike the ground several inches behind the ball—a sobering thought for us lurchers and swayers to whom the ball so often appears to be moving rapidly backwards.

And the position with the other clubs? The same, except that the ball should be one inch further back with each descending club, bringing it about to the middle of the feet with a 5- or 6-iron.

That, I think, will be enough for the PGA committee—and the reader—to ponder upon for a start.

27 April 1961

One Born Every Minute

No one in the world is a bigger sucker for gadgets and short cuts to proficiency than the golfer. Some of them help and some don't, but all are innocent fun. I cannot pronounce upon which category Len Job's invention comes into because I have not hit a shot while wearing it. I did strap myself into his 'harness' and make a swing or two and there is no doubt that it helps to keep the right arm where it should be. By emphasising the right side, however, it seemed to me that it might tend to take one's attention off the left, which is held in the best circles to be the really operative side in golf. It struck me that it would be interesting to manufacture another set of harness with the glove on the left hand and the strap set at such a length as would cause the left arm, when stretched against it, to be fully straightened at the moment of impact.

Perhaps the most celebrated harness was created by 'Sapper' in his immortal story 'Uncle James's Game of Golf'. I have tried to put my hand on it in order to refresh my memory, but, alas, cannot find it. I remember that Uncle James's contraption was made mostly of elastic and was liable to 'twang' at crucial moments. It is a story that should find its way into any anthology of golf.

At the same time I was sent details of a putting aid by a member of Moor Park, Mr A. G. Gullan. He uses it indoors for practice, with three hoops, four inches, and two inches wide, and declares that from five feet he can now pass 60 to 80 per cent of five-foot putts through the two-inch hoop. I remember seeing other aids of this kind, mostly made of wire, all calculated to make one swing the putter along the correct groove. They may well serve a useful purpose. It all depends, I suppose, on how well you can recapture the movement when hypnotized by the presence of a hole and a ball.

The most gadget-prone golfers in the world are, of course, our friends the Americans, as a mere glance at the advertisement columns of their golfing magazines will show. I was once sent a great box of tricks called the Stroke-o-Matic Golf Stroke Trainer, an apparatus containing the ball positioning tape, the foot positioning tape, the erecting tape, grounding pins, clips, coloured bands, and I don't know what else.

Many American gadgets are calculated to reveal the range of the second shot. The fact that they are strictly against the rules does not in any way deter advertiser or buyer. Incidentally, I noted on one of the more celebrated courses in the Californian desert that they get round this in a more subtle way. On the side of every fairway you will see a small cypress tree. It is pure coincidence, of course, that it happens in every case to have been planted 150 yards from the green.

Some Americans unashamedly use the sort of range-finding device which one used for cameras in the days before they were built in. Another simple gadget which I was once given is called the Golfscope and consists of a card, about the size of a playing card, with a sort of curved space cut out of it through which you 'sight' the flag, making it just fit the space. Opposite this point you take a reading and find out how far away it is. There are two readings, one for flags six feet high and the other for seven.

Many 'head still' devices have found their way on to the golfing market. Johnny Revolta, pre-war American Ryder Cup player and the short game king of his day, has a sighting gadget that you hang from your cap. You peer at the ball through it and when you move your head the ball vanishes from sight. I recall some time ago being sent some blackened glasses with little slits in them which served the same purpose. It is not until you wear devices like this that you realise just how much you do move your head. The ball is practically never in sight!

Then there are the Strokoscope and the Smashie, of which I have seen only advertisements. The Smashie is a leather-enclosed weight which you wear on the back of your hand. 'Either hand. You decide' say the makers, adding modestly that it 'has been scientifically designed to aid all golfers control the swing from start to finish'. How it does this is not disclosed.

The Strokoscope is a thing like a draughts 'man', about the size of a penny, which you cement into the face of the putter, and this, as Dr Johnson said of the man who was to be hanged in a fortnight, 'concentrates the mind wonderfully'. Since the deadliest putting weapon is an ordinary carpenter's hammer, it occurs to me that the Strokoscope may 'have something'. Whether it is legal, however, is another matter.

Only one thing is certain, that in golf there is 'one born every minute'.

9 May 1963

The 'Square' Method

I have never known precisely what is meant by a 'square' method, though there is no doubt that the expression has gone into the game of golf, at least in this country. It is obvious that, if you are to hit a ball in a given direction, the head of the club must be facing in this direction as it strikes the ball and must remain 'square' for as long as the ball is in contact with it. What happens before and after that can hardly matter. What I take the so-called 'square' method to mean is that you try to take the club back square for longer, and keep it square for longer after hitting the ball, whereas the 'roller' trusts to instinct that the club will come in square just at the moment when it meets the ball.

In my earliest days I used to have lessons from the late Jack Seager, who was at Bedford at the time, but left to spend most of his life as professional to the Rothley Park Club at Leicester. He was succeeded at Bedford by J. W. Moore, and I had lessons from him too. I am quite sure of Seager, and pretty sure of Moore, that they taught what would now be called the 'rolling' method. I can see Seager now, demonstrating how the club-face must be opened on the back-swing and closed on the way down, and I remember consciously opening it as I went back, probably too much, too soon.

There seemed nothing unorthodox in this sort of instruction and I am sure that it was generally accepted at the time. Nevertheless I am equally sure, on looking back, that, maybe because I overdid it, it contributed to the slice that haunted my game for the next thirty years. I remember Moore saying perhaps forty years ago—that the ideal position was reached when you could fairly and squarely read the watch on your left wrist at the top of the back-swing and another on your right wrist at the end of the follow-through.

Experimenting at my desk and using a pen as a club, I cannot now persuade myself that this is right. It seems all right for the follow-through but only an arch 'roller', surely, could read a watch on his left wrist at the top of the backswing. He must be swinging flat as a pancake, with the club almost horizontally behind him. This is what I have been doing for years.

As there are no golf schools or driving ranges in my part of the world—and the more's the pity—and as I have long passed the age when I am prepared to walk up and down a practice fairway picking up a couple of dozen muddy-looking balls, my only chance has come twice a year on visiting St Andrews for the spring and autumn meetings, when I could walk down to the golf school and get sorted out by John McAndrew.

Alas, he has died since I was last here (I am writing from St Andrews now), but I remember how he was always saying that one should start with the back of the left hand facing the hole and then, as one took the club back, *feel* that one was turning it downwards. This in fact brought it—and the watch—facing the tee box and the top of the swing. This seems to represent the ideal mean between the over-roller and the over-square, and I believe it to represent the methods of Henry Cotton and Harry Vardon, though I am, of course, open to correction on this matter, at least from the former.

Geoffrey Cotton infers, according to his observation at the Lytham Ryder Cup match, the Americans hit farther through the ball after impact than the British, and I find this of particular interest on account of an experience at the 1951 Ryder Cup match at Pinehurst, NC. Ben Hogan, who was then in his prime, mentioned this very point. He said that it was his impression that, as a whole, the British players 'came up' much quicker after hitting the ball than do the Americans.

'We reckon to have a straight left arm on the back-swing and a straight right-arm following through,' he said. I remember this so well because he then seized me and demonstrated. I got past the 'straight left arm on the way back' reasonably well, but, when it came to the 'straight right arm on the follow-through', he nearly dislocated a number of my ribs. If anything was needed to convince me that all good players not only do not, but cannot, play alike, this was it. I do not presume to class myself, in however distant a past, a good player in this sense, but I realised that there were many really good players of my own build who were physically incapable of keeping their right arm straight in this manner. Try it and see!

James Adams has always been comparatively 'tubby', yet he was so built as to be able to take his left arm back beyond his head and still keep it straight—and not let go with the last two fingers. If some of us were forced into such a position by a complicated system of pulleys, joints would be cracking all over the place and we should be in the infirmary!

No, of course the great players don't play alike, and what a dull game it would be if they did! What is more, they don't think alike or feel alike. So which of them are the rest of us to look to? I dare say that in the end the local professional would do us more good than all the experts combined.

11 January 1968

The Basic 'Grammar' of Golf

I am reasonably sure of one thing, namely that although there will never be a 'correct' way to play golf, we are getting nearer and nearer to a set of standard principles on which nearly all the most proficient players would agree. One of my literary pleasures in golf is to browse through books of instruction written before the first war, and occasionally just after it, and to see what little distance they had travelled along the road towards an accepted style of golf.

Making every allowance for the fact that they had not the benefit of instantaneous photography (if indeed that *is* a benefit!) and that they may not in fact have played in the manner in which they thought they played when they posed for the static photographs, making allowance for all this, it is still clear that enormous progress has been made in the last fifty years towards finding, I will not say the perfect, but the most effective way of hitting a golf ball. Some of the attitudes in which even (dare I whisper it?) the great J. H. Taylor allowed himself to be portrayed in static photographs are nothing short of grotesque. Either he never saw the proofs, which would hardly be in keeping with so correct a character, or, having seen them, he still thought that that was what he did.

In the higher spheres of golf the day of the individualist has surely gone, especially now that Harry Bradshaw has retired from the competitive game—Harry who had most of the fingers of his right hand hanging down from the club, who swayed about a foot to and fro as he swung, and was good enough to tie for the Open. You still get, of course, the occasional one who is different, and I think of the two Americans, Doug Sanders, who, although slight of build, stands with his feet wide apart and takes a very short swing with practically no visible wrist action, and Gay Brewer, the present holder of the Masters. His right elbow flies up and points directly behind him at the top of the swing, but that is due to an accident when he was eleven. As most modern teachers point out, all that matters is that the club should come down and through the ball dead square.

Then, of course, there was the young Irishman, James Bruen, a member of the winning Walker Cup team in 1938, leader of the qualifying rounds in the 1939 Open and Amateur championships in 1946, perhaps one of the most exciting players of them all, till, alas, one of his wrists gave way—and little wonder! He twice to my knowledge broke iron clubs at the grip end—once, I believe, before it had so much as reached the ground. With this powerful whip-cracking action he hit the ball tremendous distances and there is no telling what heights he might have reached.

The point is that there are two distinct ways of getting the club into what we will call the orthodox and correct position at the top of the swing. One is the one used, allowing for minor variations, by every-one today and indeed in Bruen's day. The other was the one used by Bruen, which it might amuse you to try next Sunday. It is very simple. You turn your body in the ordinary way but, as you raise the club, you keep it pointing at the tee box. Furthermore, at the top of the swing it is horizontal but still pointing over the top of the tee box. You then loop it till, still horizontal, it points at the hole.

Teaching, I think, *must* be superior to what it was in my earliest days and here I do think that orthodoxy has a lot to be said for it. Rather like spelling, grammar and punctuation. There is no substitute for having the orthodox rammed into you at an early age.

Given the 'average' young pupil, neither excessively fat nor excessively thin, neither short and stumpy nor tall and willowy, how would one set him going? What would one teach him as the basic 'grammar' of golf? I suppose one would make him catch hold of the club with the two V's of thumb and forefinger pointing at the right shoulder; club and left arm roughly in a straight line; ball opposite the left heel. Right hip to turn rather than move backwards; left shoulder to point at the ball at the top . . . etc.

We then move into the area of controversy, reintroduced recently by Max Faulkner, sagely commented upon by Henry Cotton, and of particular interest to myself. Faulkner's point was that the upright back-swing was a snare and delusion.

From time to time I avail myself of Jack Busson's advice at Walton Heath—though I am afraid I am what they call in criminal circles a 'recidivist' and within a day or two am back to my old ways—and he describes the back-swing with complete lucidity. If you were trying to hit a shot off a wall, exactly opposite your eyes, he says, your swing would be in a completely horizontal plane. If you were trying to hit a ball from a position, in theory, between your two feet, your swing would be in a completely vertical plane.

It therefore follows that for actual golfing purposes the club should say in the same plane as that from which it starts—somewhere midway between the completely horizontal and completely vertical. I am not alone, I suspect, in starting the club back in this way and then, just towards the top of the swing, letting the whole thing go haywire. At the top, it is generally agreed, the right hand should be in the 'waiter carrying a tray' position. Mine, at the crucial moment, tends to throw the tray towards the tee. This is much easier, particularly if your wrists are not very supple (Snead can still bend his fingers back to touch his *forearm*) but of course it gets one into a position from which all hope can be abandoned and from which there is no way down. It occurs to me therefore that the average club golfer would do well to join the 'flat' school of thought—in which case he would not really be flat but just about right.

CHAPTER TWO

I Was There

22 July 1954

Thoughts on the 1954 Open Championship

It is always nice to feel that you have something in common with the great. Thus, it gives me satisfaction, as I settle down for my afternoon nap, to think that Sir Winston Churchill is at that moment for a certainty doing the same thing. In more humble spheres I take satisfaction from the thought that the Open champion and I use the same putter.

This is a hideous brass affair, with a sort of curved, upturned projection behind the shaft which has at least the merit of crooking ideally in the right forefinger to turn the apparatus into a walking stick when not in use. In shape, it is more like the things you rake out the boiler with and is now widely known, on account of the curious nature of the instrument as a whole, as the Farouk putter. One of them, or something like it, one feels, must almost certainly have been found in that ex-monarch's collection.

Why such things should ever have been legalized for golf I cannot imagine, for anything more unlike a golf club in the traditional and accepted form could hardly be conceived. Nevertheless, in my own case and, it goes without saying, in that of the Open champion it has proved a potent weapon and I willingly endure the ribald comments it causes in return for what it does for me on the green. I was given it in America three years ago during the Ryder Cup match at Pinehurst and, touching wood—no, indeed, *without* touching wood!—I declare that I have not had the jitters on the green since that day.

My main impressions of a great championship are of the series of dramatic finishes, which could hardly have been better stage-managed if they had been arranged on purpose, and of the efficiency with which the whole thing was run.

The Americans, of course, make pairings which they think will create the most excitement, while we draw the names strictly out of a hat, but could anyone imagine anything much better than to put Locke in the last couple but one and then have him come up to the last green, in a natural arena thronged with thousands of people holding their breath while he has 'this to tie'?

As to the management it could hardly have been better—or so I thought—and the credit for this shall be shared jointly by the club and the championship committee. Birkdale from long experience and through the club spirit of so many of its members, not least the women, who cheerfully volunteer for all manner of duties, are uncommonly good at this sort of thing, while the championship committee of the Royal and Ancient have shown themselves over the last three or four years to be as alive and 'on the ball' as any in the club's history.

While those of us who speculated on the scores being high presented a somewhat sorry appearance, one could not blame the championship committee for rubbing their hands with delight at the dead calm and sunshine on the final day, with the car park, at five bob a time, looking more like Ascot, and the people, at ten bob a time, pouring in in thousands—9000-plus on the final day alone, to say nothing of the season ticket holders. From these people's entrance money—and they surely had their money's worth—comes the prize fund for the future. Already it stands at £3500.

Finally, the broadcasting was, I fear, somewhat inaccurate this year, though they did give us quite a reasonable amount of time. In one transmission I remarked how curious a game was golf, in that Rees and Demaret had each finished in 71, yet, while Rees had had 28 putts, Demaret (according to his own admission) had had 40.

It was not long before someone, I think it was Gerald Micklem, observed that it must indeed have been a notable round of Demaret's. If there were four short holes and he had had 40 putts and had still gone round in 71, he must have got on one of the greens in nought!

2 September 1954

The 1954 Canada Cup

If anything were needed to complete the extraordinary success saga which will make 1954 stand out for ever in the minds of Australian golfers, it was that their team should win the Canada Cup. They did—and, having seen the manner of their doing it, I lift my hat to them.

The Canada Cup, briefly, was presented by John Jay Hopkins, an American industrialist who is president of the Canadian company in Montreal, for the promotion of international goodwill through golf. The tournament began last year with seven teams. This year there were twenty-five, perhaps the most remarkable international golfing array ever assembled. Each team consists of two professionals and they play 72 holes medal. As it is the custom, so far, to send them out in fours, you can imagine how long this takes. Four and a half hours is quite good going.

Laval-sur-le-Lac is a nice course on the usual transatlantic lines—up and down between the trees—situated in the lushest residential district of French-Canadian Montreal. In the clubhouse the service and cuisine were as good as you will find in any golf club in the world. All announcements were made in both languages, French first, though I was once brought up short by the unmistakeable Edinburgh accent of one of the waiters who with nice judgment passes the summer at Laval and the winter at Tommy Armour's course in Florida.

Though the limelight fell naturally on Thomson, I think the best performance in the entire tournament was that of his partner, Kelvin Nagle. He has, I believe, made one trip to England but this was his first to the American Continent and he might well have been afflicted with the forebodings natural to one so obviously the second string. In the circumstances his rounds of 68, 73, 69, 69, for a total of 279 was worthy of the highest praise. Only four players in fact beat this total.

Over here they like to work up the interest by pairing the leaders together and sending them out last. Thus Argentina, the holders

(Cerda and Vicenzo), were playing with Australia, two strokes ahead with one round to go. Scotland (Brown and Haliburton) were one stroke behind and the United States (Snead and Demaret) and England (Alliss and Weetman) one behind that. With two players involved three or four strokes meant nothing.

It was the first nine of the last round that did it. Thomson shot out in 31, Nagle in 34 and between them in those nine holes they gained nine strokes on Argentina, ten on the US and seven on Scotland and England. Thomson started home 3, 3, 4, 3, 4, and all that remained was to see whether he could break the record of 65 and whether he could win the 500 dollars offered for the best individual score. Leading in this was the Canadian professional, Stan Leonard from Vancouver, with 275—a fine player whom I hope we may see in England one day. In the end Thomson required one par and one birdie, a 3 and a 4, for 274 and a last round of 63—but the rest, alas, was anti-climax. He took five to the short hole and then, having hit a magnificent second to the last green, left his uphill putt short and missed the next.

Still, Australia won, pulling up, by four shots with a total of 556 and they thoroughly deserved their success. On all sides I heard comments complimentary to Thomson and especially to his demeanour on and off the course, which is always cheerful but never descends to clowning.

Of the four home teams Scotland did best—fifth with 571. England were seventh with 574, Ireland twelfth with 579 and Wales seventeenth with 598. Eric Brown had a magnificent 67 in the third round but the first nine holes after lunch were his undoing and 40 saw them out of the hunt. Alliss and Weetman played steadily and well but not quite well enough—both exciting favourable comment. Daly had a 67 for Ireland but with it went three rather moderate 75's, and the going was too hot for that. For Wales, Rees finished with a pair of 69's, but his partner, Harry Gould, could not quite make the grade in this company.

In my opinion this is already a great tournament. Properly handled, it may become the greatest in the world. No one knows yet what its future is to be. Shall it stay permanently in Canada? Shall it stay for a little longer to 'settle down' and then travel the world—or start on its travels next year? Opinions vary. Mr Hopkins started it on his own. Now he has formed an International Golf Association with funds raised at first from industrialists in Canada, though soon he will tap the United States. This year's promotion, bringing players from all over the world, cost 100,000 dollars. The tournament need not always be so lush in the 'trimmings' as it was this year but it will always, necessarily, cost a lot of money.

For myself, I have great faith in it and as I said on the local television (they give it a full hour: the BBC won't even televise the Open), I look forward to the day when we shall see golfers from twenty-five nations, all brought together by the common language of golf, playing for the Canada Cup on the Old Course at St Andrews.

16 September 1954

The 1954 Curtis Cup

The Curtis Cup match of 1954, which might easily have been one of the most exciting in the series, was in fact somewhat the reverse. The occasion had everything in its favour. The weather, especially as one was receiving letters from home describing it as 'worse and worse', was sheer perfection. The Merion course was in lovely order and our team all felt at home on it and professed to like it. My colleague, Leonard Crawley, rated it 'the best park course he had ever seen'—rather like Stoke Poges or Moor Park with white silvery sand in the bunkers.

The club is one of the oldest in the States—it used to be the Merion Cricket Club, but the cricket part broke away some years ago—and is more steeped in golfing history than most American courses. Bobby Jones, for instance, played in his first championship here at the age of fourteen; he first 'broke through' here after his seven lean years by winning the Amateur, and it was here that he finished the fourth leg of his great Grand Slam in 1930.

Such was the background to what might have been such an excellent match. That it was not so was due to the fact that it was virtually over at the end of the first hour of the first day. From then onwards it was as close as could be. It always seems to be the same story in these matches. Certainly it was so in the last Ryder and Walker Cup matches.

In the first foursome we were three down after seven holes and in the other two we were three down after four. Left at the post, in fact. After this the Stephens-Price combination played excellent golf. Indeed for the remaining eleven holes they were one under fours and you cannot ask for anything better than that—but they were still three down. Their opponents, Miss Faulk and Miss Riley, were round in 75. In the afternoon it was the same story—the first two holes lost; five down; all hope abandoned.

In the second match, Miss Doran and Miss Lesser were altogether too good for Mrs Valentine and Miss Garvey. Round in 74, they forged steadily ahead and won in a canter. As to the third match, one does not wish to be censorious. A person can only do his or her best and, if you strike an unhappy patch, it does not help matters to have it rubbed in in print. So let us say that Mrs Peel did really play rather badly and leave it at that. Or rather, by contrast, let us say how uncommonly well her young partner, Janette Robertson, kept up her end of the partnership. In every way she is the model golfer—serene, almost demure, determined without being 'hard', possessed of a controlled temperament for which many a great golfer would have cheerfully given thousands of pounds. She won all hearts at Merion.

Mrs Beck, an admirable captain, put a brave face on it for the singles, as a captain should, but to suggest that there was any possibility of winning five out of six was too much of a good thing. That we should halve them at three-all only made the events of the first day more aggravating. The only decisive victory was that of Miss Riley, the stocky little Texan, over Miss Price, who, it must alas be revealed, took 86—a large proportion of them on the greens. Still, never mind. Miss Price rendered immortal service in helping to win the cup two years ago at Muirfield, so she shall be willingly forgiven. Had she beaten Miss Riley she would have been the only person to do so in four Curtis Cup matches.

Miss Bisgood also caught a tartar in Claire Doran. There was nothing in it at lunch time, at which point the American girl completely changed her attire. It certainly had the desired effect. She went out in 37, came home 4, 3, 4, 3, 4, 3, and needed only the par figures for the last three holes for a 70. She rolled in huge putts on the 9th, 11th and 15th—the last a 14-yarder that she confessed she was 'hoping to get close'. Altogether a magnificent display.

There was also little enough in Jessie Valentine's match against

Mrs Smith, who played in the last match as Grace de Moss. For twenty-seven holes their figures were level—80 and 42—though the American was in fact three up. 'Wee Jessie' hung on, but could make no real impression.

Miss Garvey and Miss Kirby were also level as could be —80 and 41—this time with Miss Garvey one up. She won the 10th, lost the 15th and then played two magnificent holes—the 16th a par four with a terrifying second over a quarry and the 17th a full shot with a wooden club. She played them in 4, 3, won them both, and was home.

The top match between the two champions was a corker. Both were round in 78 in the morning and, though they fell from grace in the afternoon so far as the figures were concerned, it became a wonderful match to see, working up to a climax where both were perhaps 50 yards from the flag at the long 18th in two. Miss Stephens played first and I thought it would be very short. However, it ran on and on to within nine feet. Miss Faulk followed with one which I thought was going to be shorter still, but this ran on to within two feet. Oh dear, oh dear, one thought. The same old story—but not a bit of it. Miss Stephens rolled her putt right into the centre and it was the American, of all people, who gave the quick nervous prod. It was one of the shortest putts I have seen missed in such circumstances, but I must confess, with malice towards none, that it gladdened our hearts.

And so finally to Miss Robertson, one down at lunch to Miss Ziske with 81 apiece, Miss Robertson having started 6, 7, 4, to be two down. With nine holes left to play she was still one down, whereupon she came home 4, 3, 4, 3, 4, 5, 4, 2, rolling in a beauty on the 17th to win by 3 and 1 a match that she will remember with a thrill of pride to the end of her days. Her last ten holes were played in one under par, by far the best figures of any of the British team and an excellent testimony to the wisdom of introducing youth to international teams.

Whether she will become one of the golfing 'greats' I cannot say. She has certainly made a wonderful start.

28 June 1956

Opens Remembered

It seems to be a characteristic of growing, I will not say old, but at any rate older, that you remember the people and events of long ago a good deal more sharply than those of today and yesterday, and furthermore that the figures of the present seem to lack the glamour of those of the past. This is probably all nonsense, but the fact remains that 'colour' lies largely in the mind of the beholder, and, as I cast my mind back over the Open championships I have seen, I have no possible doubt that it is the early ones that carry the glamour. Indeed, I 'remember' some of the championships I never saw as clearly as some that I did.

The year 1926 was much too early for me but I can see that finish between Jones and Watrous at Lytham as though it were only yesterday; and I can see Hagen battling twice round Muirfield in the gale three years later in 75, when there was only one round of 74 and only three or four other players broke 80 twice in the day, and finishing by missing a five-footer which he would undoubtedly have holed if he had not had about 'seven for it'.

The first champion I saw win his title was Gene Sarazen in 1932, and as I watched the Curtis Cup match the other day at Princes it all came back to me. One particular shot stands out in my mind—I wonder if he remembers it himself? It was the long 17th, which is now the first, and in the last round. He was almost home and dry and only a major disaster could deprive him of the title. He was well down the fairway and could just get up in two if he could steer a brassie shot along the narrow opening to the green without sliding off into the deep pit bunker on the right. He had to wait for the people in front. Suddenly, almost when no one was looking, he seized a 1-iron from his bag, gave the ball a fine two-fisted slam short of the green, and marched after it. His five became a certainty and with it the championship.

In the ensuing years the most colourful entrant was, of course, Henry Cotton. For nine long years, up to 1934, the championship had gone to the Americans and the history books record that it was Cotton who broke the succession. This was not strictly so, for in 1934, there were no worthwhile Americans to beat. Cotton's true triumph, the time when he really did break the full American challenge into small pieces, was yet to come.

Still, 1934 was a glamour year if ever there was one and Cotton set an entirely new standard for professionals to aim at. He came to St George's and opened with a 67. Next day he came to the 17th needing two fours to do it again. He hit two perfect drives, two rifle-shot seconds, one putt of 10 feet, another of four—65 and a never-since-approached total of 132.

There was a magnetism about Cotton in Open championships which to me has never quite been equalled, except possibly in 1953 when all that people wanted to know at Carnoustie was 'What is Hogan doing?' Cotton faltered in the last round at Sandwich, though he won easily enough in the end, but in 1937, also at Carnoustie, he faced the full forces of the victorious American Ryder Cup team. It rained so hard that you could not hear the clatter of typewriters in the Press tent and in these conditions Cotton holed Carnoustie for a last round of 71—possibly the best single round I ever saw. Here is the true 'colour' in golf. As Sir John Cradock-Hartopp is fond of saying, 'The acid test is the figures'. Primrose pants are all very well in their way. They are no substitute for 65's.

Nevertheless, the outwardly uncolourful may in their moments of triumph imprint ineffaceable memories and one of these to me is the victory of Alfred Perry, at Muirfield, in 1935. He had, if I remember, two fives, or even a five and a six, to win. Muirfield finishes with two pretty long holes and the way to take six at either of them is to cut the corner too much on the left and finish in the bunker. Perry's finish was one of the finest I ever saw in a championship. He banged his drive past the bunker within 10 yards at the 17th, and followed it with a wooden shot on to the heart of the green and two putts. And at the 18th, he precisely repeated the procedure, just as though it were a summer evening fourball.

Perhaps the most memorable day, as against player, in Open championships history was the final day of 1938 at Sandwich. We opened with a couple of flawless summer days, with three players tied at 140 and the record of 283 almost certain to be broken, and no hint of what was to come. The first inkling I had of what was to happen on the last day was when I was woken by the curtains of my hotel bedroom at Deal flapping wildly and the sound of the sea pounding on the beach just outside.

When I got to the course a truly remarkable sight met the eye. The vast exhibition tent, like an eight-masted ship riding helpless before the gale, was about to founder with all hands. The canvas was billowing and groaning and occasionally splitting like giant calico. Stalls costing hundreds of pounds were already smashed to smithereens, steel-shafted clubs were twisted grotesquely into figures-of-eight, cashmere sweaters and such like had already reached Princes clubhouse three-quarters of a mile away before making their way out to sea. Alfred Padgham drove the 11th green, 383 yards away, and got a two. In the reverse direction it took three full wooden shots to carry the Canal at the 14th. Four, five and six putts were commonplace; so were totals of 90 and 100.

It was a day for a short swing, fourteen stone, and two feet on the ground—a day, in fact, for Reginald Whitcombe. In the end it was a duel between Whitcombe and James Adams, drawn together. At some holes, like the 9th where Whitcombe took four putts and Adams holed a chip, no fewer than three strokes changed hands. Only 11 scores in the whole day broke 80. As Whitcombe waited in the clubhouse, news came that his old enemy, Cotton, who had pipped him at the post the year before, was again on the war path, again wanting 71. Rumour had it, and believe it or not it was true, that Cotton was three under fours for twelve holes. The long run-in was too much for him and Whitcombe added a name without which no roll of champions would be complete.

26 June 1958

Bobby's Classic Stroke

In the ninety-eight years of the Open championships this will be only the third to be played at Lytham. The last was in 1952, when Bobby Locke won it for the third time. What I chiefly remember was the morning of the final day when players and spectators alike battled their way round against the elements looking like a lot of multicoloured mushrooms as they crouched beneath their umbrellas. On the first day 70 had been broken only three times and on the second only twice. Fred Daly, former holder, had done it on each occasion with 67 and 69—each of them the lowest round of the day—and was out on his own, four ahead of Locke and five ahead of the promising newcomer, Peter Thomson.

Daly's 77 in the rain and wind was by no means bad, though I seem to remember that it contained a wretched seven at the 11th, and Thomson could do no better, but Locke came up to within one stroke with a 74. Things improved a little in the afternoon, but Daly could never quite recapture the touch that had given him such a wonderful early lead. He holed a four-yarder for a three at the last and a little later Thomson holed one from double the distance—they did not play in the reverse order of merit in those days, with the leaders going out last—but it was only to nose out Daly for second place. The winner was Locke, and if ever a single shot won a championship it was his at the 14th.

Having failed to reach the green in three, a six was a distinct possibility. I was not at the green at the time but I have seen the shot dozens of times since it appears in a film of 'Great Golfing Occasions' which I compiled from the Movietone newsreels. As the ball nears the hole, he sways to the left with his body to help it along and finally nearly falls over sideways as the chip drops in for a four.

The other Lytham championship in 1926 was one of the most exciting of all time and those who go to watch there this week will see two tangible momentos of it to this day. Bobby Jones was only twenty-four at the time, but had already been an international golfing figure for at least ten years, since at the age of fourteen he had reached the third round of the US Amateur and given past champion Bob Gardner a severe run for his money. Then he had his 'seven lean years', but had at last broken through and by now had won the US Amateur twice and the Open once. The British Amateur still evaded him and he had been beaten at Muirfield by Andrew Jamieson, a capital Scottish golfer destined to wear for ever the label of 'the man who beat Bobby Jones'. I have always understood that, had he won the Amateur, Jones would have gone straight home. As it was, he came to Lytham, or rather, first, to Sunningdale, where in those days two qualifying rounds were being held.

His 66 on the Old course is often held to be the nearest thing to a completely flawless, flukeless round. He holed a putt for three at the

5th and put an iron shot in a bunker at the 13th, chipping out clear and getting his three, otherwise all was complete perfection.

At Lytham, Jones was drawn with Al Watrous and, as luck would have it, it developed into a personal duel between them. With five to play Jones was two behind, but the strokes came back and as they stood on the 17th tee there was nothing between them. The hole is a dog-leg to the left. Watrous drove safely to the right side of the fairway; Jones hooked into a bunker. Watrous played safely to the green some distance from the flag. For Jones the situation was now desperate. Between him and the green was a rough, sandy waste stretching for 170 yards. On the other hand the bunker was comparatively shallow and he was lying well back in it. He decided it was worth the chance and took out his hickory-shafted mashie iron, equivalent in lift perhaps to a 4-iron today.

The ball flew straight from the trap to the heart of the green—one of the classic strokes of golfing history—Watrous took three putts and Jones won his first British Open. At the back of the bunker you will see today a little 'tombstone' commemorating the feat.

21 August 1958

The 1958 Curtis Cup

I do not remember when I enjoyed watching a golfing event more than the Curtis Cup match this year at Brae Burn, Mass. The LGU selectors had come in for a barrage of criticism, in which I did not feel learned enough to join one way or the other, but really it was difficult to fault their choice when they did arrive at it and I feel that they would have been very proud of their selections had they been able to watch them at Brae Burn. They not only played with great heart, and seventy-two holes in two days in a humid climate when so much is at stake requires no mean stamina—but they also comported themselves, if I may say so, with a happy combination of feminine grace and golfing determination.

The slim lead in the foursomes on the first day was, of course, invaluable. The Americans had a very young team—some of them still in, and others hardly out of, college—and many had never played a foursome in their lives before. As anyone who has done much of it will agree, there is quite an art in this form of play and it was soon clear that Miss JoAnne Gunderson, the American champion, who is nineteen, and her slim teenage partner, Miss Anne Quast, were a little out of their depth in hitting alternate shots. Both in fact went on to win their singles. Nevertheless it was not they who lost their foursome, it was Miss Robertson and Mrs Bunty Smith who won it. They were round in 76 against a stiff par of 73 and this was the best completed round of the day.

Miss Jackson and Mrs Valentine caught a real draught against Miss McIntire and Mrs Johnstone. They were round in 79—and five down. The Americans made a complete mess of the first hole, Miss McIntire nearly driving into the swimming pool, but thereafter they played shattering golf. They were home in 35—one under par—and for the whole of the day, apart from the first, were only two over fours.

So that left the Bonallack-Price versus Riley-Romack match. The British girls were round in 77 and two up, but gradually their lead was whittled away till with six to play they were one down. The 13th is a long hole. Mrs Bonallack drove into the rough and Miss Price, who was steady as a rock all day, hacked it out and now came the shot of the day by Angela Bonallack—a 3-iron, no more than a foot from the pin. They went on to win on the 17th, a really fine effort.

The first hour or two of the singles was really maddening—the old, old story we have seen so often of British teams being left at the post—or so it seemed. They rallied, as it turned out, just in time, but the excitement towards the end was really desperate. Little Anne Quast beat Miss Price by 4 and 2, and a notable scalp for her at that, and Miss Romack did the same to Miss Jackson, who could not reach the hole with her approaches, though she did get back to only one down at lunch. On the other hand our Miss Robertson, trim and neat in her LGU 'uniform' of white blouse and grey skirt, was giving the hammer to Mrs Johnstone to the extent of five up. Here surely was one point we could count upon—but where were the other two coming from? When Miss Gunderson won the last two holes to defeat Mrs Valentine, it became increasingly difficult to see.

Mrs Bonallack, who had lost the first three holes in the morning, got them back, gone to four down in the afternoon, got them back, and now had lost them again, four down with eight to play. It is impossible to praise too highly her effort over these last eight holes, more especially as Miss McIntire, at much too early an age, has been infected with the American 'four-hour' mentality and plays terribly slowly. The net result was that it was Miss McIntire in the end who had to hole a downhill putt of about eight feet to halve the match.

So now all hung on Bunty Smith and Polly Riley, replaying the crucial match of two years ago at Princes and this time with Mrs Smith one up at the 18th. Only this match to come in and a half at this hole will give us the Cup to take home. What a wonderful temperament Mrs Smith has! Right up the middle in one, bang on the middle of the green with a 3-iron, uphill all the way, in two, and down in four. As at Sandwich, Miss Riley could not match it. Her drive was in the short rough, her second in the bunker. So Mrs Smith had played her fifth Curtis Cup single and notched up her fifth win, a record not approached on either side. What a wise move by that most excellent captain, Miss Daisy Ferguson, to set her to play last in case a situation just such as this arose!

4 December 1958

The 1958 Canada Cup

With the best will in the world and in no possible spirit of criticism of our hospitable Mexican hosts, I cannot but think that Mexico City was not the best choice for a worldwide 'goodwill' tournament like the Canada Cup. It is a wonderful city with an unlimited future, but for a great many of the competitors, to say nothing of promoters, writers and other camp followers who help to make up the general pattern, it suffered from two disadvantages. These were known in advance, though only one of them to me.

The first is that Europeans (and a great many of the teams came from Europe) are liable soon after arrival, however careful they may be about the food and the water, to go down with a form of dysentery. More than any other ailment, 'tummy trouble' is calculated to reduce a man's ability both to play golf and to be good company. From the British Isles teams, Panton, Hunt and Thomas were the chief sufferers, while for a day or two it was 'nip and tuck' with O'Connor.

The second was, of course, the altitude, which is 7350 feet. People who habitually ski at well over this height may be inclined to scoff, but the truth is that the very fittest of the golfers including the two South Africans, Player and Henning, who play at 6000 feet at home, found their energy greatly reduced, while older players were almost overcome. 'I don't believe there is a single 100 per cent fit man playing in the tournament,' Player said.

I do not wish to give the impression of the world's leading golfers tottering about the place half unconscious for lack of oxygen. Nevertheless no record of the proceedings could be true without emphasising these non-golfing difficulties.

Now for the play, which towards the end became really exciting, more especially as Spain were in with a great chance of capturing both the team and individual prizes and were paired last with their immediate rivals, Ireland. The course was desperately long—7216 yards to be exact—and, although the ball goes a good deal farther at that altitude, the par for the normal professional was not a stroke under 72. Indeed, the leading players of thirty-two nations were able, between them, only to break 70 twice in four rounds. On the first day the pencil-slim Sala from Columbia did a 69—he putts standing bolt upright and was described by an American writer as a 'two-iron with ears'—and on the second Henning did a 68.

The first day saw the following position: 142, Australia; 143, Ireland, USA; 144, England, Argentina; 145, Scotland; and, away behind, Wales, 16th with 153. For Wales David Thomas had been very unfit and there was nothing to be done about it. They never became serious contenders.

On the Friday Harry Bradshaw had a second 70, running an eight-footer into the last hole for a birdie; O'Connor had another 73, and Ireland slipped into the lead. The position now was: 286, Ireland; 288, USA; 292, Australia; 293, England; 294, South Africa, Scotland.

On the Saturday morning, Sam Snead appeared on the course in considerable distress with pain round his ribs and back. He tried a couple of shots with a 9-iron on the practice ground, but there was clearly no question about it. He had to give up and the first to press him to do so was his partner, Ben Hogan, who suffered the same ailment a year or two ago and took weeks to get over it. Snead's withdrawal took some of the sting out of the tournament, but I still doubt very much whether he and Hogan would have caught the Irishmen.

The third day really belonged to Scotland. It was now a question of Ireland v. The Field and it was the Scotsmen, Brown (70) and Panton (74), who sprang up in pursuit of them. I happened to lunch with them that day and I am sure that Brown, who had one fantastic stroke of luck in chipping in for a three at a hole which might well have taken him seven, would be the first to agree that Panton's round was almost as meritorious as his own. Having eaten little or nothing for some days, Panton looked pale and positively frail. Ireland and England had their bad day, but Wales their good one, and the position now was: 436, Ireland; 438, Scotland; 440, Spain; 442, South Africa; 444, Australia; 445, England; 447, Wales.

In the meantime, Flory van Donck led the individual totals with 213. Brown was one behind at 214, Bradshaw and A. Miguel 216.

On the final day a huge crowd turned out, the biggest seen in Mexico, they said, and, of course, Ireland and Spain were the main centre of their attention. I must say that I hand it to Harry Bradshaw, forty-five years old and carrying fifteen stone. To get round in 70 for the third time in four rounds was a wonderful achievement. O'Connor had his usual 73 and Ireland for the third time a total of 143. This made them 579 and they held off the Spaniards by three shots. The two Scots each took 75 and their challenge faded.

Thus Ireland brought the massive Canada Cup across the Atlantic for the first time, the final placings being: 579, Ireland; 582, Spain; 584, South Africa; 588, Scotland, Australia; 593, England; 594, Argentina; 595, Wales.

It only remains to recount that at the end of this long business, with each round taking anything up to five hours, Bradshaw (70, 70, 76, 70) and A. Miguel (72, 73, 71, 70) tied for the individual trophy and were sent out, accompanied by a really enormous crowd, to play off by sudden death. They halved the first in a par four. Bradshaw looked like losing at the long 2nd, but pitched up within an inch or two of the hole. Then at the short 3rd he was stone dead in two, while Miguel was just off the green in one. Whereupon Miguel holed it for a two and amid many 'Oles' was carried shoulder high to the clubhouse.

19 November 1959

The 1959 Ryder Cup.

I thought that the Ryder Cup match went very much according to the book of form. Any team, whether amateurs, professionals or women, who get three points in America are doing by no means badly and Dai Rees and his men got three and a half. A few failed to do themselves justice but then that always happens. The truth is that American teams have always proved unbeatable at home in the past and are likely to continue to do so in the future.

The Eldorado course, though laid out in what had been flat desert before it was converted into a citrus ranch and thence into a golf course, was quite a stern test of golf, if only because of the artificial water hazards from which there was no recovery except by picking out and losing a stroke. Seventy was only broken six times in the singles and it needed only a few slips to take a man into the upper seventies.

In the foursomes both Alliss and O'Connor played with great distinction and they were four under fours when they beat Ford and Wall. Bernard Hunt seemed to me far from well and there is no doubt that he played rather listlessly for the first thirteen holes. His partner Brown after this started missing holeable putts and it was soon clear that against so strong a pair as Rosburg and Souchak they must be written off.

The rest of the foursomes story turns on the 18th hole. By the time the whole affair was over I was left with the conclusion that this is one of the finest finishing holes in the world. It is 470 yards long. The drive has to be placed in a narrow gap between a large water hazard and the rough and the professional is then left with a long iron or a 4-wood to a green flanked by two more water hazards. It thus becomes a combined test of skill, nerve and intelligence.

Finsterwald and Boros came to this hole one up on Rees and Bousfield. Finsterwald took out a wooden club but at the last moment common sense prevailed and he changed it for a 4-iron and played short. Bousfield had no alternative but to have a go for the green and in doing so he hit it into the water. The match between Weetman-Thomas and Snead-Middlecoff was a different affair altogether. The British were one up and Thomas hit a tremendous drive right up the middle. Middlecoff hooked slightly, just into the rough, leaving Snead a real teaser. He took a 1-iron and tried to draw the ball round through the gap. It went into the water.

Snead thus declared, in effect, 'I guarantee that we take a minimum of five'. I am afraid Weetman's shot will live with him for many a long day. Instead of playing short and thus making victory a certainty he seized, with hardly a second's consideration, his 5-iron and before anyone could stop him had hit it into the water. I was standing just behind him and could hardly believe the evidence of my eyes. Anyway the Americans got down in two more; we didn't; the match was halved, and we became one down in the foursomes instead of all square.

The singles began as they have so often done against Americans before—though notably not at Lindrick. Nearly all the British got off to a slow start and after the first half hour were anything up to three down. You simply cannot concede this sort of start to Americans. The only man to win the first hole was the redoubtable Eric Brown against Middlecoff. He went on to hole the course in 68 and, winning by 4 and 3, to create the extraordinary record of winning four Ryder Cup singles in a row: against Lloyd Mangrum, Jerry Barber, Tommy Bolt, and now Middlecoff. In these days when professionals will do almost anything to avoid match play it is refreshing to see a man who relishes every moment of it.

O'Connor, who had been playing better than anyone, suddenly seemed to lose his form and he never had any chance against Wall and the same I think can fairly be said of Weetman against Rosburg. Snead holed the course in 67, the lowest round on either day, and steadily drew away from Thomas but Thomas's turn, I am sure, will come. He made a considerable impression in America and with fifteen years of good golf in him there is no limit to what he may do.

It seemed at one time that one might reluctantly write off Rees, six down; Bousfield, five down; and Drew, four down. All three made magnificent recoveries, though in the first two cases they were just that little bit too late. Bousfield looked very much a lightweight by the side of Souchak, a burly ex-footballer and incidentally a very fine young man. In the afternoon however Bousfield went out in 32, got back to two down and was six under fours when he had to give in on the 16th. Rees too made the most exciting comeback against Finsterwald, all the way from six down to all square. Finsterwald rallied to dormy two but Rees had a spectacular three at the 519-yard 17th. Finsterwald went over the 18th and Rees, all out, hit a wonderful 2-iron to the heart of the green. Finsterwald pitched stone dead, Rees's eight-yarder just slipped by and that was that.

Norman Drew, the first British player to play against America both as an amateur and a professional, came out with tremendous credit. Fighting back from four down to all square he eventually found himself one down with one to play. He too hit a beauty to the heart of the green and what is more holed the putt for a three and a 69. Altogether his stature has grown in every way during these last two years.

'You know who I like on your side?' innumerable Americans said to me. I knew the answer would be Peter Alliss and it always was—even though he was announced for most of the match as Percy Alliss, of Berlin! He played beautifully on both days and if he only halved his single that was greatly to the credit of his opponent, Jay Hebert. Alliss finished with a majestic four to win the last hole and square the match and his two rounds were 71 and 70.

The general picture remains in my mind of the Americans being just that little bit better all along the line, especially in reading the difficult greens. This is not to repeat the old cry that the British can't putt. I saw a great many perfectly struck putts that missed because the striker had not quite judged the line. Another three days of practice instead of junketing all over America first might have made all the difference.

25 November 1959

Monarchs of Muirfield

My first memories of Muirfield are not of the Open, but the Amateur. The championship of 1932 was the first I ever saw and the only one I ever played in. I was defeated in the first round—I believe by a member of that distinguished family of Scottish golfers, the

Burnsides—and, since my job from then until the war was concerned with an evening paper, I was never able to enter again.

In the previous year the winner had been, to his and the general surprise, Eric Martin Smith, who had only just left Cambridge. Equally surprising to many was the appearance in the final of John de Forest, who is now Count de Bendern. This view proved to be far from just, for in the following year John appeared in the final again—the first player to do so in two successive years since Harold Hilton in 1900 and 1901—and this time he won. He had a great heart for match-play golf, but his play was at that time a little tedious to watch since he was afflicted by that ludicrous and entirely invo-luntary golfing disease of 'getting stuck'. He would stand gazing at the ball as though hypnotized and quite unable to make the first movement of the back-swing.

The Honourable Company of Edinburgh Golfers started their career—I will not enter into controversy as to whether they are the oldest club in the world—at Leith, where I believe they had five holes. They later removed to Musselburgh and finally in 1891 to this present links at Muirfield. It was at first only 5200 odd yards long, but has been progressively increased and without undue walking between green and tee, to 6800.

In the following year the Honourable Company were accorded their first Open championship and it was on this occasion that Andrew Kirkaldy, riled perhaps by the fact that the winner, Harold Hilton, was not only an amateur but, what was a good deal worse, an Englishman, uttered his celebrated dictum that the course was nothing but an 'auld water meadie'. It may have been. It certainly is not now.

'Water meadie' or not, Muirfield from that time was on the exclusive championship rota, which meant that the Open turned up there every five years or so—and what a notable array of champions it produced! In 1896 Harry Vardon and J. H. Taylor tied. 'J. H.' has in his room today, sixty-three years later, a sepia-tinted picture of the two of them posing outside the front door of the clubhouse, each attired in workmanlike boots. He was hoping desperately to make it a hat-trick, but it was not to be. Vardon, with the then fine score of 157, beat him by four shots.

Muirfield's next turns came at five-year intervals in 1901 and 1906 and on each occasion James Braid was the winner, and then, in 1912,

Ted Ray. He won with 295, the first man to break 300 in a championship on that course. After the war other courses came on to the rota and the Open did not return to Muirfield until 1929 and this was a vintage American year. Three of them took the first three places and eight finished in the first ten. The winner, by the length of a street, was the one and only Walter Hagen.

In those early days rounds under 70 were still comparatively rare. In the second round, on a calm day with the course running short, first Percy Alliss, broke 70; then Leo Diegel and then finally Hagen did a 67. It was this round which inspired the famous telegram to the Honourable Company from, I fancy, the late Robert Harris on the London Stock Exchange: 'Suggest play off back tees for remainder of championship.' On the final day a tremendous gale blew and Hagen proved himself the complete master. With a special mallet-headed driver he kept the ball within 30 feet of the ground, boring through the wind with a control that left the others standing. Among the first ten players, Barnes managed a 74 and Watrous a 75, but Hagen was twice round in 75 and when he casually missed a four-footer on the last green he had in fact seven strokes in hand to win. No one doubted that, if he had had 'that for it', the putt would have gone in.

And so to 1935 and a memorable win by Alf Perry. He turned out to be what one might without offence call one of the minor champions, but the manner of his victory was truly great. He spreadeagled the field with a 67 on the morning of the final day and, when his one great chance came, he took it without faltering. With a six and a five to win he scorned the safe line at the two long final holes, and I can see him now, rolling along with his nautical gait, stopping from time to time to slam a long second shot on to each green and to roll the putt up dead as though he were playing with a few friends in a summer evening fourball.

The only championship I have missed since I began was Cotton's at Muirfield in 1948, when for some unremembered reason I was in America—but in a sense I remember it better than most people, for I have so many times shown scenes from it in a newsreel film taken at the time. King George VI came to see the play, the first reigning monarch I believe to do so, and it was typical of Cotton's inspired greatness that he should lay on a 66 for His Majesty's benefit. In one round, I am not sure which, Cotton sliced into the bunker beside the last green and half socketed his recovery shot against the bank, so that it bounced back. He holed a noble putt for his five and won his fourth championship, and even now possibly not his last, fourteen years after his first.

16 March 1961

Memories of Troon

The first Open championship to be played at Troon was, so to speak, 'before I came in'. This was in 1923, but I have always been aware of that championship because for so many years afterwards, when I had started writing about golf, it was 'the last time that a British player had won the Open'. The hero was Arthur Havers and we had to wait eleven long years before another British victory turned up in the person of Henry Cotton.

The 1923 championship was memorable for the fact that Gene Sarazen, the youthful Open champion of the United States, failed to qualify—an episode about which I have often read in that most admirable book *Thirty Years of Championship Golf*, which he wrote in conjunction with Herbert Warren Wind. He had coasted round the municipal course in 75 on the first day, but when he set out at Troon itself early the following morning there was such a gale that the fishing boats could not go out and the waves were dashing up almost on to the course.

His umbrella was at once blown inside out and at the 2nd hole he buried his drive in the face of a bunker and finished with a nine. He battled on and reckoned that his 85 would be good enough, but at noon the wind blew itself completely out and people who would have been blown into the eighties came in with scores in the low seventies. Poor Sarazen failed to qualify by one stroke. He endeared himself to people in this country by saying, when Bernard Darwin sympathised with him, 'I'll be back even if I have to swim across'. He kept his promise, but the Open evaded him until 1932.

Two Amateur championships have been played at Troon—I have always thought of it more as a course for amateurs than professionals: I do not know why. The first was won by the irrepressible Charles

Yates, who beat Cecil Ewing in the final, but one incident will always stand out in my mind. In the first round Yates was drawn to go out almost first against his fellow American Walker Cup player, Johnny Fischer, and by about twenty past eleven on the first morning there they were, on the 19th green, one of them destined to go out almost before the championship had started. Fischer lay a couple of feet from the hole, whereupon Yates missed his putt for a half and left his man the deadest of dead stymies. It was a cruel finish and set me against stymies from then onwards.

The other Amateur at Troon was won by the infant prodigy, John Beharrell, who played with an air of calm and detachment that I shall always remember with admiration. He was, if I remember, still seventeen and was by a long way the youngest winner.

Nevertheless the most exciting golfing event ever seen at Troon was clearly the 1925 final between Miss Joyce Wethered and Miss Cecil Leitch. Miss Wethered, the reigning champion, remained three down until a comparatively late stage of the game and there are many who say that the concluding stages were the greatest match they have ever seen. Miss Wethered won on the 37th and both, I believe, were completely exhausted. Between them they dominated women's golf in a way which only Miss Pamela Barton might have done since, had she not, alas, lost her life in the service of the Royal Air Force in the war.

The last Open at Troon was in 1950 and I always look on it as an occasion in which Bobby Locke proved himself to be one of the best 'bad' players in the world. Let me say, in case any South African friends should feel their hackles rising, that this is intended as a compliment! The fact is that all great players must from time to time play, according to their own standards, badly. Anyone can play well. The really great man acquires the art of playing badly well. Locke's winning score was 69, 72, 70, 68. How he squeezed his second round down to 72 I shall never really understand. I am sure that anyone else would have been satisfied to get out of it with a 76, and that, of course, would have lost him the championship.

It has often been said that Troon is on the short side for a championship course and it was perhaps with this in mind that they made certain alterations last year. I had a most pleasant round there during the summer and, so far as I could judge, the changes were all for the good.

26 October 1961

The 1961 Ryder Cup

As I cast my mind back to Lytham, reflections come thick and fast, but the first and strongest is that in all the years that I have been watching golf, these two days represented the finest exhibition ever put before the public. This was partly due to the wonderful and, as I am sure the Americans thought, 'un-English' weather; partly to the trouble which the club had gone to in the way of organisation; but mainly to the innovation of playing two series of 18-hole matches each day. This gave the spectators twenty-four finishes in the two days and of these no fewer than ten went to the last green.

It is my personal opinion that the Americans always *ought* to win—for reasons into which we need not go at the moment. I am the last person, therefore, to make excuses if the British don't. So it is not in that spirit that I point out that the final score of 14½–9½ by no means reflects the narrowness of the gap between the two teams. As a number of correspondents have pointed out, of the published figures each side in the foursomes scored seven over fours on the day, but the United States led 6–2. In the singles the Americans were twenty under fours for the day and the British nineteen under, and the Americans led by 8½–7½. In other words there was only a single stroke between the two teams on the whole of the two days!

A remarkable analysis published by the *Daily Mail*, showing how many times each side hit the fairway with the drive, or the green at short holes; how many single, double and treble putts each side took, etc., pointed to an incidental conclusion. Scores in match play, as I am well aware, must on some occasions be approximate but there can be no suggestion that the approximations—which were few and far between, so close was the contest—in any way favoured the British. I still think that the home team did uncommonly well and that the Americans won largely through three or four superhuman efforts on the last hole, for which I most sincerely lift my hat to them.

If we are to have 18-hole matches, which I most devoutly hope, then *either* the order for both morning and afternoon must be announced overnight *or* we must have a non-playing captain *or* the captain must not play himself in the morning *or* the captain, if he plays in the morning, must have a sort of assistant-cum-adviser with whom to consult at lunchtime regarding the team for the afternoon. In the foursomes Dai Rees had hardly got in when the first match was due to go out in the afternoon, and this threw an impossible burden of selection upon him. He could have seen nothing of the other players; he had only minutes to decide; and he had to get his own lunch and rest. He thus made what most critics deemed an error of selection, which he later defended on the ground that the player concerned 'could hardly play so badly twice running'. His opposite number Jerry Barber, significantly enough, did not play in the morning.

As to the selection of Rees himself as captain no sooner had this splendid match ended than Weetman, of all people, issued to the Press a prepared statement (presumably prepared, since it was identically worded in all the papers I read) to the effect that the choice was made behind the backs of the tournament professionals and that they did not agree with it. In view of the fact that it was a thoughtless comment by Weetman (and have we not all made them in our time?) which turned the victory at Lindrick so sour, this seemed supremely the moment at which he should have remained silent.

Having said that I agree with the principle expressed by the dissentients and remember expressing this view in conversation with Arthur Harrison, the chairman of the PGA, long before the match. I do not think Rees should have been captain—*simply because he had been captain before*. I have always held that no one should twice (much less four times) be captain of any Ryder Cup, Walker Cup, international, county or university team. Each is an honour according to its degree and as many individuals as possible should be able to tell their children 'I once captained so-and-so'. After all, the job is not all that difficult.

Finally I come more and more to the view that, now that golf is a considerable 'spectator' game, either St Andrews alone, or St Andrews and one course in England, or St Andrews and one other Scottish course and two courses in England, should, provided the members agree, be selected as venues for the truly great events, and considerable money spent on them for the handling, comfort and good viewing of large crowds. The financing of this, and the paying back of the money from later receipts, should present no problem.

The Royal Lytham club, under the captaincy of Sir Robert Adcock, spared no effort. They even installed no less than three miles of chestnut paling. They could not, however, alter the fact that much of the terrain is flat and, with 15,000 spectators there, I do not know how many times I heard people say, 'You can see more of it on the telly'. When you think of the miracles worked to create the modern Turnberry from a wartime airfield, you realise how easily modern earth-moving equipment can create 'natural' ridges, set well back from fairways and greens, from which all could see. Though I have not mentioned it to him, it occurs to me that that keen golfer, Bernard Sunley, would get it done in a flash.

30 August 1962

The 1962 Curtis Cup

I understand that a veteran lady golfer wrote in a Scottish paper before the Curtis Cup match to the effect that it was monstrous that the team should be all English and that it was to be hoped that they would lose every game. Since I did not see the paper, I will not name either it or the lady, but if it is correct—and a colleague of mine had a cutting of the article sent to him at Colorado—well, I can only say that the wish nearly came true, and only Mrs Diane Frearson prevented its doing so. Personally I could not see where a point was coming from on either day, but I confess that I should not have seen one from an all-Scottish, all-Irish or all-Welsh, or all-mixed team either.

I have often said that one foursome and two singles represent par for any visiting team in America, but this is, of course, a stiffer proposition with six a side than eight. However, it looked at first as though we were going to hit the target in the foursomes when Miss Irvin and Miss Vaughan were out in 37, the lowest opening nine on either side, and two up. They slipped up with a couple of sixes on the way home and by the 16th the Americans, Miss Creed and Miss Gunderson, had caught them. From that moment onwards the two Americans produced what must surely be the best golf seen in any

Curtis Cup match. In fact they proceeded to do the next sixteen holes each in exactly the par figure. There have been occasions when such a performance might have won them a point in the Walker, or even, let it be whispered, Ryder Cup match.

The first match, Mrs Bonallack and Mrs Spearman against Mrs Decker, the reigning US champion (who used to be Miss Anne Quast) and Miss McIntire, was close enough for nine holes, which each played creditably in 38, but was decided on the second nine when the British started home with five consecutive fives, which is three over par, while the Americans had four fours and a three, which is two under, and won the lot. Another for good measure at the 16th made it six down at lunch—and you don't recover from that—not at any rate in that company.

Mrs Frearson and Miss Porter took a hammering from Miss Ashley and Mrs Johnstone. I saw less of this game than of the others, but I gathered from the referee that Miss Porter, though she holed a couple of good ones, had one of those agonising days when every putt seems to stop an inch short of the hole, dead straight. Let me add that the sloping greens seemed to me tremendously difficult.

The foursomes were played in a temperature of 95 degrees, in which thirty-six holes a day, on foot—whereas most members and visitors would not think of playing more than eighteen, and with electric carts—is asking a lot. At any rate, probably because of a 'touch of the sun', Miss Irvin was completely incapacitated next morning and Mrs Spearman was nearly so. Miss Jean Roberts, who as English champion in an all-English team may well have been distressed to have been left out on both days, even though she was manifestly not in the form that had won her her title, came in for Miss Irvin. Meanwhile Mrs Spearman, due out first with Mrs Decker, was put back to last so as to judge the effect of prescriptions from the hotel drug store. In the end she played and, seeing that after losing the first two holes she finished 2, 4, 4 against a par of 3, 5, 4 and was round in 77, no one could say that the captain's decision to let her 'have a go' was wrong. Mrs Decker, however, was round in 74, and only one over fours when she won on the 13th in the afternoon.

Mrs Bonallack, five down at lunch against her old rival, Miss Gunderson, made a spirited come-back to one down, but was beaten by a cruel two, her opponent's second of the day, at the 16th. Miss Sally Bonallack was six down at lunch to Miss Creed, an 'unknown' to most of our side. When I saw her drive off the first tee in the foursomes, I thought this slim and by no means tall girl had one of the most beautiful and completely professional swings that I had ever seen. She has been taught, it transpired, by her father, who is professional at a remote little course in the heart of Louisiana. Miss Bonallack could do little against her.

Miss Vaughan drew Miss McIntire, who with Miss Bell runs a sportswear shop in the hotel and must be one of the two best players in the world at the moment. Miss Vaughan had a poor outward nine and was five down. She held on well enough after that and did the next eighteen holes in 77, but it was too late. Miss Roberts, determined to show that she should not have been left out in the first instance, clouted a tremendous drive off the first tee but came to the 18th four down. Here her first putt ran with gathering speed down the slope and, rather quickly I thought, she missed the one back. 'A pity,' I remarked to my neighbour. 'You may get four holes back, but you can't get five holes back.'

As a matter of fact she did get five holes back, with four to go, but I was a true prophet in the end. She lost the next two, won the 17th but could do no better than halve the 18th. For fourteen holes she had been level fours—a wonderful score.

Finally, the heroine of the entire outing, eighteen-year-old Mrs Frearson. Faced with Miss Judy Bell, who is in partnership with Miss McIntire, and knows every inch of the course, I should not have given her much chance. She won the first three holes, was two up at the turn and then, giving her a rather charitable two at the 12th, came home in 35, winning hole after hole to finish seven up. As her opponent began to falter, she rubbed it remorselessly in—an essential ability in match-play golf, for who knows what may happen in the afternoon? In fact, she went on in just the same way and when she had won she had had, including the 'charitable' one, no fewer than four twos. A day she will certainly remember for the rest of her life.

25 October 1962

What a Finish!

In common with many other people, I find that as the years advance, I tend to remember more distinctly events of the distant rather than the immediate past. While I could rattle off the Open and Amateur championships for the years 1930-9, I should have to stop and think before I could do so for 1946-62. For the Open, apart from Faulkner and Daly, one would be pretty safe in saying Locke or Thomson, but for the life of me I could not tell you which of them won in what year.

Allowing for all this, and also for the fact that one's capability of being excited is reduced by having seen it all before, I am still in no doubt that the two most exciting finishes I remember occurred in 1936. The first was in the final of the Amateur championship.

Everything conspired to make this a grandstand finish. Firstly, it was at St Andrews, which is in itself the perfect grandstand, as all who have seen the last hole on the television will appreciate. Then there was a Scotsman, Hector Thomson, in the final, playing the burly Australian, Jim Ferrier, who has since had a successful career in the States as a professional. Furthermore it was a Saturday, and a fine one at that, and Thomson was one up with one to play.

I do not think my imagination runs away with me when I say that never since that day have I seen such a crowd at St Andrews, even for the Centenary Open. Every window was packed and people were thick on the rooftops, hanging on to the chimney pots. Both players hit good drives, and Ferrier, playing first, hit his second shot to within a few yards of the flag, leaving himself a longish but obviously possible putt for a three. I remember thinking what lonely figures they looked, just the two players, their two caddies and the referee, alone in the arena.

There was a hushed silence as Thomson played. It was as perfect a shot as he had ever hit. The ball flew high, pitched on the short edge of the green, bounced two or three times and a moment later about 10,000 voices, including my own, were shouting 'It's in! It's in!' We were not quite right, but as near as no matter. The ball came to rest no more than about three inches from the hole. Ferrier, with a weary smile, walked over and shook hands.

Thomson at that time was vying with his contemporary and compatriot, Jack McLean, for the honour of being reckoned the best player in Britain and it was McLean who was concerned in the other exciting finish in that year. The Walker Cup team had been 'whitewashed' at Pine Valley—in other words they had not won a single point—and we had all proceeded thence to Garden City for the US Amateur.

McLean reached the final—I like to recall that I was at one point two up on him in an early round (what a travesty *that* would have been!)—and he was playing Johnny Fischer. After thirty-three holes McLean was one up. On the 16th he was virtually dead in three, certainly no more than two and a half feet away. Fischer had a ten-foot putt for a four. It faded to the right, rather ill struck, and stopped level with the hole laying McLean an absolutely dead stymie. If ever there was injustice in this world, that was it.

Neither could reach the 17th in two, but one after the other they chipped up and holed their putts. The 18th is a short hole over a pond. Both hit excellent tee shots, McLean about six yards away and Fischer five. McLean putted up stone dead, so Fischer had this one last putt to save the game. As he stood over it and was just about to strike, the silence was broken by some idiot with a newsreel camera. It sounded, at that moment, almost like machine gun fire. Fischer drew himself wearily up, walked away, and started all over again. Surely he could not hole it now!

Fischer did hole it though, and we all rushed up to the first hole again for the third time in the day. Fischer was on in two, ten or a dozen yards away—and hang it if he did not hole that too, so the portion meted out to poor McLean over the last four holes had been a stymie and three successive birdies.

The finish at which I personally got most excited and should again today, though the risk of being exposed to it is, I am afraid, infinitesimal—was not in a final but in a team match. The stage once again was St Andrews and the occasion was the Walker Cup match of 1938. One cannot pin down the excitement to a single incident. It built steadily up over about an hour. Rumour sped all over the course, often only to disappoint, but gradually it became evident that we did at last really stand a chance.

All, it seemed, might depend on Cecil Ewing and Ray Billows. Breaking the barriers the crowd surged round the last green, engulfing the players. As they prepared to putt, the atmosphere was as tense as anything I remembered in golf and then, suddenly, it vanished. Leading a small crowd advancing from the neighbourhood of the first green was Alex Kyle. He had won his match and all was over.

22 November 1962

The 1962 Canada Cup

The Canada Cup is an event that needs a tremendous amount of organisation, and the fact that it is run so well year by year in countries which have never seen it before is due partly to the expert knowledge of Mr Fred Corcoran, who has handled it since its inception ten years ago (when eight countries took part: now there are thirty-two) and partly to his ability to charm the captain, committee and members into producing something better than their best. This was certainly true this year of the Jockey Club at Buenos Aires under the general chairmanship of Mr Kenneth Gordon Davis, president of the Argentine Golf Federation. Those who attended the 1935 British Women's championship at Newcastle Co. Durham, will remember the appearance there of the elegant Brown sisters from the Argentine. One is now Mrs Gordon Davis; the other Mrs Roberts, who reached the third round at Worplesdon to be beaten by the eventual winners.

We were treated to four days of the most glorious weather, and what a colourful scene it was! Lots of tents with striped awnings, everyone eating in the open, and such a galaxy of gorgeous girls that the more impressionable players—which means most of them—were hard put to it to keep their minds on the business in hand—just like the British Open in fact! (Interval for laughter.)

Our own contingent, though none were ever in sight of winning, were really a little unfortunate. Jimmy Martin, playing for Ireland for the first time, failed to appreciate the strength of the sun and found his arms burnt to the appearance of raw steaks and, though he

did play, it made a difference. Eric Brown for Scotland caught the
bug known generally as 'Gyppy Tummy' on the eve of the
tournament and, though he managed five holes under an umbrella,
eventually he had to pack it in.

Of the rest Peter Alliss was immeasurably the best. He had the
most tantalizing third round, playing quite beautifully but never
holing the longer 'doubtful' putts and, in fact, missing two very short
ones. This added a 72 to his 68 and 70, but on the final day he came
into his own with another 68—this in a really strong breeze and the
greens hardening every day—and his 278 gave him a tie for second
place in the individual contest with Arnold Palmer.

Wales, never really in the hunt, though Thomas also started 68,
70, were finally ruined by the 10th hole on the last day which, now
that all is over, leaves an element of farce to the memory. The fairway
is lined by trees and the flag was tucked away impossibly, almost
farcically on a plateau behind a deep bunker on the right. Thomas,
hitting a high 8-iron through the left hand wind, saw a tall fir tree
bend sideways in the wind, catch his ball in the topmost branch and
retain it there. A caddy shinned up the tree—but it turned out to be
the wrong tree, and there was much argument as to what was the rule
if it had been the right tree and he had dislodged a ball that had 'come
to rest'.

Meanwhile Rees, for the first time in his life, was taking six
putts—or at any rate six shots with two putters. One from under the
trees—right across the fairway; another from under the opposite
trees, to behind the bunker. From here he pitched over and took
another putt back, down the branch behind the bunker, by which he
was effectively stymied and had to putt up sideways. Two more putts
made eight.

As so often, it really boiled down to a question of whether anyone
could match that formidable combination, Snead and Palmer, for
the United States. Australia, aided by a 65 from Nagle in the second
round—which only matched that of Snead, anyway—were well in
the hunt for a time, but a sudden lapse by Nagle in the second half of
the third round (he actually took 42) put them out. So now it was left
only to the Argentine.

Vicenzo played magnificently—71, 68, 69, 68—to win the individual title—but the whole thing was settled quite clearly in my own
mind by one shot by his partner, Fidel de Luca, at the 6th hole in the

third round. The opening par is 4, 4, 3, 4, 4, de Luca started 3, 3, 2, 3, 3. Successive cheers of the large and very well behaved and well marshalled crowd reverberated over the course, increasing hole by hole. Level par for a 29!

De Luca drove well up the 6th where the green and flag were an almost exact replica of the 10th. With a strong left hand wind no man in his senses could play direct for the flag: he must play left for the centre of the green. But de Luca, fired by five birdies, the clamour of the crowd and perhaps by the well-known 'Latin temperament', fired straight at the flag, fell short into the bunker, failed to get out—and was gone. What might have been a 63 or 64 turned into 72.

Even so, he holed for a three from 20 feet on the last hole of the tournament, and Vicenzo followed him in from ten feet and it meant that the Americans, an hour behind, could afford no mistakes, especially with Snead no longer at his best. They had to pull out their best efforts, and in the end got home by only two shots in a total of 557.

This is a fine tournament, I cannot wait for it to come to St Andrews.

I am not sure that my vivid memory of the Canada Cup of 1962 will not be that of the daily 40-minute drives out to the course. At times the traffic is four abreast in each direction. In order to cross it, with neither traffic lights nor policemen, you edge into a gap in the outer line. This forces the oncoming traffic to squeeze four lines into three, with much hooting and squealing of tyres. You then move into the second line, forcing three into two with similar results, while the outer line now goes past behind you.

Fred Corcoran incidentally has an idea to promote a world long-driving championship, mainly to see whether anyone can hit a golf ball farther than George Bayer. His chief 'hope' was a tall, magnificent built young Adonis called Franco Marciani, who is attached to the pro's shop at the Jockey Club. Invited to give a demonstration, he went out and hit a ball 375 yards. What an event such a 'championship' would be!

7 March 1963

The 1963 Singapore Open

Professional golfers are fortunate fellows—or perhaps I should say professional golf players—for I am sure that the average club professional in Britain would utter a hollow laugh to see himself described just now as one of the lucky ones. For the itinerant players, however, there seems no limit to the number of people queueing up to provide money for them to play for and the latest place in which they can come and seek their winter picture is the Far East. Here in the short space of a year or two there has grown up a 'circuit'—horrible word!—of six tournaments, each taking a week and offering between them some £25,000. The trek begins in Manila and carries on through Singapore, Kuala Lumpur and Hong Kong to finish with two tournaments in Tokyo.

Readers of *Golf Illustrated* will doubtless gnash their teeth with envy to find that I have managed to wangle my way on to this congenial bandwagon, at any rate from Singapore to Hong Kong, and I am now sitting in balmy sunshine, reflecting on the Singapore Open, which has just finished, and fortifying myself upon reports of further cold weather on the way at home. It must be terrible for you all!

The British contingent this year is all too small and it is clear that a good many professionals at home ought to think seriously about how to beg, borrow or steal the price of the fare for next year. This is admittedly expensive, but it is all that they have to find, as their meals, caddies and accommodation are all free. For a young fellow it is a wonderful way to see the world and the experience alone makes it worth the money.

David Thomas is our leading player here—he did his national service in these parts and is renewing many old friendships—but he has unfortunately had laryngitis. The change of climate in less than twenty-four hours, which is all that it takes to fly here nowadays, often knocks people out and I was myself a victim for the first three or four days. Guy Wolstenholme is in better order, having spent some weeks here and in India.

The Singapore Open alternates between the Royal Island Club and the Royal Singapore at Burkit Timah, and this year was at the Island. It appears, incidentally, that some form of semi-compulsory merger is planned, largely for political reasons, so that Burkit Timah, so long the leisure home of countless Europeans, will lose its identity.

The Island course is thickly lined with trees, and with the fairways hard and rather bumpy was a test for accuracy and nerve rather than distance. It proved too much for the British players and showed how far we are falling behind the Australians, South Africans and Japanese. Nor can one see it becoming otherwise until the better young British players can manage somehow to 'follow the sun' rather than kick their heels in the cold, cold snow at home.

Thomas did achieve one thing which is surprisingly rare in tournament golf—indeed, analysis shows that he was the only man in the field to do so. He had four rounds—77, 74, 73, 71—each lower than the one before. In the Open championship this has only been done once by the winner. This was Hogan in 1953. With his health recovered, Thomas has still four tournaments in which to pay his way.

Wolstenholme is clearly still in the very difficult interim stage between amateur and professional, and it may be a year or so before he really establishes himself. It often happens that, when a man turns professional he goes through a period when he does not really play so well as a professional as he did as an amateur. Wolstenholme's rounds of 77, 77, 74, 74—302—left him 28 shots behind the winner, and that is a lot. Let us hope his time will come.

One of the most enthusiastic young players in Britain is George Maisey, who is professional at Robin Hood, near Birmingham, jointly with his father. They tell me he would practise all night if it were not dark. He finished on the same mark as Wolstenholme with rounds of 79, 74, 73, 76—302.

After three rounds, the 21-year-old South African, Alan Brookes, who had broken the record with a 67 in the second round, led by one stroke from Tomoo Ishii, of Japan, and by two from Alan Murray, of Australia, and the three of them played together in the final round. The physical contrast between Brookes and the Japanese was quite remarkable, as Brookes must be every inch of 6 ft 5 in.

The latter will remember this round for the rest of his life. Not only did he play magnificently but it was one of those days when nothing could go wrong. After nine holes he had picked up one stroke on Ishii and two on Murray, and then at the 10th he drove into the trees on the right and had to pitch out short of the green. He chipped into the hole for a three, gaining another stroke on each, and then at the 14th holed a 20-footer for another birdie. He clinched it by putting a half-blind second within two feet at the 17th and, coming home in 31, finished with a 64 to win by seven shots from Ishii and eight from Murray. Then came another Australian, recently turned professional, Bruce Devlin, followed by two more, Woodward and Nagle.

A feature of both the Singapore courses and the lovely Selangor course at Kuala Lumpur, from which I am writing, is that they have long practice tees accommodating anything up to thirty-five players at once. At any moment of the day you can wander along, pick up a basket of 50 balls for half-a-crown, and hit away to your heart's content—leaving somebody else, of course, to pick them up. When I called at Burkit Timah the tee was packed, and Cyril Horne, late of Littlestone, told me it is the same every evening. The practice ground is floodlit till nine at night and Horne told me that he has 3000 balls in use. May the time be not long delayed when we have something like this in England. I would almost take up golf again!

20 April 1967

The 1967 US Masters

It seemed only just that Gay Brewer should win the US Masters, if only because he so nearly did so last year, when he put his second at the 72nd hole away up at the back of the sloping green. He judged the distance of the long putt back to a nicety but it swung away at the last minute and lay seven feet from the hole with a most fiendish degree of borrow. He hit the next one really well but it just fell away at the last moment and he was forced into a losing play-off with Nicklaus and Jacobs.

How many times he must have relived that scene on the 18th green since then!

This year he made no mistake and in what they called a 'cliff-hanger' finish he beat his old friend and travelling companion, Bobby Nichols, by a single shot with a 67, the second best round of the tournament. Palmer and Nicklaus having dominated the tournament for the past nine years, it made a nice change. The huge leader-boards have ten names on them. It seemed quite astonishing that at one time neither of the two great men were on them at all.

As to Tony Jacklin, who eventually finished 15th with a slightly disappointing 77, he was at one time leading the field with four under par, and only a select few can tell their grandchildren that they were once leading the field in the Masters. My own view is that it would be doing no service to Jacklin to start writing him up as the new white hope for Britain. On the other hand if one were to pick a young player—he is only twenty-two—as being the most likely to succeed the present leaders, one would certainly look no farther than Jacklin. Whether he will find it worthwhile to take up his residence as a taxpayer in this country, where the point is comparatively quickly reached when it is no longer worth one's while to try, remains to be seen. It might pay him better to reside somewhere in the sun and become a visitor to British tournaments like, for instance, Peter Thomson.

As a result of the system by which the Ryder Cup is chosen we are faced with the faintly ludicrous situation that Nicklaus does not qualify, though until last week he was the holder both of the Masters and the British Open. I quite agree that, when one's living depends on success at golf, it is only fair that those who have won most points in a regular schedule of events should have preference. It might be reasonable to stipulate, however, that a player from one country should be eligible for the match if he currently holds the Open championship of the other. The British Open will have already been played again before the Ryder Cup match in October. My point is that any American who wins it should automatically receive a place in his own Ryder Cup team. Similarly any British player who wins the US Open should qualify for our team. And if you believe that, you will believe anything.

There seemed to be a good deal of controversy at Augusta about the fairways, which, owing to the warm spring, had to be mown twice a day. Even so, a good many people, including Gary Player, held that they were unduly lush, as a result of which he hit a 7-iron right over the back of the last green—208 yards. The ball, it seems, comes quicker off the lush grass and you do not get the same bite on it. Hogan on the other hand said the fairways were quite in order— but then he had just gone round in 66.

Talking with him at the airport—where as usual he was the least conspicuous member of the entire company—I was glad to hear him confirm my own theory that there really is a limit to placing the pins in positions where it is physically impossible for the best of players to get close to them. Some of them on huge greens were tucked away merely a few feet on the green and behind a bunker. Others were placed so close to the front edge that if you had a longish putt back down the slope you were in grave danger of putting right off the green. There were some, said Hogan, to which he could get no nearer than 40 feet.

I was glad though, to see them take a really stern line about slow play. They issued an edict that there would be no warning. Players who seemed to be playing unduly slowly would be specially scruti- nized and if found guilty would simply be told, there and then, to add two strokes to their score for the hole. It certainly seemed to work at Augusta, so presumably it would work elsewhere. Anything to get a move on.

When all was over, I came back more than ever convinced that this tournament has something that none of the others have got and I only hope I am spared, as they say, to go and see it again.

27 June 1968

The 1968 US Open

The running of the Masters tournament at Augusta, Georgia, is often a matter of complimentary comment, and so indeed it should be, but I am not sure that the US Open, from which I returned recently, is not the most remarkable of them all.

The Masters, after all, is run always on the same course and they have only to set the well-tried machinery in motion again, adding a few little refinements year by year. The Open, however, is played on different courses, on some of which it has never been held before, and maybe 3000 miles from the USGA headquarters in New York. The amount of work put in by the volunteer members of the USGA, who come from all parts of the country, is simply tremendous and, as for Joe Dey, the executive director, and his No. 2, Frank Hannigan, the amount they get through, to a basically idle fellow like myself, is quite appalling. I believe that 4000-odd clubs are affiliated to the USGA, which leaves a great many who do not support an organisation which is alone responsible for having kept golf on the rails, so to speak, across the American continent and thus, indirectly, made it the worldwide game it is today.

Of the new Open champion, Lee Trevino, I will say only that he has immensely brightened up the professional scene and, all being well, will continue to do so for many years. A man who can do four rounds, for the first time in Open championship history, all in less than 70 is no flash in the pan and, as to the fellow himself, I would say 'It couldn't have happened to a better man'.

He figured in the picture at Baltusrol last year and I remember seeing him and remembering him as a completely new name, but I was not to know, of course, that he only had 60 dollars in his pocket and only earned 30 a week plus what he could make from teaching at a dusty little club in Texas. The 6000 dollars that he won by finishing fifth set him going on the tournament tour and without winning a tournament he arrived at Rochester having made, he said—incautiously perhaps, for the tax man listeneth—some 90,000 dollars, including 56,000 in prize-money alone. To this he added the 30,000 dollar first prize last week, plus the prospects of immensely lucrative contracts to come.

The amount of money involved in golf in America is almost frightening and one begins to wonder, with a tinge of jealousy perhaps, whether it can be a 'good thing' and whether it has not become out of all proportion to the basic business of hitting a little ball from A to B. Still, it is more reasonable, I suppose, than when four youths with long hair can be promoted into millionaires by flogging gramophone records which the public later learn they did not even make. All the same, 90,000 dollars in a year without winning a tournament really does seem remarkable. The answer is that the total money is so big—they have played for more than two and a half million dollars this season already and it will probably reach five million—and the prizes, if you can keep steadily in the first six or ten, are so large by our standards that you can become hugely wealthy without ever winning.

Rochester was the scene of the Amateur championship of 1949, in which the British Walker Cup team played. The late president, Dr John Williams, sent each member a number of acorns from a handsome pin oak which stands outside the clubhouse, but the soil of the players' home clubs proved most unsuitable. Laddie Lucas was the British captain and, suitably enough, two of his did take root at Sandy Lodge. One still flourishes, but Lucas's brother, who is secretary there, told me that the Gas Board inadvertently uprooted the other in laying a new main!

Rochester was the scene also of what is to me one of the most poignant moments in golf when in 1956 Ben Hogan seemed set to become the only man to win five Opens. He had got as far as the 71st hole and was three feet away in three. He stood over the putt for a while, and then walked away. He came back and then not only missed it but he undoubtedly 'twitched' it. 'Once you've had 'em you've got 'em'—and from that moment the great man was never the same again.

On a slightly less elevated level I played recently for only the second time since the anti-twitch croquet putter was banned and the result was so pathetic and so distasteful and so ridiculous that on Saturday next, in congenial company in the heart of the Vale of the White Horse, I intend to be playing my positively final game of golf. It will be forty-seven years since I hit my first stroke on the common at Yelverton, in Devon, and became a martyr to the game. I shall always be grateful for what it has given me and am only sorry that we shall not part better friends!

26 June 1969

The 1969 US Open

This was my third trip this year to America, the previous two having been to Atlanta, and there is no doubt that flying is a tremendous bore—or at any rate should be. We don't want any excitement, touch wood! One strip of concrete; eight or nine hours in a narrow seat;

another bit of concrete; get out and sign in with your passport; wait an hour or so while they put in a few thousand gallons of paraffin, or whatever it is; in again and down on another bit of concrete, having seen positively nothing on the way.

What it will be like with these jumbo jets for which an entire English county may well be sacrificed by the Phillistines, defies description. Incidentally, I am the only person who seems to know the true solution of 'London's third airport'. The answer is 'Don't build one at all. Tell 'em to make do with what they've got.'

This is all perhaps a little unkind to Pan American, who took me with great courtesy and despatch on all three trips, since in any case it is true of all airline flying. It is a great help, of course, if you can get a plane that goes the whole way, so that you only have to get out and back into the same one at the intermediary stops.

I went to the US Open on Pan-Am's Flight 59, which leaves at the very civilised hour of 2.15 in the afternoon and goes straight to Chicago and thence to Dallas before stopping at Houston, Texas.

For myself I am able to travel first class in the United States, where the difference is comparatively small, but not over the Atlantic, where it makes a difference of about £6 an hour, and this, simply to sit two abreast instead of three and to get free drinks, is simply not 'on', though I wish it were, for the difference in comfort really is enormous. If I were the boss of a big company and had a man going to represent our interests on the other side, I should send him first class and damn the cost.

Another great difference is that on the way over you may get there in the early hours of the next morning but you put the clock *back* six hours. This means that you can have the odd drink with welcoming friends and then go to bed.

Coming back is the killer. You get in from most transatlantic flights at around 2 a.m. which means you have had just about enough of it, and then put the clock *on* six hours, making it 8 a.m., with everyone expecting you to start a jolly new day just when you would give anything to get to bed. Even for those younger than myself, this takes a couple of days to get straightened out.

Noel Coward had a celebrated line, 'Very flat, Norfolk', and I can only say the same of that part of the huge State of Texas which encompasses Dallas and Houston. Thousands of square miles of flat, still almost virgin territory, broken only by the occasional town or city sprawling out to the very edge of the bush. The Champions club is in the forest, twenty miles out of Houston which perhaps accounts for the small crowds on the first two days—and the holes run up and down, completely cut off from each other by the trees.

It was created by two great golfers, Jack Burke and Jimmy Demaret, and I could not help imagining the pride they must have felt in having the Open there when their creation was only about eleven years old. The Open is one of the tournaments run by the United States Golf Association and they take an unbelievable amount of trouble over it, starting two years in advance. As the British Open increases in stature once again, a similar task falls on the R and A, which they also handle with great competence.

The Champions weather was always in the nineties with hardly a cloud in the sky. For those who, like myself, could afford to take things quietly and keep popping in and out of the air-conditioned clubhouse or Press room it was easy enough, but it must have put a considerable strain on those who had to play a round in the full heat and taking a minimum of four hours. As the final round drew to its close the pressure must have been almost intolerable, and no wonder one or two broke down under it.

This particular clubhouse was not lavish by American standards, though it would be by ours. Where they tend to outdo us so emphatically is in the locker room and ablutions. The locker room here had a charming bar with excellent service, and you could sit gossiping and talking rubbish to your heart's content.

Occasionally a man would wheel by a whole trolley load of shoes, having just cleaned them, and would seem to remember to whom every pair belonged.

All this, however, has to be paid for, and prices are, by our standards, high. As at all tournaments in America, they used 'scrip', in other words, books of tickets, instead of money, and there must surely be much to be said for this on these busy occasions. A small whisky or gin, including tip, will cost you the equivalent of 12s, and lunch about 26s, though of course these figures are conversions at the devalued rate and the sums involved do not hit the Americans as hard as they hit us.

My hotel, the Warwick, was one of the best I have ever stayed in, but the room was reduced, I gather, to £12 a night (modest breakfast about 25s) only because of the vast number of rooms booked by the

American Broadcasting Company, who were covering the Open and for whom I worked. ABC have also bought the rights to the British Open for a very large, though undisclosed sum, and this has had a considerable influence in enabling the R and A to raise the prize money to an unprecedented £30,000.

CHAPTER THREE

Fairway and Hazard

28 October 1954

Don't Muck About

I think it undeniable that golf has become progressively slower in the past fifty years. Of course, with changes in balls and clubs we have to walk farther, particularly between green and tee, and this must account for many minutes per round, but I have a strong impression that people get on with the job more slowly anyway. To go round these days in a single in two and a quarter hours excites favourable comment. There was a time when it would have excited comment of an opposite kind if you took more.

We should differentiate, surely, between tournament golf and club golf, and, in the former, between sponsored tournaments and championships. I hope I shall not be thought sarcastic if I suggest the sponsors who want the best players to take part in their tournaments can hardly 'fine' a player like Locke for being a little slower than the rest—more especially as the first thing a man who plays competitive golf in America has to do is to *learn* to play slowly.

I have had a basin of this, as they say, myself, and if it is anything like as difficult to speed up as it is to slow down, then Locke and Thomson, who habitually play in the States, deserve sympathetic tolerance if they are a little slower than the others when they come here—though I do not hereby go on record as saying that they are. To play to a pace of four to four and a half hours requires an adjustment both of mind and stomach if concentration is not to be lost.

When the messages begin to come up saying 'It must be about

lunch time. What are we going to have?' you have to send back, 'dialling TUM', as Nathaniel Gubbins used to put it, the discouraging intelligence that we are only sitting on a bench on the 11th tee, that there are four more waiting to drive off anyway, and that we shall be lucky if we get our hands on a gin and tonic for the next two hours.

The championships are different and here the ruling body, by being adamant, can set the general standard. They have warned players in the past and for flagrant offences would be sure of public support if they one day went the whole hog with a penalty of two strokes or disqualification.

As to the general pace of the course in a tournament, this baffles me. In the Halford Hewitt sometimes, even after waiting for each match to get off the first green before starting the next, four and even five matches pile up on the third tee—from which players have even been known to step back to the clubhouse and have another Kummel! Other times the whole thing goes smoothly on. Depends on the wind, the experts say. Perhaps it does—but why so extraordinary a difference?

Apart from the tiny percentage of golfers who actually witness tournaments, it makes little difference whether the professionals take three hours or four. The real curse is slow play at the club. At least, I take it that I am right in saying that it *is* slower? Certainly, it seems to me the innumerable club golfers, who before the war, age for age, would have played two rounds a day, even in winter, now play only one and that the main reason is the time it takes.

Of course, lack of caddies is one cause—but not everybody had caddies before the war, and still the pace seems to have been quicker. Personally, I prefer to carry seven or eight clubs in a light canvas container rather than pull fourteen on a trolley, and therefore am not an expert trolleyman, but people assure me that trolleys have added twenty minutes to the average round. As it is only roughly a minute per hole, they may well be right, and, of course, forty minutes on a winter's day may well mean the difference between two rounds and one. If the trolley theory is right, the difference must be made up partly by more intelligent anticipation by trolley-pullers—never leaving them on the wrong side of the green for the next tee, etc.— and partly by speeding up in other ways.

Of these there are many, of which the principal and most elementary is *Don't muck about*. An incredible number of club golfers are born 'muckerabouters'. If you watched the average four-ball, pretending to be that well known time-and-motion man Mr Bedaux, you would find countless instances of not-getting-on-with-it, when they could perfectly well do so without introducing any sense of artificial hurry.

'A' drives off. What is 'B' doing? Cleaning his ball . . . lighting a cigarette . . . continuing a story he started on the way to the tee . . . arguing whether they are two up or three up . . . blowing his nose . . . anything rather than stepping on to the tee the moment 'A' has finished. And we have yet to hear from 'C' and 'D'. Multiply this lot by 18 and we may have a formidable total. And this is only on the tees. The mucking about on the greens would prove an even more fertile field for Mr Bedaux.

As to the incessant 'marking' of the ball I have already had my say. I now add to the objects of my rancour the fellow *who is given the putt and then holes it*. My dear departed friend, Eric Martin Smith, used to say 'I will give you that putt so long as you don't try to hole it'. I commend this to one and all.

Coupled with the above I direct public scorn on the fourballer who, having a yard putt for nothing, plays it out with the mental reservation 'If it goes in, I holed it. If it doesn't, I would have done, if it had mattered, so I will give myself a four.' This is the sort of thing that gets golfers bracketed with fishermen.

Sarazen used to say 'The time to be thinking about the next shot is while you are approaching the ball, not when you are standing over it'. This is wonderful golfing advice, quite apart from slow play. Just try it and see. Sarazen also once told me 'When I am playing slow, I am playing bad'. If it is good enough for him, it is certainly good enough for the rest of us.

20 January 1955

The Joys of Winter Golf

Whatever anyone may care to say about golf, at least one thing is mercifully certain, namely that it is a voluntary affair. Mad though it may well make you when you do, you need not play if you don't want to.

When I am asked whether winter golf is worth while, there does not lurk in the mind a vision of a sunny January morning at Rye, with the white sails of the local yacht club's Sunday morning race gliding along within two or three hundred yards of the fairway, the golden weathercock on the 600-year-old church glinting three miles away across the marsh, and one or two people even playing in shirt-sleeves—a happy combination of sights and circumstances which have more than once been witnessed in the President's Putter.

No. What is envisaged is a perishing cold morning with an east wind and just not quite enough rain to justify 'packing it in'. The course is on clay, well churned up and with plenty of wormcasts, and some of the greens are temporary ones, hastily mown pieces of fairway and quite 'unputtable'. How well I know it and with what purring contentment I sit in front of the fire, with the rain pattering against the window, and reflect that never, never, never will I go through it again!

Do I therefore look with a slightly patronising air upon people who do choose to endure it? Certainly not. The truth is, as I see it, that it all depends on whether you go to a regular place of work during the week or whether you belong to that select, undisciplined, though as I think favoured, section of the community who lounge about at home and do their work either when they feel like it or, as is more likely, when publisher or editor will wait for it no longer. If you repair five days a week to an office, then of course you look forward in a different way to your weekend of leisure and exercise and are determined to get it, come what may. Having at certain stages of life had to catch the same train every morning myself, I sympathise with the feeling.

The pleasure or otherwise of winter golf depends also on your figure. We whose shadows grow no smaller with the years are less favoured than our slimmer brethren. It is said of women and I pass no comment on the justice of the observation, that one of the main disadvantages is that you cannot live with them and cannot live without them. The trouble with golf in the winter is that you cannot play without three sweaters on and you cannot play with three sweaters on. It occurs to me that if W. J. Cox should find himself short of a question to answer, he might enlighten the more corpulent among us on this subject. He would be speaking, in both senses, from experience.

Speaking from memory—and despite the foregoing, from a

memory not so distant as all that—I have always felt there to be one or two elementary principles by which winter golf can be made a great deal more enjoyable. They are so simple that people are apt to dismiss them on the ground that they 'know that already'. Even so, I venture on one, namely 'Why not *be up*?' Most people are 'not up' all the year round, largely because they select a club which will get them up if they hit a good one and seven times out of ten they don't so they are short. They still maintain, of course, that they had the 'right club'. In winter the whole thing is intensified. With frozen fingers, in a chill wind, and off a bed of wormcasts, they are liable to hit only one really good one in twenty, and even this one, what with atmospheric conditions, reduced force, and so on, will not have the full value of spring and autumn. So what used to be a 'good No. 5' becomes not a good 4, but something like a good 2, and, as no one broadly speaking ever hits a 'good 2' in winter, you might as well make it a good spoon and have done with it.

Finally, if there is a handicap golfer who can afford in winter not to play with the larger ball, I have yet to meet him. This is perfectly legal for all purposes, though the manufacturers, for reasons of their own, do not encourage its sale.

3 May 1955

No More Bad Lies?

The 'manicuring' of golf courses is part of the pattern of standardization, which older golfers think has taken much of the essential character out of golf, so that the player is exposed no longer so much to adventure, as to an examination in skill. And examinations above everything else have to be fair. Every candidate must be set the same questions. It is manifestly unfair if, in the exam on iron play, I am asked to hit a 2-iron off a carpet of lush, green grass and you are asked to hit it out of a divot mark.

The Americans, of course, although they are great manicurers of golf courses, have a more logical approach. They don't play it out of a divot mark. They give it a nudge, and tee it up. They take the view that, having driven on to the fairway, they are entitled to a fairway lie and there is, as I say, an awful logic about this. When you come to think of it, they are! If the divot marks were marked with little sticks visible from the tee, one could say that they ought to be avoided, like the bunkers—but no one knows where they are. Is it therefore my fault if I drive into one?

Of course, this does not apply to every American golfer, but it does to most. They have not been brought up with the game as we have. They can sympathise with our being moved by a sense of tradition, but it is our tradition, not theirs. They know golf principally, and again logically, as a scoring game, not as a match. The American country club golfer goes out with a view to playing 18 holes and seeing how many he can do them in. For him the luck cannot 'even out'. The fact that the other fellow will probably get in a divot mark too, before the round is out, leaves him unmoved. The point is that *he* is in one now and it is going to affect *his* score.

Thus followed—and I hope I am right in 'accursing' our American friends of its invention—the idea that a bunker must be manicured in the same way as the fairway. Once in the bunker you are entitled to a fair bunker lie just as, when you have driven on to the fairway, you are entitled to a fair fairway lie. You are also entitled to use a club with a broad, flat sole, with which to take all the terrors out of bunker play, and give you an easier shot *from* the bunker than from just behind it. The finest inland course in the world is probably Pine Valley. To the skilled player, with a good nerve, it is nothing like as difficult as they like to make out, but one of its main terrors to the more humble is that the bunkers are great wastes of sand, often with small scrub growing in them, and are so large that you don't even trouble to smooth out your own footmarks. However bad they are, there is a worse place within a yard or two!

The main reason for the incredibly high standard of upkeep which we demand, and indeed take for granted today, is in my opinion due basically to a desire to eliminate luck. Readers may conceivably remember my writing recently of playing in the desert at Tripoli and Benghazi, where everything bar the greens, or 'browns', is completely rough and ready. Here one is going back to something which, I imagine, must resemble the orginal pre-Tom Morris golf where you took a pinch of sand or earth from the actual hole and teed up with it within six feet of the hole. Golf was a simple matter of starting at A and holing out at B, encountering the manner of hazards on the way and overcoming them as best you might. You played among the whin bushes on the foreshore, and carried with you a 'rut-iron'. In this sort of game the luck must surely have evened out in the end. No use coming in and saying 'I got in a heel mark at the 17th'.

Not that people do not still try it on. I remember in our Halford Hewitt days, putting John Morrison on the beach at the 6th at Deal. This is part of the vast pebble ridge which stretches for miles on either side and contains, I suppose, some billions of pebbles. He tried to 'splash' it out with a niblick but nothing much happened.

'Very unlucky,' he said, 'got a stone behind it.'

Anyway, once a bad lie becomes a comparative rarity instead of the normal thing it is only natural if people want to eliminate it altogether. In America this is easy enough by playing 'winter rules' at 100 in the shade. If you stick to the old diehard maxim of 'Play the ball where it lies', the only thing to do is to keep on trying to make the fairways almost as good as the greens. And if it costs a fortune—as it does—do not blame the rise on the cost of living.

So it seems to me in the end that it is a case of all or nothing. You either go back to playing on the common—as I started golf, with three home-made holes on the common at Yelverton, Devon—complete with rut-iron, lofted putter, and no complaints; or else you say 'If I am going to have fairways and greens and green-keepers and motor mowers and lead arsenate and fusarium patch and leather-jackets, let us go in for it all in a big way'. (Three bad lies in a single Sunday and sack the secretary.)

21 July 1955

The Charms of the Old Course

The fact that the Old Course is indisputably a 'classic'—and its bitterest enemies must at least concede it that—does not necessarily make it good, nor is it a reason why anyone should necessarily like it. The works of Sir Walter Scott are widely held to be classics, or so I have had impressed on me since my schooldays, but despite this assurance I find them totally unreadable. To read them is, to me, the golfing equivalent of playing a very slow fourball in boring company on a clay course on a wet afternoon in February. On the other hand the fact that I personally can do nothing with the works of Sir Walter Scott does not in the least degree diminish their reputation as classics.

As with any work of art first impressions of the Old Course are of interest but of little real value. I cannot believe that Professor Richardson or Ernest Newman would be prepared to state confident opinions on the world's accepted classics of painting or music if they were seeing or hearing them today for the first time. They would ask to see and hear them again and again before they committed themselves.

If, however, the most experienced critics over a period embracing the whole of what we may call 'modern' golf are almost unanimous in declaring that the Old Course has 'something the others haven't got', we are bound to suspect our own judgment rather than theirs if we cannot see it.

In the days when I was playing on a great many courses every year for the first time I used to judge them by whether I could remember the holes afterwards. After playing at Pine Valley in 1930, I remembered every hole in every detail and six years later was able to leave a hole-by-hole description with the paper for which I then worked before leaving for the 1936 Walker Cup match. It was incorrect only in the sense that I said the 14th was an island green completely surrounded by water—which, of course, it was not, or you would never get on to it or off it!

The very complexity of the Old Course makes it the only exception to the rule about 'remembering the holes'. After my first round on it I could remember practically nothing. I did not know where I was going, and could not remember where I had been. Incidentally, I was playing rather well that day and drove almost exactly where my partner, Gerard Fairlie, directed. As often as not the ball finished in a concealed pot bunker and it was only later that I realised that he had been doing it on purpose. At any rate the whole thing put me in mind of the early stages of a jigsaw puzzle, when all one has done is 'a few bits of sky'. I knew enough about the business not to make derogatory remarks but in my heart I suspected that all this veneration for the Old Course was probably a bit of a pose.

It was not until I had played half a dozen rounds on it that I began to catch the magic. After twenty rounds or so I began to know something about it, and to perceive the almost limitless extent of what remained yet to be found out. I still do not really know it, and never will—during the last medal I got into an enormous bunker at the 7th, and not far from the hole at that, on which I had never consciously set eyes before—but at any rate I have reached the stage where, instantly and with complete sincerity, I should concur with the great Bobby Jones when he said 'If I were set down to play on one course for the remainder of my life, I should choose the Old Course at St Andrews'.

Some perceive the qualities of the Old Course more quickly than others. Morty Dutra, for instance, who was over for the Open as the US professional 'Senior' champion, told the editor of *Golf Illustrated* that there was nothing he would like to do so much as to spend two or three weeks at St Andrews plotting and planning how to play it to the best advantage. Bill Campbell, captain of the last US Walker Cup team, wrote perceptively that a match between two people on the Old Course was in effect a question of each of them matching himself against the course and seeing who did it best. While some of the professionals were saying what must by any standard be judged rather stupid things about it, John Panton hit the nail on the head by remarking, on the conditions that prevailed during so much of the Open, 'The trouble is that in these conditions you don't have to use your head'.

The second-rate player always has to use his head at St Andrews but the truth is that there are times when the first-class player doesn't. One such was the match-play championship last autumn when the professionals could pitch nonchalantly up on to the 17th and as likely as not halve it in three. Another was during certain parts of the Open, though as Locke drily observed, when somebody who had not got to play it remarked how easy the course was, 'The bunkers are still there'. The essence of golf on the Old Course is that you normally have to stop before every shot, be it a drive or a 40-yard approach, and say to yourself 'Now just a minute. What is it exactly that I am trying to do?' If those conditions do not prevail, then the Old Course is not itself and it is no use its most devoted adherents maintaining the contrary.

It was not wholly itself during the Open, though heaven knows nobody made a fool of it, and we cannot blame those who were seeing it for the first time, whether young professionals from this country or some of our distinguished visitors from afar where, as Byron Nelson put it, they would 'bulldoze the humps and turn it into a municipal course', if they did not gather quite what we are driving at when we go into rhapsodies about it. You judge things in this life as you find them. If people assure you they were different yesterday and will assuredly be different tomorrow, you are prepared to agree. It does not alter what you see today.

If we could experiment with holding the Open in September, instead of July, I think it would be a splendid thing. If we could hold it on the Old Course for ever, it would be still more splendid.

24 July 1958

Setting a Tougher Paper

One of the great charms of the historic championship links in Britain is that year after year they have set the same problems to successive generations of golfers. The 17th hole at Lytham, for instance, was pretty well identical with that on which Bobby Jones made his famous stroke in 1926 and, as David Thomas walked forward through the bushes and over the sandhills to survey the same stroke, one could almost see the figure of Jones making it thirty-two years before.

Nevertheless, in conditions which were admittedly exceptional, Lytham set the world's leading players a common entrance instead of a scholarship examination—golf at what today is called, I believe, 'O' level as against 'A' level. It still sorted out the best player—I think that is unquestionable—but somehow it seemed to leave something to be desired. Lest this be thought to be in any way critical of the club itself, let me say that one of the reasons the course was comparatively easy was that it was in such flawless order.

In America the ordinary run-of-the-mill circuit courses are made as easy as possible so as to induce sensationally low scores, but for many years the USGA, who have to fight an incessant battle against a variety of undesirable influences in a way which is not widely appreciated over here, have determined that, whether the tournament pros like it or not, they shall be set a stiff exam for the Open. Thus two years before the championship a sub-committee and a golf architect, normally Robert Trent Jones, visit the course and plan it for the Open. Fairways are narrowed; the rough is allowed to grow; crafty pin positions are decided upon so that you cannot get near the flag from 'anywhere', but must position your drive; and bunkers are set at a distance from the tee which will catch the drives of champions. This almost inevitably results in protests and gnashing of teeth, but it has retained for the US Open a degree of respect shared only by the Masters tournament where the same outlook applies.

Should we go some distance towards this in Britain? In America, of course, so big is the country and so many the claimants for the honour of staging the Open that the championship tends to be played on a different course each year, i.e. where it has not been played before. For this distinction the club does not object to having its course 'mucked about'. Over here there is a natural tendency on the part of the older clubs who form the limited championship rota to regard their courses as sacred. Nevertheless, barring the Old Course at St Andrews, which *is* sacred, a case could be made out for 'stiffening' operations before the Open.

The 18th hole at Lytham was a case in point. This really did play to its full value, for the distant back tee brought right into play the bunker set in the fairway on the left and gave only a narrow opening between this and the bushes on the right. One or two could carry the bunker; all could drive into it. If they were short, it left as much as a 3-iron to a tightly trapped green. Without the bunker the hole would have been a pushover: with it it became real scholarship golf. So the point arises: if the bunker had not been there, should it have been put there for the championship? Needless to say, it would be removed afterwards—at the championship committee's expense!—if the members did not desire to retain it. Quite a number of holes at Lytham would have been much strengthened by a strategic bunker of this kind.

On the other hand many would have been strengthened by the removal of bunkers round the green—of which there are much too many in any case. With the beautiful sand—the best he had ever seen, Thomson said—the top-class player was more disappointed if he did not get down in two from a bunker than relieved if he did, and I cannot think that this is as it should be. If those bunkers had been grassy hollows, with nice thick grass for which no club or technique has yet been perfected, the man who was on the green would have a distinct advantage over the man who was just off it.

Indeed the more I see of golf the more fatuous it seems that inland clubs in the old days dug little pits all over the place and filled them with sand, merely because sand was a natural part of the original golf by the sea. There is a thought here for many clubs who find it difficult to make ends meet. Cut out two-thirds of the sand bunkers and let them revert to grass, heather, or whatever comes naturally. The saving would be considerable and the quality of the course much improved. As to the championship courses, I should not wish to be dogmatic, but it does seem that there is a case for making a rather closer preview and by mutual consent closing some of the gaps that have opened up as the years go by on some of the most revered championship courses.

23 July 1959

Taking to the Waters

Splosh! One of the finest sights in the world: the other man's ball dropping in the water—preferably so that he can see it but cannot quite reach it and has therefore to leave it there, thus rendering himself so mad that he loses the next hole as well!

The greatest of all water hazards is, I suppose, the sea but somehow that is not quite the same thing. One could never, however, fail to mention that most photographed of all golf holes, the 16th at Cypress Point in California, where to hit the green involves a carry of 200 yards directly over the Pacific Ocean. 'Porky' Oliver took 14 there in a professional tournament, while lesser mortals have taken 30 or more. The beach is littered with balls and the novice cannot resist going and picking them up, little knowing that if they have been in the water for more than a few hours they will have been bitten into by crabs. Any more indigestible meal than the cover and elastic of a golf ball it would be hard to imagine.

Incidentally, one of my most regular dreams—probably after eating crab—is of finding myself on a pebble beach (sometimes it is a chalk pit) looking for my ball. I find it, and then another and another, till there seem to be almost more balls than stones. Is this a regular golfer's dream? I have never had such in reality.

Some of the greatest normal water hazards are at another famous American course, Pine Valley. One short-hole green, the 14th, is entirely surrounded by water except for the little path to the next tee and it is a case literally of being either 'on' or 'in'. The next hole has a huge carry over the lake and at the short 5th, actually a full shot with a driver, a topped shot sees you in a pond, deep among the turtles.

At home the most notable water hazards are surely the Swilcan Burn at St Andrews and the Barry Burn at Carnoustie, of which the most wonderful and intimidating use is made over the last few holes. I sometimes think the Swilcan is one of the greatest hazards in golf, water or otherwise. Completely invisible, about six yards wide, it crosses the fairway just in front of the first green and the first un-teed shot of the day has to carry it.

There is a great story of a man upon whom the entire result of a team match depended, playing it at the 19th. He went in with his second, picked out, went in again, picked out and went in again. Beckoning the caddie, he took the clubs from his shoulder and threw them in. Then he threw the caddie. Then he jumped in himself.

Water hazards induce a degree of anger and frustration out of all proportion to their golfing consequence. A man may lose his ball in the forest or the furze and march composedly to the next tee. To see it disappear into the water will often render him beside himself with rage. Was there not an Oxford player before the war who slung all his clubs into the lake at the 16th at Stoke Poges? I cannot remember the details but it always seemed well authenticated at the time.

I do remember seeing a Cambridge player, now no longer with us, during the trials at Mildenhall missing a putt on the 5th green, whereupon he flung his putter away in disgust. It twirled slowly through the air and pitched with a splash in the very centre of the stream, whence he had the mortification of having to take off his shoes and socks on a cold winter's day in order to retrieve it.

I suppose the earliest water hazard I can remember was a dewpond on the Eastbourne Downs course, from which it was always said that the boys used to retrieve vast quantities of balls. In those days I do not think I hit it far enough to hook into the Great Ouse on my home course at Bedford: they had not then made the excellent short hole from which it is now comparatively easy.

My most recent acquaintance among water hazards is also among the very best. That is the trout stream which dashes merrily along through the course at Moretonhampstead in Devon. You can, if I remember aright, get in it six times—or rather at six different holes, for there is, of course, no limit to the number of times you can get in it at each. I made two visits, I recall, but the stream itself, and indeed the whole scene, is so delightful that one felt no pain at all.

20 August 1959

Playing at Home

Only the other day by a coincidence I received notice of a Press Golfing Society meeting at Sunningdale. It was to be a Stableford competition and anyone who happened also to be a member of the club was to 'deduct two clear strokes from his handicap'. This is the usual practice, of course, yet I remember wondering at the time whether it was right. If your heart were set on winning this competition, for instance, would you choose to be a member with a sound local knowledge of Sunningdale and pay two clear strokes for it, or would you choose a strange course and your full handicap?

In any case, why two strokes? Why not one—or three? The practice has grown up over the years and two it always seems to be.

My own first thought is that 'playing at home' can sometimes be a mental handicap. When you do a good round, anywhere, it comes from playing good golf more than from 'knowing the course'. You can know the course like the back of your hand and still play execrably, but it is very uncommon to play well and still score badly, whether you know the course or not.

I often feel that professionals must feel almost handicapped when a tournament happens to take place on their home course. 'So-and-so ought to do well', I should imagine, and possibly overhear the members saying . . . 'knows it like the back of his hand . . . round in 64 last week . . . never takes more than 68 . . .' etc., etc. When the great day came, I suspect I would give a lot to be playing almost anywhere else.

Goodwill can sometimes be a hard load to bear. Relating to this I was intrigued with the comment, after the Walker Cup match, of Herbert Warren Wind, who is America's leading golf critic. 'You will win it in America before you win it over here,' he said, and upon my soul I believe he may be right. The load of goodwill towards the British team; the unfortunate publicity in some of the papers to the effect that the match was virtually in the bag; 'this would teach the Americans', and similar nonsense, was more almost than any team could reasonably carry.

Of one thing I am quite sure after a lifetime of watching and playing golf, namely that you are almost certain to play better on a course first time—always excepting the Old Course at St Andrews—than any of the next, let us say, half-dozen times. This is elementary psychology—and psychology plays a bigger part in golf than any game in the world. If you have no thought in your mind but of hitting the ball on to that large patch of fairway, you are almost certain to do so. But supposing you know that, invisible just off the fairway, is a whacking great pit, and if you go into that heather on the other side you are almost certain to lose your ball—what a different shot it becomes then!

I always remember years ago when I first played at Hillside, Southport. I forget the number of the hole, but I know that I was doing quite well and making no great difficulty about it. I was just preparing to drive over a direction post—it was a hole facing somewhat in the direction of Southport and Ainsdale—when my caddie, in a strong Lancashire accent, which I cannot render on paper, said: 'You've an out of bounds on the left.' 'Ah,' I said. 'I see.' I prepared to play again. 'You want to keep away from the right,' he said. 'It's very thick out there.' 'All right,' I said, 'I'll do my best.' I was actually addressing the ball when he said: 'And it's very bad in front of the tee.' I forget where I hit the thing, after the laughter had subsided, but the stroke had by that time become virtually unplayable.

I have no doubt, too, that some courses are friendly and others hostile—some to the world in general and some to particular players. Of the championship courses I have always thought of Hoylake and Carnoustie as being thoroughly hostile. I do not mean anything unpleasant in this, but simply that they are going to give you positively no help, that they will yield up a good score with the utmost reluctance, and that they each reserve a series of potential knock-out blows for you, however well you may be doing, right at the end.

Among the essentially friendly courses on which tournaments, if not Open championships, are held, I should class, say, Porthcawl and Ganton. I know, of course, that they are a great deal easier, but it is not only that.

We all have individual holes which we can, or cannot, play. In my early days I went for two or three years without taking five at the 4th hole on my home course at Bedford—and it is by no means a 'push-over' par four. On the other hand it does not so much as occur to me that I shall get a four at the 4th at St Andrews, even when my drive, as sometimes happens, leaves me within easy reach of the green. On one or two occasions I have even been putting for a three. 'And three putts, five.' It is indeed an 'umbling game!

21 January 1960

Cold, Wet, but Happy

People often wonder why we continue to play the President's Putter in the first week of January and I think I know the answer. It is true that conditions are sometimes, though not by any means always, appalling—I remember on quite a few occasions playing in shirtsleeves and Rye is then absolute heaven—but the fact is that by coming to Rye in mid-winter we have this wonderful little town virtually to ourselves. This is a privilege in return for which I myself would put up with any amount of evil weather.

Both from within and from afar Rye appeals more strongly to my own emotions than any comparable place in the world. It has no counterpart. Seeing it from the links, you realise that you are gazing at a spectacle which has comforted the heart of the wayfarer across the marsh almost unchanged for several centuries. The town is perched on a hill and surmounted by the same square-towered church that was there when the French raided the town and stole the bells exactly 600 years ago this year. I believe in fact that they did it three times and each time the men of Rye sailed across and got their bells back again.

No one should visit Rye without visiting the church. Two blue and gilded figures strike the quarter hours and inside the church a huge pendulum, 18 ft long, hangs down through the roof and swings gravely to and fro above the heads of the congregation. This belongs, believe it or not, to a clock which was put in by a man from Winchelsea in 1561 and still has its original works exactly as he installed them.

In summer the narrow cobbled streets are choked with tourists and cars. In winter we have this little paradise to ourselves—and long may it remain so, even if from time to time we suffer for it on the links.

This year I was abroad when the entry forms came round, so I failed to enter, thus saving myself at least one round of agony, but I can say with hand on heart that I did do my fair share of watching. In conditions which one would have thought would make golf well nigh impossible there was in fact some extraordinarily good play, though how they did it I do not know. The Saturday, with a wind blowing directly from the east, was almost the coldest day that I can remember and weird and wonderful was some of the headgear to be seen, notably on the heads of Crawley senior and junior.

At one time in the afternoon a great darkness descended over the marsh and this turned out to be a fast-approaching blanket of driving snow and sleet. Through it, when it arrived, one had a vision of the town still bathed in pale winter sunlight. Then this too was enveloped and even the most conscientous correspondent could be excused for retiring to the clubhouse.

Of my other memories of foul weather it so happens that no fewer than three are connected with Hoylake, though I am sure this is pure coincidence. The first was the University match of 1929, when the bunkers became flooded and, despite the best efforts of the Hoylake fire brigade, remained so. It was astonishing to see how many bunkers there seemed to be, once they had got water in them.

The two captains, Bob Baugh for Oxford and Eric Prain for Cambridge, held a last minute consultation and made up some rules of their own. Afterwards they were hauled over the coals on this account by one or two weighty traditionalists who held that 'By gad, sir. You play the Rules of Golf, sir,' but I always thought this to be somewhat unfair. After all, the Rules of Golf said stroke and distance for out of bounds, but the local rule at Royal Liverpool said distance only.

At any rate we had our own set of rules for the bunkers. In some cases we were to hit another shot from the original place, in others we could pick out without penalty, and in others we played the ordinary rules. My only criticism years later is that few of us really knew which was which—and that my opponent at a critical stage fluffed twice running into one bunker, picked it out each time and then holed his third! It rankles still!

Seven years later, during Padgham's championship of 1936, we were back at Hoylake in delightful July weather. I forget whether it was the first day's play or one of the qualifying rounds, but the course suddenly became completely covered with snow and play had to be abandoned. I remember it well because I had to do a ten-minute Empire broadcast on play that had not taken place. This did not worry me a bit in those days (it would today!), but I remember that I was in full spout in a little glass-windowed box behind the luncheon tent when a waitress came out with an enormous pile of plates, tripped over a guy rope within a few feet of me, and went down with a crash that reverberated loudly throughout the entire Empire.

Finally at Hoylake we had Thomson's championship of 1956, when it blew half a gale and the rain came down in torrents. We had a television tower out by the 13th, on which our platform had been protected on three sides by some tarpaulin. The gale had swept it away in the night and now we had nothing. I do not know how many hours we sat up there, but it seemed more like days. The scorer, on whom almost everything depends in golf television, did his best, but when we turned the sheets to read the scores they simply peeled away in our hands. In the end we got almost as much sympathy as the players!

14 April 1960

Golf on the Common

I suppose that the principal reasons why I so much enjoy playing golf on the common is that that is, so to speak, 'where I came in'. It was at Yelverton, in Devon, I should hate to admit how many years ago. My parents had gone there for a holiday and stayed in a hotel overlooking a triangle of rough common ground. My father played golf, but I myself so far as I can remember had never handled a club in my life. I was ten years old and there were two other children of the same age in the hotel.

They each had a club or two and they used to go out before breakfast and play three 'holes' on the common. There were, of course, no tees or greens and certainly no flags. Soon I got a couple of my father's clubs cut down by the local pro and joined in the fun. It was a thrill comparable only to riding one's first bicycle and proved later to have determined the whole pattern of my life. My loftiest ambition at that moment was, I recall, to become a good enough classical scholar to pass into the Indian Civil Service. I wonder what sort of job I should have made of it!

Later on I remember having a lesson with the pro at Yelverton and when we came home I had regular lessons throughout the holidays. The game became my abiding passion. Starting rough like this is, I think, a good beginning, for it tends to turn you into a traditionalist. You realise that golf is basically an amusement and that the whole point of it is to start from one point and hit the ball along to another, encountering and endeavouring to overcome all manner of hazards on the way. You did not expect good luck on the way or a decent lie: you were grateful if you got either. You did not feel 'entitled' to a fairway lie on the fairway (there wasn't one anyway) and it never occurred to us to move the ball if it lay in a hole or a hoof mark.

The common still seems to me the supremely 'natural' place to play golf, sharing it with people engaged in other pursuits such as riding horses, shooting bows and arrows, playing cricket and the like. Without mentioning names I should say that common courses are not in such flawless order as many of the better known courses where the club owns its own land. There is more rough to take with the smooth, and that is how it ought to be.

I often think that the perfect order of the best courses is one of the reasons why golf is so expensive. We have become spoilt. We expect fairways good enough to have passed in our grandfather's day for greens, and greens almost good enough to play billards on. A lot of people even expect to get a good lie in a bunker and therefore to have the sand raked. Most American club golfers expect, logically enough, to get a good lie if they succeed in driving on to the fairway, hence the almost universal practice of playing 'winter rules' in mid-summer and indeed throughout the year. It is, as I say, perfectly logical to say 'I have driven on to the fairway and I find my ball in a divot mark. I am entitled to a proper lie,' but I think this attitude springs from the fact that fairways are on the whole so good that a bad lie becomes a rarity. In my own earliest beginnings it was the normal thing and you turned your attention to doing the best you could with the ball as it lay. You wasted no effort in blowing off steam.

The logical 'progress' in golf has been, in my honest opinion, progress in the wrong direction. Given the conception of the game of golf, but no clubs, balls or courses, what sort of game would you create? Would you, for instance, walk 8250 yards, which is the length of most championship courses, including the walks from green to tee, or, say, 6000? Would you create a ball that gave the best players testing second shots with every club in the bag or one which goes so far that on the West Course at Wentworth in summer they often cannot even take a driver from the tee? Would you, having decided on your ball, permit changes in it that altered the architectural value of every golf hole in the world by going farther?

Would you, I wonder, allow so many clubs that a reasonable healthy man found them impossible to carry and became reduced in the end to wheeling them round in a perambulator? Would you, indeed, have 'sets' of clubs at all or would you have individual clubs, as we did when I began, and restore to people the immense thrill of making up your collection one by one? I wonder if younger people have any idea what fun this was—going automatically into the pro's shop when you visited a strange course and trying out mashies and cleeks and jiggers and new-fangled patent clubs for chipping and running-up, and just from time to time finding the object of one's dreams—7s 6d.

This is not, perhaps, such a digression as it may seem, for to tell the truth this sort of golf did exist and I am old enough to remember it. I can think of no better description for it than golf on the common. I would willingly swap it for the expensive and luxurious pastime that the game has become today.

3 August 1961

My Perfect Course

Designing one's composite, or eclectic, golf course has been a favourite pastime with golfers since the game began, but curiously, in the course of effusing what must now amount to several million words on the game in general, I have never done it before. No wonder it is popular. It is the greatest fun in the world. My own was designed during a long train journey with the result that a journey which is normally far from inspiring passed almost before it had begun.

The game is full of both limitations and temptations. One would like, for instance, to design two perfect courses, one seaside and the other inland, but presumably one must mix them up. Then again one cannot know every golf course and one tends from sentiment and experience to develop special favourites. My own are the Old Course at St Andrews and its nearest inland equivalent, Mildenhall, and I would cheerfully take fourteen holes from one and four from the other and call it a day.

I set off on the principle that the perfect course will be made up of four long holes, four short and ten two-shotters of assorted lengths. Of the four long holes I would make two of them really long, where if you miss a shot you are hard put to it to get a five. The other two are what you might call chance-of-a-four holes. Among the four short holes I like to see one long one—a full go with a brassie, say—one very short 'chance of a two' and two of ordinary length. As to the ten two-shotters, these will include a number of very severe par fours and two of the chance-of-a-three type.

I reserve the right not only to switch from course to course but also to change the weather and even the time of year from hole to hole.

Let us start with the four long holes—and if you do the lot in 19 you will have had a good day. We open, of course, with the 14th at St Andrews, on the day of the autumn medal, with the wind against and slightly from the left, strong enough to ensure that you can drive into but not past the Beardies on the left and have to finish in the narrow gap between them and the wall. Indeed the wind is strong enough almost to make it worth while playing the second on the top level, in the Elysian Fields, and perhaps risk everything with a spoon for your third.

Elsewhere I throw in the 14th at Birkdale, again with a strong wind. I once saw Bruen pitch his second on this with a spoon, and still would not believe it if I had not seen it. No one will do it on the day I have in mind!

Now we want two 'par four and a half' holes and here we instantly put in the Road Hole at St Andrews, which stands on my course, as it does there, as the 17th. Mr Tom Simpson says that a great hole is one which begins to operate on the mind of the player long before he comes to it. In this sense the Road Hole is about the greatest in the world.

We want one more of these 'four and a half' holes and after much searching and with many alternatives in mind I take the 4th at Rye at the time of the President's Putter, with a perishing wind nearly blowing you off the high tee in the sandhills, but just enabling you to reach the edge of the green with—unlikely thought!—a perfect drive and a brassie.

Now perhaps for the short holes. It is time we went inland; for the long short hole we go to the 13th of Addington on a fine sunny day with the heather in bloom and a full shot with a brassie soaring up against the blue sky and down through the green background, to land with a plop on the upper terrace of the green and roll down towards the flag. For the very short hole I think we might go to Formby, to the 16th. Not a breath of air ruffles the flag, the green is well watered and we are in shirtsleeves. We tee it well up, knock it off the peg with a seven iron or some such, and, hey presto, there is our putt for a two.

As to the two orthodox short holes—orthodox in length, that is—the 5th at Mildenhall goes in as automatically as the Road Hole. There never was one to beat this, with its diabolically narrow green sloping sharply away on both sides and the green itself like the dome of glass in the fairy tale. On the day we play it there is a fresh wind from the left and the shot is a held-up 3-iron to a target about six yards wide.

Now we have room for only one short hole, and perhaps twenty or thirty candidates for the honour. It shall go to one which possesses that quality which the architects call 'indestructibility', the power to survive changes in the ball and the weather and everything else—the 'Pulpit' at Rye, once the 8th, now the 5th. We play it with the same tremendous left-hand wind nearly blowing us off the tee, and the shot is a 4-iron. Interesting to note that this and the 5th at Mildenhall do not possess a single bunker between them.

Now we turn to the two-shotters, the bigger ones first. What a choice lies before us! Half-a-dozen could easily come from Hoylake, but we will ration that great course to two and take the 1st, that wonderful right-angled dog-leg round the Field, a drive and a spoon today with the wind against off the tee, and the 17th, one of the great finishing holes in golf where the wind has miraculously changed and it plays as a drive and a 3-iron.

We cannot leave out Sandwich, so we will have the 15th, reachable today with a drive and a spoon, and then go inland again for another of the late J. F. Abercromby's masterpieces, the 16th at Addington, one of those holes which is completely useless as a three-shotter, but reaches the heights when you know from the tee that you can just reach it in two.

North again to Lytham, where I take a hole I dislike with the most cordial respect, namely the 8th—about a drive and a five perhaps, with a breeze blowing towards the railway line—another hole which begins to operate in the player's mind, or at any rate in my mind, on walking towards the tee.

From Lytham I dodge back to my third favourite course, Huntercombe, where we find it to be Bluebell Sunday and the whole course is ablaze in the May sunshine. Resisting a temptation to take the 7th for the sake of the view across the Thames valley almost to Oxford, which enfolds itself suddenly as you leave the tee, I take instead the 13th, partly because I think it to be a really great hole, and partly as an excuse to inform the reader that I once did it in two! The green, only about eight yards in depth, is above a steep terrace with a sort of 'spine' facing the player, so that you must approach it deliberately from left to right, dead centre being, broadly speaking, impossible. The second shot, as we play it, will be a 2-iron or spoon.

For the last two medium-length holes I take the 3rd at Mildenhall on a brisk autumn morning with cock pheasants parading the adjacent stubble, and the 1st at St Andrews on the same sort of day with a stiff breeze against the left shoulder. With all the world to drive into, and so get the players away, and the Swilcan Burn waiting to sharpen you up for the second shot, this is the perfect opening hole, and I therefore make it No. 1 on my ideal course.

Now we are left with the two drive-and-a-pitch holes, and after much shilly-shallying I pick first the 6th at Deal at the time of the Halford Hewitt, with a strong wind behind—almost reachable from the tee, although it needs a fluke to stay on the green, but with every kind of hazard lurking on the right and left. And finally another 'indestructible' hole—the 1st at Prestwick. A tremendous wind is blowing and the slightest letting up will see your ball sailing away like a seagull's feather across the down platform of Prestwick station.

Well, there we are. A fine course—but such is the variety of golf, unique among games, that one could at once sit down and construct a dozen equally good. I don't know how long my course is. Nothing, indeed, could matter less. But I do know that if you can do it in my par of 71 you will have a good chance in the next Amateur championship.

My card reads as follows:
1—1st, St Andrews; 2—1st, Hoylake; 3—3rd, Mildenhall; 4—5th, Rye; 5—14th, Birkdale; 6—1st, Prestwick; 7—13th, Huntercombe; 8—5th, Mildenhall; 9—4th Rye; 10—15th, Sandwich; 11—13th, Addington; 12—8th, Lytham; 13—6th, Deal; 14—14th, St Andrews; 15—16th, Addington; 16—16th, Formby; 17—17th, St Andrews; 18—17th, Hoylake.

7 December 1961

Out of the Rough and into the Trees

The first time that the idea of having no rough on a golf course came upon my own consciousness was some time before the war, in connection with the two public courses at Richmond Park. Naturally enough, they attracted a good many novices and it was found, so I remember being told, that a round might take as much as three and a half hours. This was held to be largely on account of people having to look for balls in the rough—as a result of which, and I trust I have the facts correct, some eccentric genius said, 'Why not cut the rough and make it all semi-rough?' As a result of this, play was speeded up and all have golfed happily in the Park ever since.

No great golf course can do without rough, whatever form it may take. On the other hand not many courses can aspire to be great, and very few golfers really aspire to play on a great course. If, as I surmise, Henry Cotton's course in Essex is going to cater for a lot of comparative newcomers to the game, I am entirely in his favour in doing away with the rough.

As a matter of fact, I have held this view for a long time. The truth is that, for the longer handicap player and for all beginners, the game of golf is *difficult enough in itself*. (I could name others, nearer home, for whom it is also difficult enough these days, but that is another point!) Anyway a fellow who finds it difficult to hit a drive straight or more than 170 yards at his best, does not need to find it in a sandpit or thick grass or heather. The next shot is going to be just as difficult as the one before, without that.

A vast number of English courses were laid out 60 or 70 years ago, when the game spread across the country from Scotland. They were designed for conditions and equipment which have long since gone out of date. A reasonable drive with a guttie at the turn of the century went, what—160 to 170 yards? Cross bunkers were set as 'carries' and a fairway 40 yards wide was a big target. Nowadays the expert will drive 280 yards or more, with the result that the 'guttie hazards' do not come into his reckoning at all and his 40-yard target at that range, if my rusty recollection of the theory of equal triangles is correct, is equivalent to a fairway 24 yards wide for the man with a guttie.

To the expert, indeed to any single-figure handicap man, the first 150 yards from the tee simply do not count. With a steel-shafted club anything but a downright 'top'—which from a peg tee is pretty rare—will carry the first 150 yards. On my ideal course, therefore, the first 150 yards would be absolutely clear of any form of hazard or impediment whatever. If a man cannot carry that far, the game itself forms hazard enough.

If I ever became captain of a golf club, one of the first things I should do would be to review the bunkers and, between tee and green, ruthlessly fill in all those which no longer impede the single-figure man. Ask your local 'ace' to describe all the bunkers on your course within 150 yards of the tee and I will bet that he will be completely unaware of at least three quarters of them. He never goes into them. It is probably twenty years since he so much as noticed them. Indeed, one could do worse than formulate a rule to fill in every bunker that the local scratch man cannot identify from memory.

Reverting to the original question, of rough rather than bunkers, the idea of almost eliminating rough is not only nothing new in America but is common practice in the average country club. Generally speaking, you will find that if you miss the fairway you will be impeded not by long grass but by trees. This makes for a certain lack of adventure by our standards but it has much to be said for it. Nothing in the whole world of golf is so tedious as losing your ball. Hunting around in the rough, wondering whether to let the people behind come through, ruining a medal card, losing the hole in a match without even playing it—nothing so completely ruins the fun of golf.

I suppose some of the most 'comprehensive' rough in the world, if that is the right word, is at Pine Valley, near Philadelphia. It consists mostly of forest, in which it would at first sight seem hardly worth while venturing in search of one's ball, yet strangely enough one almost always seems to find it. In this case one does not mind setting about bashing one's way to freedom through the trees and scrub. Better to find it and take three to get out than lose it and play three from the tee.

15 June 1967

Bigger and Bigger, but not Better and Better

When Gene Sarazen (65) and Jimmy Demaret (57) were at St Andrews in the recent past, so it seems, in order to compere a filmed television match, they set out to play the Old Course with guttie balls and a set of pre-1900 hickory-shafted clubs lent to them Laurie Auchterlonie, senior member of the famous St Andrews honorary professional to the Royal and Ancient. I would to have seen this but, alas, it is too late now and all that I can gather about it is that both players needed two full woods to set themselves up to pitch over the Swilcan Burn at the first (374 yards) with their third shots.

Sarazen got safely over, but Demaret's ball pitched in the Burn and for a while was lost. This caused great anxiety, as it appears that they only had one guttie each. All was well in the end, however, when a spectator discovered Demaret's ball some fifty yards down the Burn and floating merrily towards the sea. More than this we do not know, except that Demaret is quoted as saying 'This is the only way to play the Old Course. It is sacrilege to play with steel shafts and a rubber-cored ball.' Whether he meant it, again we do not know. I suspect not!

Be that as it may, it would be a wonderful experience to go back to the guttie and to the wooden-shafted clubs of, say, the twenties, when they still bore their own names and Sarazen had not invented the broad-soled sand iron. One must imagine, of course, that no one possessed anything else nor did they know that in the future they would, in fact, have the clubs we use today. I cannot help thinking that the game would be great fun. You could of course 'do' things with a guttie, such as imparting backspin or cutting it up into a right-hand wind, in a way that is impossible today. On the other hand a bad shot with a guttie and a wooden shafted club was liable to be a complete loss, or so I gather.

I do not, of course, go back to the guttie, but I do remember vividly my first shot with a steel-shafted driver. This was hit right off the toe of the club and would have been a pretty poor effort with a wooden shaft, but with the steel one, the ball, to my astonishment, went perfectly straight and ran a considerable distance. It stung a bit, but it was one of those shots 'as good as a better'. Still, if we all played with the same implements, a bad shot would be a bad shot and we should expect it and know no better.

I have always felt very strongly that golf has grown too big, in the physical sense. With land more and more difficult to come by, people still seem to think it essential to have 150 acres or so, and inter-national architects of courses round which real estate developments are to be based inevitably make them 7000 yards or more because this, to Americans, is the definition of a 'championship' course, irrespective of whether a championship has ever been played there.

One need not go off the back tees, it may be said, but the tees on these courses are nearly always the modern elongated affairs, sometimes as much as 100 yards long, and it injures one's pride, and to me takes a lot of the fun away, to have to go right forward and be made aware at every hole that you are not playing the real 'men's' course at all.

I have for years been in favour of a shorter ball—together, of course, with 'smaller' golf. This will never be permitted, but it is nice to think about it. A shorter ball and smaller golf might in certain circumstances make courses *play* longer, and this really would be marvellous. To take a drive and a biggish iron instead of, say, a 7-iron, and still walk 20 or 30 yards less, would be a joy.

What is now known as a 'bad length' hole, say 320–340 yards, would become a drive and a jolly good iron. We could get a really good long hole or par five (no, no, dash it; bogey five) in 400–440 yards. The longest short hole could be 150–160 yards—and none of these 250-yard horrors rated so optimistically by the golf unions as par-three's—and the shortest could be an intriguingly tricky little job of 120 yards to a suitably small green.

If we had four long holes averaging 400 yards, four short ones averaging 140 and the ten others averaging 350, we should have a course with quite a stiff bogey of 72—yet only 5560 yards to walk: a distance that would be positively sneered at today. Yet what a splendid game of golf that would be, and how cheerfully, after plenty of time for lunch, we should set out on our second round of the day. And later on, perhaps, for nine holes, or a one-club match after tea.

Other advantages present themselves. On the really 'long' courses, say 6300 or 6400 yards from the back tees, even the wretched professionals would get a challenging game again instead of being constantly penalized for hitting the ball farther than other mortals. Round the ludicrously named 'Burma Road' course at Wentworth—so tough, so testing etc.—it is quite common for a player like Peter Alliss to be able to take a driver only three times in the round. Off most of the tees he is playing as though with one arm tied behind his back.

Huge courses lead naturally enough to huge fairways, huge greens and huge expense. Only the other day, by a coincidence, I had a letter from Mr J. Hamilton Stutt, the golf architect, mentioning among other things the extraordinary degree to which these vast courses push up the costs of construction and maintenance. In golf, as in daily life, everything gets bigger and bigger. This does not mean, alas, that it gets better and better.

15 August 1968

Companions of the Links

'The good players get the best caddies'. This, I believe, is not so in America, not at any rate in the big events. I am pretty sure I am right in saying that, so great was the advantage to be derived from a first-class caddie-companion, as I will call him, that the authorities some years ago decided that caddies must be drawn for.

This obviously is the fairer way when so much is at stake—just as it would be fairer if all competitors played with the same kind of ball—but it does to my mind take an awful lot of the colour and personality out of the game.

Over here our smaller and more intimate rota of championship courses, all of which a professional caddie may get to know intimately, and the long tradition of the golfer being accompanied by a caddie from 'Big Crawford' down to a snivelling, hiccupping boy, together have made the long succession of British caddies the most varied and the most eccentric in the world.

Doubtless there have been many exceptions in America and my mind goes at once to 'Stovepipe', the immensely tall negro, so called because of the battered silk hat he was accustomed to wear when caddying, who was carrying for Gene Sarazen when in 1935 he holed his 4-wood second shot at the 15th for the 'double-eagle' that enabled him to tie with Craig Wood and later win the play-off. 'Stovepipe' lent much moral support to Sarazen, to which he pays tribute in what is one of my favourite golfing books *Thirty Years of Championship Golf*, which Sarazen wrote with Herbert Warren Wind nearly twenty years ago.

'Stovepipe', he wrote, 'was a very religious fellow and devoted a lot of his time to church activities. "Stovepipe", I used to ask him, "how are things going?" "Not so good, Mr Gene, not so good", he would drawl mournfully. "Collections were mighty poor today. We done got to win."' But then, just above, my eye catches the words 'I was very pleased with the caddie allotted me . . .' so he wasn't really Sarazen's private caddie after all.

I must not let Gene Sarazen and his book do all my work for me, much as I would like to, but I will venture one other quotation. He and Walter Hagen, 'my rival and my hero', are having a drink one evening in the smoking room of the *Berengaria* on their way to the British Open at Sandwich in 1928—and what a way that was to travel by comparison with today! Saracen has been saying that this above all is the tournament he wants to win before he dies, and Hagen (one can almost see and hear him) is saying 'Gene, you can never win the British Open until you have a caddie like the ones I've had. Now I'll tell what I'll do. I've won the British Open a couple of times, so winning it does not mean as much to me as it obviously means to you. I'll loan you my caddie, Skip Daniels. He's an old fellow, caddies only in the county of Kent, just at Sandwich, Deal and Princes, no other courses. He's very particular about the people he caddies for. It's got to be someone special, like the Prince of Wales or Walter Hagen. Skip expects to caddie for me this year, but I think I can arrange for him to caddie for you instead . . .'

Skip did caddie for Sarazen, who lost the championship with a lunatic 7 at the Canal Hole in the second round that brought tears to the old man's eyes. I will say no more than that the story of how they came together again at Princes four years later and how old Skip, now about 65, really did win the Open for Sarazen is one of the most charming and emotional pieces of writing I have read about golf or any other game.

Caddies have always been one of my favourite topics and one day I may write what Sherlock Holmes would have called 'a trifling monograph' on the subject. Most people go through their golfing life without ever having a caddie, any more than most of us have a chauffeur, but it so happened that, in being lucky enough to play for the University centuries ago, I fell into a way of golf where one did very often have a caddie; starting at Mildenhall, where there was a small coterie of highly individualistic bag carriers, many old enough to be one's father and a couple, Mr Whiffin and the ex-butler, Mr Munns, to be one's grandfather—if they had started early enough, which in those parts they almost certainly did. In playing our Saturday and Sunday matches against London clubs we were generally entertained to a caddie by our opponents, and so the habit grew up.

The more my mind dwells on the miscellaneous selection of boys, girls, grown-ups and veterans of all races and colours who have accompanied me on my golfing way in about thirty different countries all over the world, the more entertaining it occurs to me that my trifling monograph will be. What a dull business it would all have been by comparison, just pulling a trolley or riding round in an electric cart!

CHAPTER FOUR

Club and Ball

23 February 1956

The Rising Cost of Golf Balls

Without knowing the economics of golf ball manufacture one cannot blame the makers for putting their prices up. On the other hand, I have yet to be convinced that the costs of each manufacturer happen to be identical and that some of them do not make much larger profits than others when all sell at the same price. All prices rise by the same amount on the same day, and if this does not indicate a price ring nothing does. Only the manufacturers have the evidence. It would be a good thing all round if they revealed some of it, namely their exact costs and profit per ball. It would be interesting too to hear how they defend the practice of cutting out competition in the way of price. Perhaps I have an axe to grind here. The American-sized ball, which I always use, is now the dearest of the lot at four and sixpence!

If I have not an axe to grind, at least I have a bee in my bonnet. I think the present golf ball makes absolute nonsense of the game. Nearly every course in Britain was designed in days when the architect might assume the ball to go much less far than it does today. The result has been that some courses have been intolerably lengthened to accommodate the ball, while others, for want of money or space, have had to sink back into a drive-and-a-pitch category. It really is too ludicrous. Can you imagine adjusting all the courts at Wimbledon to accommodate somebody's new cannonball tennis ball? Or moving all the football stands to accommodate some new jet-propelled football? I often think that followers of other games must think golfers mad when they see us solemnly adjusting some 35,000 holes to fit one ball instead of fitting one ball to 35,000 holes!

The solution is such a simple one too. Each rise in the price of balls brings nearer the day when the Royal and Ancient might pluck up courage to do something about it and when the manufacturers might be forced into accepting it. At the moment it is they, not the ruling body, who rule this particular roost.

One of the main secrets of the length of the present ball lies in the thinness of the cover—nor would the makers wish it otherwise. Despite any impression I may have conveyed to the contrary they are only human! Their business is making and selling golf balls. At a rough guess I should say that a thicker cover would reduce their sales by not less than half, and if the thought makes them shudder, well, it would make us shudder too if we were in their place. At the moment a topped iron shot, or one of those head-up 'skimmers' out of the bunker, costs you four and threepence—and me four and sixpence. When we top one, we have to go and buy another ball. With a thicker cover we could go on till we lost it. Only the other day, with what I can promise to have been not a very, very bad shot—at least it finished on the green, though amid cries of protest—I not only marked an almost new ball; I actually opened it so that I could get my finger nail right down to the rubber. Four and sixpence is a high price to pay for a shot that finished on the green.

My own opinion is that the latest rise will substantially reduce the sale of golf balls. I may be wrong, but in many ways I hope I am right. I recall how a few months ago all the experts were 'proving' that tea could not be produced at less than nine shillings a pound, or whatever it was, and furthermore that the price would go higher yet. The answer to this, rubbed in every day by the *Daily Express*, proved disarmingly simple. It was—'Don't buy it.' The housewives didn't—and where are the experts now?

The better-off citizens who habitually start a round with a new ball and do not hesitate to take out another when a cut or scratch appears on the first one are, of course, deceiving themselves alive. There have been times when I have done the same, so I do not say this in any spirit of 'holier than thou'. The most humbling performance in this line is to go out with a collection of old balls and practise. Among them there will often be one or two with a monumental great cut in them, totally unfit for play, judged by everyday standards. My own experience of practising is that when you have hit them all there are one or two complete mis-hits, quite close to the starting point; then the main body fairly closely grouped, these being the 'ordinary' shots, not perfect but by no means bad; then one or two rather farther on that you know you hit really well; and finally one, just one, far away out in front in lonely glory. And is this one the best ball in the bunch? Certainly not!

Vanity, vanity, all is vanity, so far as golf balls are concerned. I do not believe that one professional in twenty could tell which ball he was playing with if they all were marked alike. As to club golfers, I do not think one in ten thousand could do so. And I am absolutely sure that I personally could not. Furthermore, if by some optical illusion a ball could have a great cut in it and act accordingly, but the cut itself remain invisible and unsuspected by the player, I do not believe he could tell the difference between playing with this and a new one.

From now on I am using the old ones. One more rise and I go on strike altogether and buy one of those repainting outfits. My word, what fun they used to be, when you come to think of it! I can smell the paint now, as we used to rub it round and round in the palms of the hands. And then we dried the balls on an apparatus of upturned nails, like the things that fakirs sit on in the East.

18 October 1956

The Romance of Old Clubs

If you have anything of the romantic in you, it must be impossible not to be thrilled to the marrow every time you putt with a putter which saw service with Harry Vardon. So I should feel anyway, and I am pretty sure that Cotton feels the same. It represents that element of continuity that is so precious in English life and history. On the other hand, to savour its full appeal, it does seem to me that one needs to have overlapped, by however few years, the lifetime of the owner. Cotton, of course, did so with Vardon. Indeed, he studied at the feet of the master and later became as indisputably the leading figure of his generation as the great man had been before him—and largely by sticking to the same methods to which some of the modern 'shut-face' exponents are just beginning to return today.

I do not, for instance, feel that I should get the same 'kick' out of using a putter which used to belong, say, to Old Tom Morris. Though I can almost convince myself that I knew the old gentleman personally, from seeing so many of his pictures and from gazing so often at his portrait in the Big Room at St Andrews, he did die many years before I was born and I should always feel somehow that a link in the chain was missing.

Yet perhaps I am wrong after all. It so happens that I have just finished a book about the Borneo Company, who a hundred years ago joined the first of the 'White Rajahs' in creating Sarawak. They also at the same time began trading in Siam and it was their manager who introduced Anna Leonowens to the King of Siam as a suitable governess for the children in the Palace. Nothing in the writing of their story has thrilled me so much as to have in my hands the actual letters written by the King in his own hand relating to Anna—what kind of house she was to live in; how much she was to be paid (150 rupees a month was a bit over the odds, he thought); and how she was there to teach the children English, not the Christian religion as the American missionaries tried to do.

The King's knowledge of English was limited but in its way remarkable. If some of the expressions are a little quaint, they are at the same time absolutely clear in meaning and his handwriting is beautiful. It gave me a feeling of smug superiority, as I watched the current film version of *The King and I*, to think that I had had in my possession the real letters of the real King about the real Anna. All of which is not perhaps so irrelevant as it may seem. After all, they were royal and they were ancient.

Reverting more strictly to golf, there is also a strong sentimental appeal in clubs which were never wielded by celebrated hands but form merely a part of our own undistinguished background. Nearly every golfer has a collection of them somewhere. I have a good many in the umbrella stand in the hall. Even this humble item of furniture has for me this same appeal of 'continuity', for it is in fact one of the chimney pots from the original miller's cottage which we removed when turning two rooms into one for our bedroom. Now, in addition to umbrellas, shooting sticks, one tennis racket, one cricket bat and one .22 rifle, the miller's chimney pot contains various putters which have been pensioned off, not perhaps in disgrace but at the best in semi-honourable retirement. Just poking its head over the top of the chimney pot is the short-shafted one with the patent lump of lead on the back, which alas was with me on the day my dreams came true, when impossible shots from divot marks flew like arrows to within a few feet of the flag and a full brassie shot, almost given up for lost, was found to be sitting on the green, waiting to be holed for a three. No such series of flukes and good fortune will ever come my way again. If I had only been accompanied by a moderate fourteen-year-old entrant for the girls' championship to do the putting, I might have won the . . . well, never mind what might have been. I'll never win it now.

To handle some of the clubs with which deeds of great renown have been performed in the past is, or should be, a humbling business for the young golfer of today. One in particular I have in mind is one which anyone who visits the Royal Lytham and St Annes course can handle for himself—the mashie iron which Bobby Jones used for the shot from the bunker at the 17th virtually to win the 1926 Open. It hangs in the hall and very sensibly, as I take leave to think, they do not attach it thereto, so that anyone can take it down and waggle it.

One feels at once a sense of awe, not only at waggling a truly historic club but at the skill which was required to wield instruments of this kind by comparison with the steel-shafted matched sets of today. Jones's shot from the open bunker must have been upwards of 170 yards. How many people today could hit the ball 170 yards with that club off the fairway? I remember the same feelings on handling the driver with which he won his Grand Slam, which is now in the museum of the Royal and Ancient Club. Beside it is the driver with which Harry Vardon won the last of his championships, with a thickish grip and a tiny head.

What fun it would be if one could assemble enough sets of authentic hickory shafted clubs and set the professors playing a tournament with them. By the time they had finished the scores of thirty years ago would take on a new meaning!

3 April 1958

Something Borrowed

To arrive at a golf tournament without one's false teeth is a splendid and memorable thing to have done, and my immediate thought is that the individual who did it possessed at any rate one subsequent advantage. He couldn't gnash them! Apart from that I feel that the exploit deserves to be brought to the notice of the Purchasers' Club—that exclusive membership-by-invitation body composed of people who have 'bought it' in ways both great and small. Incidentally, a list of Purchasers and how they bought it would reveal some most illustrious names and some more than anxious exploits.

As to forgetting the more ordinary forms of golfing equipment, I suppose we have all done it in our time, though I must confess that I myself suffer the more painful form of amnesia; that is, not forgetting to bring them with me, but forgetting to take them away. The locker rooms of the world are positively littered with waterproof clothing, shoes, pullovers and the rest of it, which I have not only left, but forgotten where I left them.

One of the finest bits of forgetfulness was that of the present captain of the Royal and Ancient, John Beck, who went down to Sandwich to play in the Open some years before the war. It was only when prolonged search failed to reveal his name that it occurred to him that he hadn't entered.

For myself, having had the good fortune to travel the world pretty widely, I have played with all manner of borrowed clubs in all manner of circumstances. In fact over the last six months I dare say I have played as many rounds with other people's as I have with my own—and often a good deal better. As a result I have come to the conclusion that, while we all have individual likes and dislikes, there are certain forms of club which indisputably make the game easier—or at any rate less difficult—for everyone.

It is also certain that many people make the game as difficult as possible with the clubs they already have, however fond they may be of them. The number of times, for instance, in which I have been given a set with impossible grips is quite incredible. Miserable little things hardly thicker than a fourpenny cheroot; hard as iron and with a highly polished glaze on the surface. Even with a left-hand glove (which to me is indispensable with any club), together with a good deal of moistening of palms and rubbing up and down, it has been quite beyond my power to hold on to some of the clubs I have been given—often by their proud owners, so that rejection becomes out of the question.

The most important clubs, of course, are the driver and the putter, the alpha and omega of golf. Next I should place the 4-wood and the 9-iron. After all, you are going to take the driver for a certainty fourteen times and each time under ideal and exactly similar conditions. Fourteen drives somewhere in play can 'make' your round. And the putter you will take, let us say, twenty-seven times—that is allowing nine conceded putts, where the club does not matter. So here we have two clubs accounting for fifty shots. It is indeed worth taking some trouble to get these two right—never mind the other twelve, which are about six too many anyway.

For myself, never having had any difficulty about getting the ball 'up' though a lot in keeping it down, I prefer a deepish, straightish-faced driver and a suitably elevated tee, but in the maid-of-all-work, the 4-wood, I am as convinced as I am of anything in golf that nearly all of them ought to be shallower in the face, and smaller in the head too, so as to fit into small depressions and make it as easy as possible to get the ball up. The average brassie today is little more than an excuse to sell an extra club and can profitably be left at home. As to the putter, I personally prefer the brass-headed, nearly centre-shafted type used by so many professionals on both sides of the Atlantic.

Another test too which I immediately put the borrowed set of clubs is 'Are the irons *sharp*?' Some of the older sets—among them the original Bobby Jones model, the ones with the yellow shafts—have soles as sharp as razor blades. The slightest touch on the ground, except with a full shot, and you are done. Similarly I cannot stand the short irons, say the 8 and 9, with noticeably rounded, or 'scoopy', soles. To me they spell disaster.

Finally, though I think it ought to be banned, the club now known generally as the 'wedge'. Given a good one—and they make some very good ones now, though none to approach the one I was given by

Charles Lacey at Pine Valley twenty-one years ago this year and still cherish—you are presented with the easiest shot in the game, whether you are scratch or 24. Yet some of the bludgeons I have found in borrowed sets—they are clubs indeed. But not golf clubs.

6 August 1959

A Few of my Favourite Clubs

In the old days, when a man broke a club, it was almost always described as his 'favourite driver' or his 'favourite mashie'. I never could understand this, for it presupposed that he had a whole umbrella-stand full of drivers and mashies, which, of course, he hadn't. Nevertheless everyone did tend to have one club in his bag more favourite, or perhaps one should say more faithful, than the rest.

This belonged to the Golden Age of golf, when clubs were individuals and had names of their own and were lovingly collected, one by one. It coincided incidentally with the Golden Age of motoring, which I also had the luck to experience, when a supercharged 4½ Bentley would whine across Newmarket Heath at 110 and only a tenth of the present cars were on the road.

No one who did not experience those days could possibly appreciate what went out of the game of golf when clubs became known by numbers and were sold in 'sets'. There was no such thing as a standard set. Your own set was simply what you happened to carry in your bag. There was always therefore the thrill of going into a pro's shop, anywhere you happened to play, picking out odd clubs and waggling them, finding an obvious treasure, resisting temptation and walking away, only to return and add it to the set.

It was inevitable that some clubs were on better behaviour than others and kept their place through the years, often lingering on into the steel-shaft era, which began in 1930, as the only hickory-shafted club in the bag. Among the most common 'favourite clubs' were those maids-of-all-work, the jigger—a lofted, very shallow-faced iron, useful for running-up and for nipping the ball out of the rough or bad lies in general—and the baffy, which corresponded to the newly discovered No. 5 wood. I preserved a devoted friend of each species.

The putter is the only club which has survived through the years as a singleton. Putting, they say, is a game within a game, and the putter is a club on its own within the set. People with handicaps of 18 or more will cheerfully buy a set of irons from 2 to 9 (for a sum in excess of £30, when they would be far better off with only four), but you rarely see anyone take a 'matched' putter as well. Putters do not 'match'. They are the last remaining eccentrics in the conforming society of golf.

So for that matter, in many ways, is Max Faulkner and, if only for this reason, I was delighted to see him finish a barren and disappointing year in a blaze of consolatory glory in Ireland. I can well imagine the inspiration that it gave him to hold in his hands again the old discarded but ever-faithful friend. 'The others may complain of the greens and not be able to putt for toffee.' I can imagine him murmuring to it, 'but you and I can'.

Among those who declare that the first cure for a spell of bad putting is to change the putter is the last American Ryder Cup captain Jack Burke, and I profoundly and respectfully agree with him. The truth is that we all have different styles with different putters and are liable to get bound up by a particular method, till we forget that putting is really quite a simple matter if you don't do too much thinking and get stuck. The obvious proof of this is the free and easy way by which you hole the putt 'second time'. No trouble at all.

A new putter, or a very old one long discarded for that matter, seems to produce not only a fresh and more elementary method but a simplified mental approach. One seems to remember again that the object is to strike the thing along towards the hole with two hands—instead of to keep the forearm in line with the shaft, or put the palm of the right hand towards the hole, or not to hold on too tight with the left hand, or whatever item of mental clutter had caused the final seize-up with the other club.

Thus, while nearly all the best clubs these days are roughly of a pattern, putters still vary to a remarkable degree. Numerically, I dare say the most popular is the one known in America as the Bull's Eye and in this country as the Golden Goose, though even these vary remarkably in weight and lie. The best holer-out of them all, on the other hand, Bobby Locke, uses an ancient rusty-bladed, hickory-shafted affair with a long shaft.

Experiments a few months ago led me quite seriously to suspect that with practice the most lethal weapon of all was Mr Gillespie's T-square, though it bore no relation to the traditional form of golf club. This was used pendulum-fashion between the legs with what, if you come to work it out, is the only true pendulum movement possible in the human frame.

The inventor, assured by the Rules of Golf committee that the club was in order, insured for £1000 with Lloyd's against their changing their mind. Within a matter of months they did so. Mr Gillespie, very properly, collected his thousand smackers, while I was robbed of the only weapon with which I have ever been reasonably dead from three feet.

2 March 1961

The Right Set

I have not the slightest doubt that *some* old clubs hamper one's golf. I have in mind in this connection a very old friend, an intermittent player but sufficiently keen to have had a single figure handicap and to have long been a member of one of the 'Royal' clubs in Lancashire. Being now possessed of a certain amount of leisure, he has taken to the game again with increasing keenness. When we last played, I noted that he was using a set of irons which he must have had for the best part of thirty years and which in my opinion were, by modern standards, virtually 'unplayable'.

With great respect, I do not think that the design of wooden clubs has improved at all since the war, partly perhaps because the designers had got them right already. The only exception is that, with four wooden clubs comprising a standard set instead of three, the brassie has gone virtually out of business, especially with the American influence causing manufacturers to forget that to hit a small ball off a close lie requires a much shallower face than to hit a large one off a lush lie.

Equally I have no doubt that the design of iron clubs has improved. Many readers will be old enough to remember the first irons put out under Bobby Jones's imprint when the great man turned 'businessman golfer' after his Grand Slam in 1930. They had light yellow shafts and the leading edge of the sole was almost as sharp as a razor. You had only to touch the ground with a chip shot and, unless you were prepared to grip like a vice, you had 'had it'. My friend's iron clubs were of this kind and it gave one the twitch even to have them in one's hands. You cannot buy an iron shot in the professional's shop, but at least you do not have to make golf as difficult as this! I am glad to say that he has now invested in some clubs with reasonably blunt soles. At least he now gives himself a chance.

I should not like to offend my manufacturing friends by saying that golfers change their clubs too often. On the other hand if you have got clubs with which you can from time to time play the best shots of which you know yourself to be capable, it must surely be both a luxury and a folly to change them. In 1930 I had a set of wooden clubs, or rather a brassie and spoon, built to my design by J. O. Lovelock when he was at Mildenhall. The brassie had practically no loft, but an extremely shallow face, equal to the width of a penny, and I could pick the ball up from almost anywhere with it. Occasionally I played with other clubs, but it only served to convince me how superior were my own. By superior, of course, I mean 'less difficult to play with'. I played with them till well after the war and only ceased when the spoon was stolen from the hall of the rectory at Appledore which we had rented for a holiday.

My irons are a set of Tommy Armour McGregor 'Silver Scot', which I acquired on the first Walker Cup tour after the war. I am convinced that they were vastly superior to anything we had in Britain at that time and here I think my old friend John Letters, who was on the same tour, would agree with me. I am equally convinced that he and others make just as good clubs in this country as any in America today. These clubs are miles easier to play with, in my opinion, than any we had before the war, especially the No. 7 and No. 9, by which I judge a set and which are the bread-and-butter clubs of the average golfer.

Before the whole pattern of golf was changed by the well-meaning but, as it turned out, fatal decision to limit clubs to fourteen, thus causing everyone to carry that number when they could do as well or better with seven or eight, one had a much bigger 'turnover' of clubs than today. Part of the joy of golf was to go into the pro's shop, whether at home or away, and waggle a few clubs in the hope of finding one that fairly beckoned to be taken into one's armoury.

I suppose the biggest turnover is in putters. They remain the individualists of the golf club world, and we all rather pathetically cling to the illusion that maybe a new putter will do the trick—or, if not a new one, at any rate a different one.

The only other club that retains a slightly individual character is the driver. I have read that Sam Snead has had the same driver almost for a lifetime and Leonard Crawley has a beautiful specimen which Craig Wood gave him. I fancy that more and more people will come round to wooden clubs with the new bent shaft, which sets back the face of the club to a position exactly below the hands at the bottom of the shaft, but, as for the irons, once you have got a good set, as I have, I am afraid that the likelihood is that you will wear out before they do.

10 May 1962

Changes in Equipment

It so happens that I am writing this in the clubhouse of the Royal and Ancient at St Andrews and I am surrounded by reminders of the fact, in the shape of clubs and balls of earlier days. How anyone hit the ball at all with some of these clubs it is difficult to imagine. In some cases the heads are four or five inches long and it would seem that the ball would have had to be almost teed up to get at it at all. Others have heads hardly bigger than a half-crown. Perhaps these are examples of the 'rut iron', a name which has always fascinated me by its graphic descriptiveness.

Fashions come and go in golf clubs as they do in clothes and often what is hailed as the latest thing is only a revival of what was all the rage fifty years ago. An obvious example is the No. 5 wood, which more and more people are coming to appreciate as the easiest, or perhaps I should say least difficult, club in the bag. This, with its small head and shallow face, is merely the 'baffy' of years ago.

Though some of the extraordinary contraptions which I see beside me in their glass case against the wall will never 'come round again', I think there may well be a return to smaller heads and shallower faces, which make wooden clubs play so much easier with the smaller British ball. After the war many British clubs were direct copies of American. The irons were in many cases magnificent, but American wooden clubs are not, in my opinion, so successful in this country.

They are designed for hitting a larger ball off lush grass and are admirable for the purpose, but only a player with great physical strength and skill can use them on a seaside course with a small ball. The No. 2 wood has become generally regarded as unplayable except from an exceptionally good lie and most people have the sense to discard it or perhaps, having paid rather more than a fiver for it, carry it round without using it.

If clubs were not sold in sets of four, no one I fancy would buy what is in effect a second driver. Few people indeed would have four wooden clubs at all. They would carry a driver, or, for those who have difficulty in getting the ball up, a two-wood together with what are now sold as a three-wood and a five-wood. In my earlier days no one thought of carrying more than three wooden clubs. Nor did many people think of carrying as many as fourteen clubs. The fixing of a maximum number, sensible as it seemed at the time, can now be seen as a wonderful thing for the manufacturers, but a bad thing for golf, in that it created as a standard set of clubs a number greatly in excess of what people would normally carry or buy. This in turn led to huge bags, which are now used by the top professionals as little more than travelling advertisement sites, and finally perambulators on which to wheel them round.

All this started from the moment they decided upon fourteen as the maximum number of clubs, whereupon it at once became the minimum as well. Incidentally Tony Torrance was telling me only recently how it all began when he and another member of the championship committee happened to be at Pine Valley in, I think 1936, together with two members of the US championship committee. They noticed a caddie staggering under a load of about thirty clubs, which they thought, reasonably enough, to be ridiculous. They turned themselves into a quorum, so to speak, and determined to set about influencing the R and A and the USGA to impose a limit. One suggestion was twelve clubs. Bobby Jones suggested sixteen. In the end they settled for fourteen.

As to golf balls I do not think we shall see many changes for years to come. The bigger ball is now 'dead', so far as Britain is concerned and I am sorry because I feel that the Rules of Golf committee were right in thinking that people would have found it more enjoyable to play with. Practically no one seems to have given it a real trial. Nearly everyone I know who has played a good deal with it prefers it to the small one.

If a way is discovered of making the present ball go even farther, I imagine that the committee would clamp down upon it to prevent courses becoming more 'unbalanced' than they are today, at any rate for good players. What we really want is two kinds of ball, the present one for most of us and a shorter one for the experts, which would make the second shots play as the architect originally designed.

3 March 1966

Equipment of the Future

It seems clear that clubs and balls must remain *basically* the same, since their form is so clearly laid down in the rules and both the Royal and Ancient and the United States Golfing Association are so obviously determined that it shall remain so. Variations in clubs are, of course, more easy to control than variations in the ball, since the latter are invisible to the naked eye. With millions of dollars involved eventually in the difference of a single stroke in a major tournament it is natural that rumours should allege the use of balls slightly heavier and slightly smaller than the law allows, on whichever side of the Atlantic it may be. Indeed, I was shown one which had been used in an international match and which, when tested, was both heavier and smaller than the law allows. I will not, however, create a 'sensation' by saying who used it and when.

Every ball maker all over the world, according at any rate to the advertisements, makes a ball which goes farther than everybody else's (except when hit by me) and from these claims we may fairly assume that, whether or not they are succeeding in making the ball go farther, they are at least trying to. The more they succeed, the more completely they change both the game and the courses on which it is played, especially by the better, and therefore longer, players.

A friend has just sent me a specimen of a ball made in America which is 'made of a form of plastic which cuts out all question of winding and soft core centres: you can cut the ball right through, as one would cut a piece of cheese. It appears to have much greater length—I would say 25 per cent—than the conventional ball . . . The great advantage to the average golfer, apart from the extra length, is, of course, that you cannot cut through the skin.' If this ball does what my friend suspects, then it will clearly alter the present character of the game and I am venturing to send it to a member of the Rules of Golf committee.

Another new ball promised within the next few months when a new plant will have made an economic price possible, is also claimed as a 'breakthrough'. This is to come from the Crookshank Company, controlled by a well-known Kenilworth engineer, Mr J. H. Onions. As I gather, one of the secrets is to cause some 50,000 air pockets to form between the elastic threads, while another is to have the weight nearer to the outside than to the core, 'thus giving a gyroscopic or flywheel effect giving increased stability during flight and much better putting characteristics on the ground'. I have studied the very well produced booklet with care but some of it is naturally over my head—which does not make it any less good sense for that!

It interests me, for instance, that 'adding weighted material to the rubber mix greatly increases the internal hysteresis of the ball'— which is a bad thing, by the way. Hysteresis sounds like a particularly nasty operation but my dictionary defines it as 'magnetic friction in dynamos, by which every reversal of magnetism in the iron causes dissipation of energy'. Now I know what has been wrong with my iron play all these years. Hysteresis!

Mr Onions is also the inventor of the semi-pneumatic 'Geodetic' grip, which 'gives' a little in the hands and is calculated to restore some of the torsion, or twisting of the shaft, which occurred when one hit the ball with hickory-shafted clubs. Those ancient enough to have played with hickory will remember vividly the harder, torsion-less feel of their first shots with steel. (*Geodesy*: A science whose object is to measure the earth and all its parts on a large scale. *Geodetic*: Pertaining to or determining by geodesy.)

Anyway, one cannot but agree with Mr Onions that, whatever the quality of modern grips—and I am sure it is very high—their lasting qualities leave something to be desired and they seem constantly to need filing, or a dose of castor oil, to keep them in condition. Mr Onions found the answer to a 'sympathetic' but not 'squashy' grip (the words this time are mine) 'by employing a principle based on the Pneumatic Formula V_1, P_1, V_2, P_2. (V=Volume, P=Pressure). To interpret, this means that by compressing air or gas to half its volume, you double its pressure and conversely, if the pressure is halved, the volume is doubled.' I should have thought it would be a case of V_1, P_2=V_2, P_1. Anyway it is a jolly good grip.

Mr Onions also invented the Crookshank woods, with which I have played for some years and for which in my opinion he should be knighted. When the principle of the 'bent' shaft was first introduced by the Castle Company at the Centenary Open, it struck me immediately that they 'had something'. The bent shaft cannot be appreciated until you lay the club behind a ball, when you immediately become conscious that here at long last the face of your wooden club is exactly where you have wanted it all these years—directly in line with the shaft. I saw that this really was, as I thought at least, a breakthrough, because I remembered Hogan, who probably took as much trouble about the design of clubs as any man who ever lived, saying that he was always 'trying to get the face of his wooden clubs *back*.' In the end the only way you can get it back to the line of the shaft is to 'kink' the shaft somewhere or other. Mr Onions has done it almost invisibly, down by the neck of the club.

If I have pulled his leg about some of his long words, let me say in return that his wooden clubs, exquisitely produced and already popular in the States, cured *instantly* a slice I had had with me for forty years. Here, if ever there was one, is a tribute from the heart!

CHAPTER FIVE

Games We Play

The Most Sociable Game

How appropriate to be writing about the camaraderie of golf during Halford Hewitt week, when the gay companionship that makes the game unique is to be enjoyed in its highest form! There is nothing quite to touch 'The Hewitt', as it is widely known, and I believe that most of those who play in it would rather cancel their whole summer holiday than miss it.

Before the war—and a generation is rapidly arising which thinks you something of an old fogey for using the term, its members being as little interested in such times as I used to be when people reminded me that beer 'used to be 2d a pint before the war', meaning of course the 1914 war—anyway, before the war a man who lived a fairly liberal sort of life had opportunity after opportunity of meeting his friends, whether at sporting events, or at any of the half dozen clubs to which he probably belonged, or at the popular restaurant or evening haunt of the day, or on golfing weekends and suchlike.

Those days are gone. Taxation has cramped and confined the roving spirits who now, since we are talking of spirits, find it cheaper to entertain at home. In some of the old haunts, so much enjoyed in the past, you can look around a crowded room and find that not only is there no one you know but there is no one you want to know.

So when a fellow realises that there will be more than 600 congenial persons gathered together under one roof for the Hewitt, he gives the office a miss, come what may, and makes the most of it.

The Hewitt, of course, turns golf into a team game. Normally I should be the first to admit it to be an individual self-centred affair like most other things in life, but here at Deal it really is our old friend the 'team spirit' *in excelsis*. Ten-a-side, and all foursomes— and is there a man born who has not whispered to Providence a small prayer begging that he may not be left with a four-footer on the last green with the fate of the entire team depending on it?

This is not the place for a long digression on the virtue of foursome play, but if you want the camaraderie of golf at its best I think you will almost certainly find it in a foursome. To share a ball with a fellow in the Hewitt, the University match, tournaments like the Sunningdale Foursomes, or for that matter with a woman partner at Worplesdon, gives you a fellow feeling that no amount of fourballs, however successful the result, could ever match. This theory is fortified by looking at the opposite end of the scale, the fourball at an average American country club, in which all four hole out at every hole, their scores being marked down by the caddies, the whole infinitely dreary business taking a minimum of four hours and being one of the greatest wearinesses of the flesh ever voluntarily imposed upon man in the name of recreation.

'Is golf,' I am also asked, 'alone among games in having such a friendly atmosphere?' On the whole I should think it probably is—not, I hasten to say, because golfers are more friendly persons than players of other outdoor games, but simply because the game itself offers more opportunity for friendly contact. The game which offers least, I should have said, is cricket. Like anyone else, I used to be compelled to play at school—not wholly without success, I should like it to be known!—but it always struck me as the *loneliest* game in the world, at any rate when one's side is fielding, which is approximately half the time. No one to talk to, and no certainty of there being anything for you to do.

In golf your side is batting, as it were, all the time. You are always 'in'. Furthermore, unless things are desperate, you enjoy personal contact with both partner and opponents all the time. So much so that there is no more infallible way of judging a fellow than by playing golf with him.

Among sports, as against games, I always thought rowing to be the least sociable, at any rate at the University, where rowing men cut themselves off from all human kind, spending their lives in hard training till the great evening when they emerged to set the college courtyard on fire and get monumentally intoxicated on three unaccustomed pints of beer.

No. I think that whatever else you may say about golf, it must be admitted as the most sociable and most friendly game in the world, if only for the fact that anybody can, and does, play with anybody else. You may meet Joe Davis, but you really cannot play snooker with him, since no handicap that he can give you would be enough to make an enjoyable game of it for both. You cannot play cricket with Hutton or tennis with Sedgman or football with Stanley Matthews, but you can play, any day of the year, with Henry Cotton or Joe Carr, and not only have an enjoyable game but, if you are crafty enough and persistent enough on the first tee, actually take their money. I once won eighty Belgian francs off Cotton and for a long time kept it with the intention of having it framed!

Furthermore you can start golf as the most junior pupil of the Golf Foundation and go on playing till you are over eighty—if you get that far. You can play with older people, younger people, and your own contemporaries. You can play with the expert or the novice, with men or with women, with amateurs or professionals, in this country or (now) almost any other in the world, and you can do it by the sea or on heaths or moors or the downs, often amid some of the finest scenery in the world.

Not a bad game in fact. Not a bad game at all.

14 October 1954

The Art of Foursomes

In America anyone suggesting the playing of a Scotch foursome, as they call it, would render himself liable to be certified. In Britain every club golfer goes on record as saying that the foursome is the 'best form of golf', while at the same time going to great pains to avoid playing one. Nevertheless, when the occasion is right, I very much doubt whether there *is* anything to beat a foursome.

To me, all inter-society matches are best played wholly by foursomes, if only for the fact that you can play four rounds in a weekend with a different partner every time and, if the captains are astute, against different opponents, thus getting the best of all worlds. All international matches that orginated in this country, and the University match and such like, are played partly by foursomes, while institutions like the Moles and the Match Club and indeed, as far as I know, all similar dining clubs play all their matches by foursomes. Some clubs also have a reputation for encouraging foursomes. Royal Wimbledon is an example and doubtless there are many others. So there must be something to it after all.

Strangely enough the best of friends do not always make the best of foursome partners. The late Eric Martin Smith and I played all through one year as partners and won our match against Oxford and then played nearly all through the next year. In the end we had to ask to be separated. We knew too much about each other. I knew that he knew that I was always liable to slice. And he knew that I knew that at any moment he might do a quick hook!

In the last Walker Cup match, White and Carr, a successful combination of the previous match, begged to be put together. If I had been captain this alone would have caused me to split them. Nor would I have played the two Scotsmen together. Put them each with an Englishman and thus goad them into going flat out to uphold the honour of Scotland. And if they rather disliked their partners, so much the better! (None of which shall be deemed to be due to playing for six years in the Halford Hewitt with John Morrison!)

Having played innumerable foursomes, not without past success, I have concluded firstly that there is a considerable art in foursome play as distinct from all other forms of golf and, secondly, that once you appreciate this you can play a great deal more effectively in a foursome than by yourself.

Perhaps the principal art is in ruling out emotion. Call it hardening your heart, if you like, though nothing unfriendly is implied. This leads to the classic foursome injunction: 'Never apologise'. As John Beck has said, 'I take it that my so-and-so is trying, until proved otherwise'. To 'Never apologise', my own foursome philosophy adds logically: 'Never praise either.' We can do all that during the post-mortem.

We are playing together and you put our tee shot at a short hole into the bunker. What should you do? The answer is: 'Absolutely nothing'. I have only one thing in life at this moment: to do the best I can with a bunker shot. I am good enough to have a vague chance of giving you a putt for a three, but not good enough to do so if anything intrudes on my mind during the process. To put it bluntly, I am not interested whether you are 'sorry'. For heaven's sake we did not expect to get round in 68 flawless shots. Still less am I interested in the thought that you 'thought you could get up with a 4-iron but ought to have taken a 3'.

Perhaps I don't get it out very well, in which case your own little world is filled, or should be, exclusively with the prospect of a putt which is rather longer than the one for which you had hoped. Are you really interested at this moment in hearing that the sand was 'a bit softer than I thought it was going to be?' Or perhaps, as you lean down behind the putt to study the line, you look up to find me leaning down and peering at it from the other end. Believe it or not, I have seen top-class professionals doing this in the Ryder Cup match!

There are two reasons why you can do yourself better justice in a foursome than alone: one physical, the other psychological. The physical reason is that you only have half the number of shots to play, and, by short cuts, a great deal less far to walk. And, of course, half the number of shots to *worry about* leaves you with extra resources—provided you do harden your heart and do not worry about your partner's shots. I remember analysing this at Sandwich one time. My partner drove down the middle. I put him on the green with a 5-iron and he laid the putt dead. I drove into play at the 2nd. He put it on the green and I putted. Never mind whether it was dead or not. That was his worry. We had two perfect fours, to which my contribution was one drive, one 5-iron, and one putt. And since he played a good tee shot, all I had at the short 3rd was another putt.

Psychologically, anyone can do better as the hero coming to rescue his partner from trouble than getting himself out of trouble of his own making. How much easier to hole a five-foot putt left short by your partner than the same putt left miserably short by yourself.

One could go on about foursomes for ever, but I must leave space for a word about the most enjoyable form of all, which is mixed foursomes. The ancient joke used to be of the man found alternately playing and kicking his ball, who was 'practising for the mixed foursomes'. Alas, that is a little thin nowadays. At Worplesdon every year many a male has to face the awful truth that he and this slip of a girl have gone round in fewer than he could have gone round in by himself.

16 May 1957

The Professionals Can't Play
to Their Handicaps Either

In the bad old days every club used to fix its own bogey and many were the absurdies that resulted. Local clubs would steadily raise their bogey to indicate that their course was a tougher proposition than that of the club next door, while Gleneagles, by cheerfully setting the bogey at 80—the only one in the country, I believe—sent the customers home positively delighted at having done 'three successive rounds under bogey'. It was all innocent fun and did no one any great harm, but the case for having some common standard by which all bogeys should be fixed as logically unanswerable and the four national Unions were invited to go ahead and do it.

They devoted a tremendous amount of work to it and, perhaps as a result, produced a scheme which, while excellent in theory, was so complicated that no club within my own experience has ever strictly applied it. It did, however—and in its amended version still does—possess one major and indisputable drawback as a method of handicapping club members. The bogey was to be fixed on the basis of a first-class player *playing in conditions in which, broadly speaking, the handicap club player never plays*—namely, from within 6 feet of the back of the back tees, all holed out, in fair conditions of spring and autumn, without wind.

If that seems rather a challenging statement, may I ask any club golfer who may read this: 'How many times a year do you, sir, play from within six feet of the back of the back tees, all holed out?' In many cases the answer must surely be 'Never!'

For years I have contended that practically no one really plays to his handicap. Put in another way, are the *majority* of the scores in a Stableford competition in your club a stroke or two either side of 36, as they ought to be? Anyone who scores 26 in a Stableford is *ten shots* worse than his handicap!

An entertaining tournament at South Herts—and a more representative club you could scarcely find—seems to prove the point. Playing with the captain, Mr Ronald Baird, Dai Rees went round in 70 and ninety members tried to beat him. Those of 60 years old and over played off the ladies' tees (quite 'wrongly' of course, for their handicap should allow for any shortcomings attributable to advancing years); the 45's and over played from the middle tees; and the under-45's played from the tees from which all handicaps are meant to be based. The day was dry, the course fast, and the greens good, but there was a bit of wind.

And what happened? Oh dear, oh dear! One over-60 beat Rees with a net 63. Two tied at 70—one from the ladies' tees and one from the middle. Two more tied at 71—also one from the ladies' and one from the middle—and Mr Baird, hats off to him, had $79-7=72$ from the 'proper' tees. Discounting the four members who beat bogey from the 'wrong' tees, he was the only one of the ninety to play to his handicap. Of the rest, thirty-nine couldn't play to their handicap from the right tees, thirty-three couldn't play to their handicap from the middle tees, and twelve, let it be whispered, couldn't play to it from the ladies' tees!

And now, having 'taken the mickey' out of the members of South Herts —and it would be interesting to know whether any club would back its members to do any better—let us turn to more distinguished victims.

The full impossibility—I will not say absurdity—of golf handicapping according to the strict standards laid down is revealed by the professionals, who really do play under the appropriate conditions; from the back tees, all holed out, in fair conditions of spring and autumn. Of course conditions are not always fair. On the other hand they are sometimes fair conditions of summer, which are presumably easier than spring or autumn. I take as an example, because I have the figures handy for reference, the Open championship won by Hogan at Carnoustie. The scratch score at Carnoustie is 74 and the weather was good throughout. On the basis by which the club golfer is meant to be handicapped, I was able with malicious glee to announce the following handicap:

Plus Three	..	Hogan.
Plus Two	..	Rees, Cerda, P. Thomson, Stranahan, Vicenzo.
Plus One	..	King, Locke, Alliss, Brown.

Scratch	..	Daly, Faulkner, Lees.
One	.. ..	Weetman, Jacobs, Hassanein, Fairbairn, Lester, C. Ward, Horne, Van Donck, Scott, H. Thomson.
Two	.. ..	Mangrum, Panton, Poulton, Sutton, Haliburton, Hargreaves.
Three	.. ..	B. Hunt, Whitcombe, Bousfield, Mills, French.
Four	.. ..	Shankland, Topping.
Five	.. ..	R. Burton, Hunt, McIntosh.

Judging by which, as I added at the time, a scratch amateur should give one stroke per round to Weetman, two to Lloyd Mangrum, Panton and Haliburton, and four strokes a round to Dick Burton. First come, first served. Let the dog see the rabbit!

Does this all prove that present handicapping is a farce? To my mind, certainly not. I think that like many other illogical and at times apparently crazy British institutions, including the House of Commons, it survives the one supreme test. *It works*. I could no more play to my present handicap (which means going consistently round Addington from the back tees, all holed out, in 75) than fly. But then with great respect, sir, nor probably could you! The great point is that our handicaps should be wrong by roughly the same amount and therefore right in relation to each other—and, so far as I can see, they are. Always excepting, of course, the captain of South Herts.

3 March 1960

Games of Endurance

I have never quite seen the point of 'endurance' golf. Many instances are quoted in that invaluable and astonishingly comprehensive publication, *The Golfer's Handbook*—some of them palpably untrue, like the claim of a Mr Robert Coy, of Peoria, Illinois, to have played 246 holes in 21¼ hours, making 51 minutes per round without any stop for rest or refreshment.

Incidentally I never see the name of Peoria without thinking of the late Sandy Herd. You may remember that he did 19 holes in one and the story went that an American was going to present him with a golden putter when he did his 21st. I must have read this story dozens of times. One evening, sitting next to him at a dinner, I asked him about it. He said that in the course of a dinner at Peoria (he could not remember where Peoria was) the man sitting beside him jokingly said that he could give him a golden putter when he did his 21st hole in one. He could not remember who the man was or what he looked like, and, of course, he had never seen him again. Alas for a good tale!

The authentic endurance record would appear to be held by a Mr Stan Gard, a member of the North Brighton Club in New South Wales, who played 256 holes in a day, beginning at 12.55 a.m. and finishing with the aid of car lights at 9.30 p.m.

He is followed by Mr Bruce Sutherland who played the Craiglockhart links, near Edinburgh, continuously from 8.15 p.m. one day till 7.30 p.m. the next, completing 252 holes and walking rather more than forty miles. 'Mr Sutherland,' says the entry recording this feat, 'was a physical culture teacher. He never recovered from the strain and died a few years later.'

For myself I have always been more amused by one-club, and even cross-country, matches. We always used to have a one-club match at Cambridge after playing the Society at Mildenhall. This was enormous fun. The course is roughly triangular and lent itself particularly well to this sort of thing. The one-club course consists of three holes—1st tee to 2nd green, 3rd tee to 4th green, and 5th tee to the 9th green beside the clubhouse.

The whole point of a one-club match is that, while every man can take whatever club he fancies, the members of the teams must play strictly in rotation, so that you may have the man with the niblick driving off and the man with the driver trying to excavate the ball from a bunker.

In the Walker Cup match just after the war I remember that John Beck, the British captain, even got the American team out one evening on the Old Course at St Andrews for a great one-club match—including the dedicated Frank Stranahan. I am sure he viewed it rather on the same lines as laughing in church.

I like the thought of cross-country matches not merely because they are eccentric in an age of too much conformity but because they seem to me to re-emphasise the original purpose of golf, which is merely to start at A and see in how many strokes you can hole out at B, overcoming as best you can what hazards may lie in your path.

I believe they still hold in Ireland the 'Golden Ball' competition, which was started as part of the national festival of 1953. Players start at the first tee at Kildare and hole out on the 18th at the Curragh, a hole of some 8800 yards—for which they advertised a million pounds for anyone doing it in one! The first Golden Ball was won, appropriately enough, by Joe Carr. And what do you think his score was? The answer, amazingly enough, is 52.

A feature of nearly all these cross-country matches is that those who fix a score and wager against it nearly always lose their money. Members of White's Club, for instance, bet in 1939 that one of their number would not hole out from Tower Bridge to the club in 200 shots and a safe enough wager one would have thought. He took his putter, and crossing the river at Southwark Bridge, holed out in 142.

People in Macclesfield bet Mr Stanley Turner that he would not hole out from his home to the Cat and Fiddle, five miles away and 1000 feet higher up, in 200. He was allowed to tee up within two clubs' length. He did it in 64.

Golf, like other games, tends to be taken over-seriously. Let us have a few more of these matches. For a start, what about the 2nd tee at Deal to the 9th green at Princes? Any takers at 50?

26 April 1962

Hidden Extras

Club selection snobbishness brings at once to mind one of the oldest golfing stories about the obstinate old Scottish caddie whose man, despite the caddie's advice to take a spoon, decided at a short hole to take his iron and holed out, whereupon the caddie said: 'You'd have done better with your spoon.'

However, I do think there is a lot of 'snobbishness', if that is quite the right word, in the matter of length in golf. Perhaps 'keeping up with the Joneses' is nearer the mark. It was first brought to my notice when, more than thirty years ago, alas, I used to play with my father. He was a typical enthusiastic but indifferent club golfer and never, if

I remember rightly, reached a handicap of less than 16, which today would probably be nearer 24. We used to play mostly at Bedford, but during the annual family holiday we used to tour the courses of North Wales. Wherever it might be, when we came to a so-called short hole, i.e. bogey three, he inevitably took out his iron. It was a short hole: therefore it must be an iron. Sometimes it was manifestly impossible for him to reach the green with his driver.

Incidentally, he often used an expression which one does not seem to hear today but which I think is rather a loss to the game, since it seems to me so particularly graphic. As he hit one of those half-hit, half-foozled shots with which we are all so familiar, he would say: 'Ach, *smudged him*!' Sometimes he would begin uttering it while the club was still on the down-swing.

At any rate he unwittingly taught me not to be a 'snob' at short holes and I have never been proud since. I do not mind what club the other fellow takes. The other day I cheerfully took a driver to the short 4th at Worplesdon. Of course, swinging quietly, I hit it straight over the back of the green, but I like to think it showed a proper spirit of humility, which was increased when our opponents reached the green easily with an iron. Nevertheless there is a certain amount of useful gamesmanship that can sometimes be practised when the opponent is due to play first and takes out an iron. An audible request to the caddie to 'give me the brassie' puts all sorts of uncomfortable thoughts in his head!

I think the mistake made by innumerable club golfers—but not by me—is that they tend to take a club with which they could reach the flag (but not probably the back of the green) if they hit their best shot with it. A man like, say, Peter Alliss knows virtually for a certainty that if he takes a No. 7 iron it will go X yards and that if he takes a No. 6 it will go X plus 15, or whatever the difference is. The rest of us are not in this happy position. Our shots with the No. 7 alone may vary by as much as 20 yards.

I do not often practise, but when I do I am often impressed by the extraordinary extra length that lies somewhere within me but is practically never revealed. I take, let us say, a 5-iron. The pattern is nearly always the same. Out of twenty balls about three will be a total loss—topped, scuffled or 'smudged'. Sixteen will be roughly in a group, about 20 yards wide and perhaps 15 yards deep, i.e. in the difference between the longest and shortest. And one, just one, will be at least 15 yards ahead of all the others. This one flew painlessly off the club and was hit with no evident force or in any way differently from the others. Yet there it is. That is what it lies within me to do with a 5-iron. All the same, in order to get that distance in actual play I should be a clot if I took anything less than a No. 3.

I know that I am always holding forth on the subject of carrying fewer clubs, but there does, I think, lie a very practical advantage in most of us doing so.

Personally I carry only the odd-numbered irons, and I do find, in so doing, that at least I am never in doubt as to what club to take. 'Can you get up with a seven?' I often find myself saying to myself. 'No, of course not. . . . Would you go over with a three? Yes, easily. Well, that settles it then. It's a five.' In the old days I should have been waving between a six and a five and a four.

I do not so much mind playing bad shots—and it would not matter if I did—but to catch myself playing a stupid one has all through my golfing life made me extremely angry. Taking a 3-wood from a close lie on the fairway and topping it, when you could not have reached the green anyway and an iron would have moved you safely along; or hitting the face of a bunker when a more lofted club would have got you safely out, and so on. And, of course, the worse you are, the less you can afford this form of stupidity.

Nobody could say that my old partner, J. S. F. Morrison, was technically a very good golfer. He hit innumerable bad shots, but in all the years I played with him in the Halford Hewitt I do not remember him playing a stupid one.

14 June 1962

Gambling Golfers

It has been suggested that our younger golfers are spending too much time in the clubhouse playing games of chance at the expense of being out on the practice ground or on the putting green. Is this fair? From my own viewpoint I think not. The only games of chance that I have witnessed, and for the good reason that I was participating in them, have been a few games of poker at St Andrews with, among others, Arthur Lees and David Snell, but they can hardly be termed young golfers and it was certainly not at an hour at which they ought to have been out practising!

Vast numbers of golfers seem to play bridge, though I am not one of them. I decided early in life that bridge was a game to be played very well or not at all and the obvious choice in my case was the latter. On the other hand I am very fond of a game of poker and certainly should not think the less of any young golfers whom I detected engaging in it. There could hardly be a better mental training for match-play golf, in which you have to learn to steel yourself against constantly being disappointed or 'robbed' by your opponent. The feeling of having a full house, aces, beaten by four miserable little twos is very much akin to having your opponent hole a chip when you are lying five feet away to win the hole, and then miss it. In golf, as in poker, the moment you get the 'needle' you are done.

Talking of poker allows me the opportunity of relating the unhappy experience of my New Zealand friend, George, with whom I used to play golf at Cambridge. He came into my room late one night, manifestly intoxicated, and kept repeating 'Four kings and a —— ace. Go home!' It was Guy Fawkes night and he had been playing poker in some rooms overlooking the market square, in which the usual high jinks were going on. They had a jackpot; somebody raised it, George raised it again, and everybody came in, to his understandable delight since he had in his hand four kings and an ace. Life had rarely seemed so good—when in marched the senior proctor with a couple of 'bullers'. 'All those not living in the house— out,' he said. 'Everybody out!' So they all picked their money up and withdrew, leaving poor George with his four kings and an ace. Someone, it appeared, had thrown a firework from an adjacent window and it had gone off between the senior proctor's legs.

However, that is a diversion. I do not know whether the best of our younger golfers practise as much as they should, or as much as our friends from the Commonwealth, who seem to come and steal the bread pretty regularly from their mouths. Certainly it seems to need an absolutely single-minded devotion to duty to reach the top today, but simply hitting thousands of balls on a practice ground will not alone get you there. For the single-mindedness that I have in mind I can think of no more outstanding example than my contemporary and fellow contributor to *Golf Illustrated*, Henry Cotton, and it is perhaps the memory of the slaving away that he went through in his early days which is partly responsible for his annual £100 award to the most promising assistant of the year today.

One thing is certain, that you cannot 'live it up' and reach the top against the tremendous competition that exists nowadays—but then I wonder whether there was ever a time when you could. Vardon, Braid and Taylor were all abstemious men—though I have always relished the remark of Harry Vardon when a woman asked him to sign the pledge—'Moderation is essential in all things madam, but never in my life have I been beaten by a teetotaller.' The only exception is Walter Hagen, to whom wine and song were certainly no strangers in his greatest days. Nevertheless I suspect that an analysis, if ever we could make it, would show that his late nights and extravagances were confined mainly to occasions when it did not really matter to him in the morning. Also he realised that the worst thing in the world before an important event is to go to bed too early, so that you wake early in the morning and start 'thinking'. I do remember him during the Open of 1937 at Carnoustie, when he was doing quite well, coming into the hotel at about one in the morning with some trout that he had been catching about sixty miles away— but then he knew perfectly well that he was not going to win the championship, so why not enjoy a bit of fishing? He would not have been out fishing when he was winning during the twenties!

6 December 1962

'They Didn't See Me, Did They?'

Our American friends, God bless them!, are universal suckers for articles beginning 'Of 825 students tested by Dr Hiram Q. Fizzenbaum, Director of Faculty of Psycho-Physico-Therapeutic-Dynamics at the University of Oshkosh, 43 per cent said that they had kissed a girl in the moonlight before the age of seventeen. . . .' All the magazines are full of them and the readers fairly lap it up.

The eminently readable magazine *Golf* had the bright idea of applying it to cheating at golf and accordingly invited five practising psychiatrists, psychotherapists, trick cyclists or head-shrinkers—

depending on how you view them—to pronounce upon the subject. There were Drs Hoffman, Wertham, Kline, Ellis and, oh blessed and unforgettable name, Salvatore V. Didato.

Dr Hoffman came out with the blinding deduction that golfers claimed lower scores than they had actually effected as a 'status symbol to elevate themselves in the eyes of their friends'. Well, well, we have all done that, but I hardly like to think I was cheating. When he goes on to add, however, that a golfer 'won't, of course, discuss his bad games!' he must, I am afraid be dismissed from the contest. If he believes that, he wants his own head shrunk.

Dr Wertham thinks that high taxation is responsible, since mild forms of cheating in other walks of life, 'such as padding the expense account, ballooning the overtime voucher and sundry other items in common business use are now considered sociably acceptable.' He may have something there.

Dr Salvatore V. Didato thinks that much cheating may be attributed to the perfectionist. 'His children must be the smartest, his wife the most socially acceptable'—so his golf must be the best as well, and if it isn't, he has got somehow to make it appear so.

The premise to all this is that a spokesman for a Long Island club with three (presumably public) courses, accommodating sometimes 1200 players a day, declared that in his experience no fewer than 75 per cent cheat in some way or another—improving the lie on the green after marking the ball; throwing the ball out of sand traps; bending back branches; 'forgetting' one or two strokes on a bad hole; and so on.

One has the impression, however, that he is thinking in many cases of mere breaches of the Rules of Golf, which does not imply what you and I mean by cheating at all. How often, for instance, have you cheated by 'testing the surface of the green', which for some unfathomable reason is contrary to the rules?

On behalf of the alleged 75 per cent it is only fair to say that a large proportion must number themselves among the hundreds of thousands of new golfers who come into the game in the United States and Canada every year, who simply do not know the etiquette and background of the game—and who shall blame them? Most of us were brought up on the inviolability of the ball's position as we find it—'the ball shall be played where it lies'—and, though this has been modified I do not know how many times in the 93 pages of rules, the thought is still in the back of our heads. I am sure that millions of golfers on the other side of the Atlantic have never heard of the expression—and again, who shall blame them?

No, real cheating, as we mean it, is in my own experience extremely rare and almost always, to the mere observer, rather entertaining. Before the war I played once or twice in the annual open meeting at Hythe, and very enjoyable it was, but why should I remember it so well now, when so many equally agreeable meetings have long since faded from the mind? Why, because it was known that one of the competitors was a pot hunter who always brought his own partner and was known to cheat.

The course was accordingly dotted with spies. A chap taking his dog for a walk here, a lady member picking wild flowers there, caddies beating the gorse bushes in search of balls, and such like. Not a stroke was played by the suspect without its being recorded by someone. I forget what score I did myself, but, being in the know, my mind was not, as you may imagine, on my own game, but on the cloak-and-dagger stuff going on in the bushes. And was the man in fact cheating? Yes, indeed—preposterously and gigantically. He was warned off and the competition was never quite the same again.

I have not the slightest doubt, indeed I know, that to a certain class of people too much money at stake (even if they can perfectly well afford it) does promote both active and despicable cheating, i.e. spare ball dropped down caddie's trouser leg through hole in pocket; ball nudged into favourable lie in rough by caddie's boot, etc.; and the application, shall we say, of a different level of golfing morality from that which the wretched man would apply in a friendly game.

Mostly, however, cheating seems to me slightly comical, and none more so than that of a Cambridge player before my day, now no longer with us. He was playing with Dale Bourn in the foursomes against West Hill and at the last hole—I never drive by on the adjacent road without thinking of it—Dale drove him into the bunker on the right, the West Hill pair being away on the left. When Dale got to the bunker he observed his partner busily teeing up the ball in the sand.

'Oh, I say, old boy,' said Dale, or words to that effect. His partner looked up and replied simply: *'They didn't see me, did they?'*

I can write in a certain lofty strain on the subject of cheating, since I am at the moment on the tenth day of my annual starvation cure, which entails no solid food and nothing to drink worth drinking. Almost every day my walk takes me past the inviting portals of the White Hart at Witley, and a small voice whispers: 'They're open.' My conscience, believe it or not, is completely clear.

6 October 1966

Golf's Oldest Joke

It seems odd to think that well within the recollection of the more elderly golfers playing today, women were confined to putting greens or to little courses with holes no longer than 80 yards, since it was reckoned unseemly that a lady should raise the club above her shoulder. The emancipation of women has items on the credit and, I trust it is not ungallant to say, the debit side of the ledger but from the golfing point of view I should unhesitatingly place the mixed foursome on the credit side. I have had some of the happiest days of my golfing life playing mixed foursomes—nor need it be suspected that one of these led to deeper things for my wife, so far as I know, has neither hit, nor attempted to hit, a golf ball in her life—and thank heaven for that!

I do not know which is the oldest joke in the history of golf but I should suspect it to be the one about the man alternately hitting and then kicking his ball and explaining that he was 'practising for the mixed foursomes'. Nowadays it would be more apposite if it were told of the lady player at alternate holes carrying her ball forward, chucking it into the rough and hacking it out from there. On the sort of courses on which the better known mixed foursomes tournaments are held, of which Worplesdon is, of course, an outstanding example, the destructive shots come not from the women but the men.

At Worplesdon, I have heard it said, if you could find a lady with an equable temperament who kept the ball in play and never missed from four feet, you were an almost certain winner. Perhaps that was an exaggeration but I retain a strong impression that when a fancied couple got knocked out it was nearly always the man who had done the damage.

From the male point of view there are certain elementary principles to be observed in the playing of mixed foursomes, one of which is: 'Always, if possible, get your partner to drive from the first tee.' The advantages here are obvious. Firstly, if anyone is going to make a fool of themselves in front of all these people, it isn't going to be you. Secondly, if you hang back long enough to vanish from sight at the critical moment, you will probably find that she has provided a new ball.

Another essential art is to discover which of the opposing pair is going to drive from the first tee. If it is the man, then, despite the principle laid out above, you must drive there too. Never in any circumstances drive against the opposing woman. Supposing, for instance, that you incautiously drove first at Worplesdon and were followed, for the other side, not by the man but by the Vicomtesse de St Sauveur. Our 'Lally' is a slim little thing who looks like someone's just-grown-up daughter but is by common knowledge a grand-mother. She has a rather full swing and does not appear to hit the ball very hard, but is the living embodiment of the old adage that great strength does not necessarily return the penny. All you have to do is to hit the ball exactly in the centre of the club and it will run on and on and on, pitching well short of where the man's pitched and finishing well past where his finished. The man is not born who can refrain from 'pressing' against one like this, and for the rest of the round he is in the heather.

In the earlier days of Worplesdon it was even more necessary to make sure of the order in which your opponents were going to drive, since sooner or later you were liable to come up against Joyce Wethered and one of her succession of partners, and by however much he might outdrive you it was the partner you wanted to be matched against. Miss Wethered in fact, won eight times, with seven different partners—her brother, Roger; Cyril Tolley (twice); John Morrison; Michael Scott; Raymond Oppenheimer; Bernard Darwin; and Hon. T. Coke, now the Earl of Leicester.

Of all these, the most entertaining was 'Bernardo', who suffered from the 'twitch' to such an extent that I can hardly bear to write about it. He had no sooner to take his putter in his hand than it might have been an electric eel. In the end he was reduced to putting with his mashie, bending it almost double and catching it down by the very bottom of the shaft, and even then prodding at the ball with little convulsive jerks. His accounts, day by day, in *The Times* of the progress of Miss Wethered and her partner 'lifting his venerable head' were among the best things ever written about golf.

9 February 1967

The Battle of the Sexes

Golf, they say—and how right they are!—is an 'umbling game. It is 'umbling in all sorts of ways, but in none quite so poignantly as when a man who fancies he can play is beaten level by a woman. There is only one way to make certain that this never happens to you and that is never to play in direct opposition to a competent woman player.

This is a mistake which I made twice, and bitter were these two pills to swallow. Neither, it is true, was in a straight single, but each in a threeball. No amount of airy pretence on my part, however, that we were merely out for the fresh air and exercise could stop the third party from keeping the score and at the end of it I had on each occasion been beaten level.

I ought, of course, to have insisted on conceding strokes, since to be beaten 4 and 3 when conceding two shots carries nothing like the ignominy of being beaten 2 up when playing level. Another mistake I made was in not appreciating in time that my powers, such as they used to be, had already begun to fade.

Some years before the war I remarked in the company of some keen golfers that, if we could play off the very back tees on the New course at Addington, I reckoned I could give pretty well any woman golfer a stroke a hole. This was not quite so boastful as it may sound, as I reckoned that off many of these tees there was nowhere that most women could drive to except thick heather. I was a little taken aback when the others took me up and produced a county champion, backing their man, or rather their woman, with a tenner. She was an awfully nice person, but the match was rather an embarrassment, and I do not know which of us was the more relieved when in fact it ended, quite honestly, in a half.

It would have been no dishonour, of course, for almost anyone to be beaten level by Miss Wethered or Mrs 'Babe' Zaharias, and I imagine the current American 'proettes' would take quite a bit of beating, too. Far and away the most splendid incident in the battle of the golfing sexes happened in 1951. The late Bob Harlow, once Hagen's manager and a shrewd judge of golf, when asked to name the ten most important events of the year, rated it No. 7. This was the match between a team of distinguished amateurs raised by General Critchley and half a dozen visiting women professionals from America. The men playing level, lost all three foursomes— the match was played in mid-summer at either Sunningdale or Wentworth: I fancy the latter—and this really put them on their mettle for the singles in the afternoon. They lost the lot.

Many were extremely touchy about it for some years afterwards, but I trust that the wounds have healed sufficiently with the passage of sixteen years to permit me to recall that my esteemed colleague, Leonard Crawley, holder of the President's Putter, was beaten level by Mrs Zaharias, and among others who fell by the wayside were John Beck, Edward Bromley-Davenport, and of course, the General himself.

A little later I was raising a laugh with Harlow about all this during the preliminaries for the Ryder Cup match at Pinehurst and revealed that I myself was originally going to play in Critch's team, but had to cry off, thus escaping the slaughter. I added blithely that I should undoubtedly have beaten my opponent-to-be, Mrs Betty Bush, and thus in a small way made history. Harlow had not been a lifelong publicist for nothing and I can see now the light that came into his eye. Muttering 'Boy, this is a natural!', he rang straight through to Betty Bush in Chicago, fixed up for her to come to Pinehurst to play the match, and planted the story in all the New York papers. It even appeared, I believe, in some over here.

I consulted the Pinehurst professional. Did he know Betty Bush? Yes, sure he did. I asked with elaborate casualness what she would be likely to do round the No. 1 course (par 71). 'Wa-al,' he said, 'I guess she won't do no better than 72.'

This sent me at great speed to the practice ground where, a minnow among the pike, I stood in line with the Ryder Cup players, receiving sympathetic hints and even a demonstration of the 'long right arm', on my own person, from the great Hogan himself, which nearly put me in the infirmary.

The eve of the contest dawned and by this time there seemed hardly a soul in Pinehurst who did not know about it. At the last moment there came a call from Chicago. Betty Bush had recently had an operation, she said, and felt she really could not make the distance. She was most terribly sorry to let me down.

'Not at all,' I said. '*Not at all*.'

6 June 1968

'Amazing for His Age'

Only a few months ago a friend from Huntercombe, where I used to be a member for some years after the war—and how wonderful it must be looking now, with the bluebells out—told me of Jim Morris, who had retired after spending pretty well a lifetime as professional there, playing against Lord Campbell. They got round in one hour fifty-eight minutes. His Lordship holed the course in 74 and was easily beaten level by Morris, who at the age of seventy-six had a putt for a 70 and just missed.

Incidentally his 'eclectic' score for Huntercombe during his years there is 44. This, however, is nothing like a record. Mr Willie Gilchrist, for instance, has an eclectic for the Gullane No. 1 course, over which it is reckoned that he has played 10,000 rounds, of 36. A stalwart of North Hants, Mr J. W. Nelson, had an eclectic of 40, but his figures for nine consecutive holes from the 8th to the 16th really are something. Here they are: 1, 2, 1, 2, 2, 2, 2, 1, 2—15!

I played in a golfing society meeting a few years ago at Worplesdon with the late Sir Picton Bagge. He was a rather frail figure and can never have been a long player, and as the afternoon round wore on he began to find difficulty with some of the carries. Little wonder, though it was not till all was over that he revealed that he was 83. Then of course, there is the renowned Nathaniel Micklem, QC, one of only two who were twice a QC, starting with Queen Victoria and coming round again, so to speak, with Her present Majesty. He was second cousin to Gerald Micklem's father and lived to be one hundred. He once, at the age of eighty-five, came in from the morning round declaring that he would play better in the afternoon, as he felt he had worked his stiffness off!

It was only a few days ago that I managed to get from Micklem himself the correct story of an historic remark of the old gentleman's, of which I had long been aware. His son was principal of Mansfield College, Oxford, and at the age of sixty-five was compulsorily retired, much to his annoyance. The father, too, was incensed. 'Just when I thought I'd got the boy settled!' he said.

I have often suspected that if you could guarantee to drive 220 yards dead straight and to hole out everything of five feet and under, you could come remarkably near to winning the Open championship, provided that for the other shots you could play to, say, a club scratch. This view seems to be borne out by some of these astonishingly successful veterans. I think, for instance, of Admiral Benson, who carries about seven clubs in an open sort of container dating from, I believe, the last century and which he carries at the 'trail arms' position. A year or so ago he had his handicap reduced, at the age of eighty-one, from 17 to 16, as a result of a round played in quite a stiff wind in the medal at St Andrews, and, of course, from the medal tees.

As to the original question of whether I could see myself playing good golf as an elderly gent, the answer is simple. 'I did once, but I don't now!' I had a handicap of scratch for about twenty years—to attain which, I hasten to say, you did not have to be as good then as you do now. Furthermore, though never long, I was reasonably straight and I did acquire a pretty deadly short game, possibly on account of getting so much practice at it through the deficiencies in my long game. Anyway, if anyone was going to move steadily towards being a really stuffy middle-aged player, still liable to beat undergraduates, it seemed likely to be me. There seemed no reason why my short game should not last—and indeed some parts of it have—so I was the sort of player who might, with luck, proceed serenely along till The Close of Play, widely regarded as 'amazing for his age'.

Exactly when or why this all came unstuck I do not really remember. Perhaps a dozen or fifteen years ago. At any rate when the rot did set in, it put in motion a cumulative process of decay. There is never any great pleasure in doing progressively more badly something that you once did well and I found myself gradually reducing my activities to those occasions when everything was right—the course, the weather, the transport, and, above all, the company. Then, of course, from lack of practice one would get gradually worse, till arriving at the stage of telling oneself to stop moaning and decide either to give it up or take it up. I still have not quite decided.

The trouble is that from time to time, either on the practice ground or in play, I hit what is, within my physical limitations, an absolutely perfect shot. Not often, but sometimes: a better shot, perhaps, than many a 16-handicap player will hit in a lifetime. So I know that, just as the world's most perfect statue exists in every block of granite, so within my portly frame there exists an ability to hit the golf ball which would get me back to a low single-figure handicap again. But what a long road back it would be, like pedalling a bicycle up a long, long hill against the wind. An interesting road indeed— but, alas, I have travelled it all before.

CHAPTER SIX

Great Players and Great Characters

'Brab'

'First of all,' says Lord Brabazon of Tara, in summing up his recipe for happiness on attaining the age of level fours, 'a one-track mind makes you a bore, and to be a bore is the one unforgivable sin. Take to your heart as many subjects of interest as you can, especially if they are original and new. There is so much in life that we take for granted. We are inclined to accept things as of no interest and without curiosity, rather as a cow views a passing train. This is a great mistake. . . .'

If ever a man possessed a multi-tracked mind and was the reverse of a bore, it is Lord Brabazon. 'The happiest man,' said some sage, 'is he who touches life at the greatest number of points.' He might have been thinking of Lord Brabazon, who by this standard must be the happiest man alive.

'Brab,' as everyone has called him for more than fifty years, was in at the beginning of the three great revolutions of our time: the motor car, the aeroplane and the wireless. When he was a boy at Harrow, in 1900, a man came driving down Grove Hill in a motor car, put the brakes on too quickly, ripped the spokes from the wheels, and was killed. It was the first fatal accident in a motor car and Brab was standing a few yards away. He *would* be! While others stood back, thinking the infernal machine would blow up, he stepped forward and turned off the ignition burners. He was the only person who knew what they were. Afterwards he gave a lecture to the school scientific society on the motor car. 'A treasure lost to the world,' he calls it.

Later he gave to his tutor at Cambridge the truthful, if unique, excuse for lateness that he 'had been ballooning'. He still maintains that it is the 'only way of going up into the air like a gentleman. The peace and quiet of it all must be experienced to be believed.' One of the first requisites, apart from the ballast, was an ABC timetable to help you come down near a place from which there would be a train home. They got special rates for balloons on the railways in those days and Brab has often told me that these same concessions apply in the bye-laws today, in case anyone cares to use them.

There was a time during the First World War when Brab probably knew more than anyone in the world about photography from the air. This is not so immodest a claim as it might sound as they were all pioneers in a new field and the 'experts' could be numbered on the fingers of two hands. Nevertheless, if he chose to claim it, which I am sure he would loathe to do, Brab has as good a right as anyone to the title of the 'father of aerial photography.' His reminscences of the curiously assorted characters with whom he worked in the First World War—Trenchard, Lord Hugh Cecil, Geoffrey Toye, Melville Gideon, and Group Captain Laws, who now runs the 'photo-finish' in horse and greyhound racing are fascinating. He also has the knack of reducing abstruse scientific problems to terms intelligible to those of us who normally would not have had the slightest idea what the other fellow was talking about.

Another point at which Brab has touched life since his early days is sailing, and here again he is the first man to explain in a manner that I can understand the scientific problems involved in an art which holds people under its spell as completely as does golf. He even adapted the autogyro principle to sailing with a vertical rotor attached to the mast. The end came when he ran adrift and the blades chewed up a dinghy like matchwood. Nevertheless the late King George V said he had never seen a boat that could sail so near the wind. All this was at Bembridge—of which I remember Brab once quoting the remark of a man who, when it was suggested that he be nominated for this exclusive club, said, 'What, me put up for Bembridge? They'd think a rabbit had been sleeping in the ballot box!'

The background to Brab's life since the First World War has been

politics. He was Minister of Transport during the blitz and to him
fell the appalling decision whether to bottle up the life of the city by
closing certain tubes or to keep them open and risk one unlucky hit
drowning thousands of people. Later he was Minister of Aircraft
Production, from which post he was manoeuvred out by a piece of
political chicanery of which it is extraordinary that he should be able
to write in such gentle terms. However, what the Commons lost the
Lords gained.

Readers of *Golf Illustrated* will not need to be reminded of the part
that Brab has played in golf—from the typical gesture of pulling the
first trolley to be seen in Britain down the sacred sward at St Andrews
(widely ridiculed at the time), to driving down the same sward (not
very far) as captain of the Royal and Ancient. 'When I look back on
my life,' he says, 'and try to decide out of what I have got most actual
pleasure, I have no doubt at all in saying that I have got more out of
golf than anything else.'

When I in turn look back on all the autobiographies I have read, I
have no doubt at all in saying that I have got more pleasure out of
Brab's than anyone else's.

29 November 1956

Castlerosse

There never was a man like Castlerosse and there never will be
another. The temptation to reminisce upon his personality, his wit
and his excesses, and to try to recapture from the past the qualities
which made him in the minds of so many people positively the best
company they ever had the luck to fall in with, is almost irresistible.
Here, however, I must confine myself within the limits of his activities concerning golf. They were, as a matter of fact, not inconsider-
able and he left behind him as an enduring monument one of the
loveliest golf courses in the world.

At one time, before I knew him, I believe he was scratch or
thereabouts. At any rate he could hold his own in the best of
company and this was despite an injury which, according to the
textbooks, ought to have kept him permanently in double figures. In

the First World War his right elbow was hit by a bullet which went in above the elbow and came out through his forearm an inch or two below. He could never again straighten his arm in any direction, though it is fair to add that it 'set' in a position ideally suited to the raising of a brandy glass.

To play so well with the right arm as a 'non-runner' was no small feat and in its minor way was comparable with Ed Furgol's extraordinary efforts with his withered left arm. As time went on, however, Castlerosse passed the twenty-stone mark and, what with this and his incessant matrimonial and financial worries, his golf fell away. It was typical of him that he should expect to play just as well as before and be absolutely furious when he didn't.

My most cherished memory of him in action is also my last. We played at Walton Heath and I doubt whether he finished a single hole. His ball would scuttle into the heather and with a lordly 'Pick it up' he would repair to the next hole. At the 18th, having driven into the heather and had his ball picked up, he called for another to be placed for a final shot to the green. He hit it to square leg into the heather, and, tossing the club to the ground, uttered to the caddie the immortal instructions: 'Pick that up, have the clubs destroyed, and leave the course!'

Castlerosse's monument was, and will ever be, the course at Killarney, on which the four-cornered international matches were played some years ago—and how I wished at the time that he could have been there to play host to them! Leonard Mosley's book *Castlerosse*, which brings Castlerosse back to life, gives me more credit than I deserve in helping to bring golf to Killarney, though it is true that I was 'in at the birth', and could, I think, point to within a yard or two to the spot where we stood gazing across the western demesne of the Kenmare estate, over the lake to the mountains of Kerry beyond, and he said, 'Do you think we could make a golf course here?' I remember as though it were yesterday replying, 'We could make the loveliest golf course in the world.' We wired for Sir Guy Campbell and escorted him to the same spot. 'This is the most exciting thing I have ever been asked to do,' he said—and to him be rendered the credit for what followed.

We took round with us Pat Lyne, the estate foreman, and two of his observations—vintage Kerry, both of them—have stuck in my mind these eighteen years. We put in bamboo stakes to mark the tees and greens, and next day found that the horses had pushed them over. 'I will come tomorrow, please God,' said Pat, 'and substantiate every one of these.'

Then we wanted to put the clubhouse on the tip of Killeen Point, jutting out into the lake. It was a question of finding room for the road as well as for the 1st and 18th fairways. 'I would not be worrying myself about that at all,' he said. 'There has been a road here before, but it has not been used for some time.'

'How long ago would that be?' I asked.

'Oh,' he replied, quite seriously, 't'would be about 400 years.'

In the summer of 1943, Castlerosse kept inviting me to spend my leave in Killarney. When I replied that only family illness or urgent business reasons would do, he bombarded Anti-Aircraft Command headquarters with wires. 'Your aunt who lives here is dying.' 'Your aunt is dying. May leave you her fortune. Come at once.' Alas, Army Council instructions required the illness of a parent! Then Castlerosse by mistake hit on the solution. In a long letter he said he proposed to spend 'another £40,000 on Killarney'. 'Sir,' said I to a, mercifully, Irish major-general, 'I am a director of this club (not mentioning that my holding was one £1 share). He will ruin me. This is "urgent business reasons".'

And so, one September evening, I found myself in the lights of Dublin, my heart almost too full for words. Castlerosse at home, and Killarney in September. I rang up a friend and mentioned where I was going.

'Castlerosse?' he said. 'Why he died this morning.'

2 May 1957

Balance and Douglas Bader

A week or two ago I was in Douglas Bader's office in the City, talking of this and that, in particular the flight which he was just about to make to Persia, when I saw on his desk some pictures of him playing golf. They were among a series of snapshots taken by friends with whom he played in Australia earlier in the year. I thought them of such interest to golfers in general that I secured the loan of them for

Golf Illustrated. I mention these preliminaries only in order to ensure that no one should think that Bader thrust them upon me for publication. Quite the reverse.

Some years ago I seem to remember reading in a book of Joyce Wethered's that the biggest single 'secret' of golf was balance, and when you cast your mind back to the first tee of your own club you may well be inclined to think that this is true, and that lack of balance is one of the main things that keeps the average golfer average. When you think of the heaving and lurching and swaying that goes on—to say nothing of the 'bellringers' at the end of the stroke—the wonder is that some of them hit the ball at all! For 'them' perhaps I should have written 'us' for I confess I have never been much of a balancer myself.

Miss Wethered was, of course, a super-balancer. Indeed, I wonder if anyone who watched her can honestly recollect a single stroke during any period of which she was not in perfect equilibrium? The same would apply to all the great stylists—Vardon, Jones, Snead and Cotton among them—but would not apply, in my humble opinion, to Hagen, who lives in the memory for his effectiveness rather than his stylishness. The only complete 'non-balancer' that I can think of was Ted Ray. No doubt he was in balance up to the split second at which he struck the ball—he could hardly have won Open championships on both sides of the Atlantic without—but he was certainly off balance from that point onwards, sometimes churning up the turf as his left foot screwed round and sometimes moving his feet altogether. And what fun it was to watch him doing it!

Bader is another super-balancer. He has to be. It seems almost incredible, though, that one is looking here at a man with two tin legs—and not posed at that, but caught unwittingly in action in the course of a normal round. His left knee is his own but the rest of the left leg and the whole of the right leg are artificial. He has neither toes nor ankles and so can make no compensatory movements for the forward-and-backward and lateral sways which pass unnoticed in the actions of most of us.

At one time his handicap was 4 but I fancy it is now 7 or 8, certainly no higher, and using an extra heavy driver he hits the ball at least as far as the average single-figure club golfer. He has, of course, developed immense strength in his hands and arms, as he is constantly lifting himself by them. All the same, balance is obviously the answer. In his early pre-war efforts at golf he used to fall over a great deal—this was faithfully portrayed in the film *Reach for the Sky*—but as time went on he went to the other extreme and can now adjust himself to the most extraordinary stances halfway up the sides of bunkers.

Bader may congratulate himself on having other points in common with the masters. He keeps his left arm straight as the club comes into the ball, and his right arm straight for a considerable distance past it. Hogan, in fact, is able to keep his right arm straight, right until the very end of the follow through. He reckons it to be one of the essentials of successful golf, though of course to the more portly among us it would simply mean being carted off to the infirmary.

This ability to stop the left arm 'giving' at impact is not so easy as it might sound. I remember having some photographs taken of myself hitting a drive years ago and thinking to myself that, whatever else might be shown in the picture, it would find my left arm straight at impact. It was extremely mortifying to find that, although the shot was rather a good one, my left arm looked more as though I were 'playing back' to a rising ball at cricket.

Finally, I think even the best of professionals would lift their hats to Bader's bunker shot. Muddy, wet sand, a downhanging stance, and no ankles or toes. When you consider the action of most club golfers in a similar situation—the sliding about and hunching down with the right shoulder and the frantic efforts to 'hoick' the ball up instead of hitting through it and letting the loft of the club do it—it really seems a masterpiece of its kind.

Indeed, one is forced to the conclusion that the best thing many of us could do would be to have our legs off!

12 October 1961

The Old Hill-billy

It is distressing to think that we shall not after all be seeing the great Sam Snead for the Ryder Cup match. Thousands of people would have taken away with them a treasured golfing memory and now they will probably never see him at all. Some may even think it not worthwhile going to Lytham after all, so great is his personal drawing power. I hope that this will not be so, for there are plenty of other fine American players to be seen and there is no doubt that this match has a thrill all of its own. I remember to this day getting up at crack of dawn and motoring from Cambridge to Leeds to see the match in 1929, and how fascinated we were with the then youthful Horton Smith.

Snead is a true 'hill-billy' from the backwoods of West Virginia and started with positively nothing. His fantastic success is the more praiseworthy for this. What he has made he has made for himself. Nor is he inarticulate, as in the 'hill-billy' caricatures. In fact, he can make a very witty after-dinner speech, sing a song, and tell stories by the hour, some of them extraordinarily droll.

How much money he has made from golf few people will ever know. The general opinion seems to be that his hoard of gold is second only to Fort Knox. He appreciated early in life the principle, for which English footballers have been struggling, that if you bring in the gate you should have your share of it. He has even been paid 2000 dollars to appear at a dinner!

Strangely enough he has never won the US Open championship, though he has three times been runner-up, once, I seem to remember, through taking an eight at the last hole and once losing to Lew Worsham in a play-off. He has won almost everything else that the world of professional golf has to offer, including the Masters three times, and ten years ago he became the first man to pass the 200,000-dollar mark in official winnings.

Much as I enjoy watching Palmer and Nicklaus, probably the two best players in the world today, you could not call them 'pretty to watch'. Not for nothing is the title of Palmer's forthcoming book *Hit It Hard!* Snead, however, represents the poetry of motion in the golf swing. He has always been a long driver, but he does not give the impression of 'hitting it hard'.

I retain a vivid memory of him practising in a line of players at the Thunderbird Club in the Californian desert before the 1955 Ryder Cup match. There must have been a dozen of them, their clubs flashing in the sun and cascades of balls flying away like white tracer bullets against the mountain background. I was standing at the end of the line and I noticed that one club appeared to be moving at about half the speed of the rest. It was, of course, Snead's.

At his home club, the luxurious Greenbrier at White Sulphur Springs, Va., he has two remarkable feats to his credit. He returned a genuine 59—the first man ever to break 60 on a full-sized course—and on another occasion went into the woods, secured a piece of a tree, carved it into a golf club, and with this and a putter holed the course in 76.

Now, together with five others, he has been fined 500 dollars—about the equivalent of fining you and me three farthings—and suspended for six months. This, though it assuredly ought not to, keeps him from representing his country in the Ryder Cup match. It is not for me to comment on the rights and wrongs of suspending the six players concerned, though I must say I have sympathy with the USPGA in principle. The circuit of highly lucrative tournaments has been built up on the basis that certain players undertake to play on them. They are allowed to cry off from time to time, but if they do so they must not play in another event at the same time. It was this undertaking which was contravened by Snead and the others.

The same trouble arose when Palmer, Player and Leonard wished to play in the Canada Cup in Puerto Rico this year. Why Snead was not involved then I do not know, but at any rate the other three did not play in the tournament, whose date clashed, but they did not risk suspension by playing in the Canada Cup either—a situation which one trusts will be taken care of in advance on future occasions.

23 November 1961

The Coming of the Bear

I am very surprised that Jack Nicklaus has turned pro and I cannot help feeling that the last year or so represents the only period in the history of golf in which he would have done so. It was widely felt in America that neither he nor his fellow amateur, Deane Beman, could 'afford to turn pro'. They were doing so well as they were. Both were selling insurance, through contacts acquired on account of their prowess at golf.

Let me make myself absolutely plain about this. The above is not a thinly disguised 'crack' at their amateur status. It is impossible, and unreasonable, to suggest that a man should not do business with people who are all the more glad to transact it with him on account of distinctions he has gained in other spheres. That applies as much to stockbrokers in this country as insurance men in the States.

Nevertheless the rewards to Nicklaus and Beman have already been outstanding. Nicklaus in his second year at the University at the age of twenty was already credited with 25,000 dollars a year. Beman, a couple of years ahead of him, had already 'turned pro' at insurance. He works at it like a beaver and he and his 26-year-old partner hope next year to make 125,000 dollars. He draws 6000 dollars a year in expenses from the firm to help to pay for the golf that brings him the business, but that, believe me, is little enough by American standards. Beman is now a dedicated insurance man who plays exceptional golf, not a golfer who sells insurance.

The rewards open to Nicklaus in the near future were, therefore, rosy indeed. It can only have been through the offer of even greater, and presumably guaranteed, rewards that he turned pro. Only in the last two or three years have such rewards been available to the three or four leading players in the world—mainly through television.

How will Nicklaus fare in direct competition with Palmer and such like? I think very well. Firstly, let me go on record as saying that, like Palmer, he is not only a fine golfer but a very fine fellow. He looks the world in the eye with a fearless sincerity and he has 'guts'. This to me was proved at Pebble Beach this year, when he was subjected to a series of 18-hole matches against opponents who had everything to gain and nothing to lose. It is easy to say 'Anyone can beat anyone over 18 holes'—though it isn't true, of course. It is a different thing to determine 'No one is going to beat *me* over 18 holes'. I believe he would have won if the matches had been over six holes.

Last year Nicklaus declared that in golf his one ambition was to win the Open and the Masters. I see no reason why he should not. Over the past two years his aggregate in the two Open championships, though he won neither, was better than that of any other player. He has all the assets. He has terrific length—so much so that he recently won a 72-hole competition without taking anything bigger than a 6-iron for his second at a par four hole. Not only that, but he is straight. All through the week at Pebble Beach you could take his drives for granted. As Palmer says in his book, the old days of 'you drive for fun and putt for money' are long since past.

With his awkward, rather cramped style, Nicklaus is an exceedingly good putter, too. If you can drive anything from 250 to 300 yards, straight, and then have anything from a 6-iron to a wedge to a watered green with a large ball, *and* are a fine holer-out, you are not often going to descend to taking 70! At Pebble Beach, Nicklaus was 20 under par for the week.

I hope that he will enjoy his life as a professional. One thing I am sure: the profession is fortunate to have got him.

26 July 1962

Joe Carr

I once wrote somewhere that a Walker Cup or any other overseas tour, on so many of which I have been lucky enough to go as camp follower, would never be the same without Joe Carr, and sadly I say again that I am sure that this will apply to the expedition in search of the Eisenhower Trophy. It was such a splendid prospect to think of Joe marching along the fairways of Kawana accompanied by a little girl caddie about the size of his golf bag! Furthermore the Japanese would have taken instantly to him, as have done the inhabitants of every other country in which I have seen him play.

Joe always carried with him, and assuredly will live to carry again, a remarkable load of goodwill. 'There's one of your boys I want to see win,' people would say in America, 'and that's . . .' All right, all right. I know the answer. It is Joe Carr. Yet on the whole the record shows that Joe has never done as well in team matches as he has done on his own and, though it may not sound like it, and before Irish hackles rise, let me record that I say this as a compliment. In team matches he has carried an appallingly heavy load of responsibility. He has always been our trump card, the one card that is expected surely to win us a trick, and I believe that this has borne heavily on him. In a championship, and I believe he has won about twenty-five in all, if somebody beats him—well, it has probably done the somebody a bit of good and the best of luck to him and there's always another year.

Nothing sorts people out so surely as going on an overseas tour together. The 'good trouper', as the stage folk put it, very soon makes himself evident. On the first tour I accompanied of which Joe was a member, in 1949, they proceeded from the Walker Cup match to the American Amateur at Rochester and I remember that a couple of large station wagons were put at the party's disposal. In the mornings Joe had to be woken, re-woken and sometimes re-re-woken and a man detailed to stand over him till he got up, before one of the cars could leave. This amiable weakness is the only criticism that I can find in Joe's qualities as a trouper, and I may say that I do not remember it happening since. He has always been the life and soul of the party, with sympathy towards all and malice towards none.

Joe, with friend and foe and spectators alike, has always been the most popular member of the team, yet I have never known him by word or gesture deliberately court popularity. As I pause to analyse why this should be, I conclude that it springs from a number of causes. Firstly, of course, he is a 'natural'; nothing artificial about him, always himself, as polite to the asker of stupid questions as to the president of the club. All over the world, too, a real Irish accent is a key to people's hearts and Joe's is no exception.

I do not know where the expression 'Have a go, Joe!' came from, but Joe Carr on the golf course certainly 'has a go'. I do not know, either, how many thousands of drives I have seen hit in my life, but it still gives me a positive pleasure to see Joe lash out at one. There are those, though not many, who hit it as far, but none in my opinion who hit it, if I may be permitted an apparent contradiction in terms, with such controlled abandon. Yet how deceptive, really, this impression is, for Joe realised at least ten years ago that the farther you hit it the straighter it had got to be—as those who can cast their minds back to the days of geometry and 'similar triangles' will readily appreciate.

So behind the apparent abandon, and I can find no better word for it, there lies morning after morning, perhaps running into thousands now, of hitting a hundred drives from his back garden adjoining the Sutton Golf Club, first thing before going off to work in Dublin. Yet still he contrives to give the pleasing impression of a fellow to whom life is too short and too full of good company to be bothered with practice.

He gives the same impression on the course. I suppose he tries as hard as any amateur has ever tried at golf, yet you do not have the feeling, when things are not going his way, that the cares of the world are on his shoulders, and he takes the outrageous fortune that so often befalls a championship golfer with neither moaning nor complaint. Who remembers, now, that in the great Centenary Open two years ago, at St Andrews, Joe Carr shot off like a house on fire for the final round and was indubitably within sight of winning the title when a sudden cloudburst flooded parts of the course and play was abandoned? Joe's brilliant start counted for nothing and next day the magic was no longer there. Here is a hard luck story on which to dine out for the rest of one's life. I wonder how many people have heard Joe mention it since?

Now at last he has been left out of a team, albeit of only four players. I remember when Francis Ouimet, the American captain, declared that he would not himself play in the 1936 Walker Cup match, his saying: 'Waal, I guess it's time some of these young boys had some of the nice things of golf', and I am sure that Joe is magnanimous enough to feel the same. In the meantime, if anyone thinks he is 'finished', let them just watch him next year.

11 August 1966

The Mogul of Sandwich

I have just been working out that, including three and a half blissful years at Cambridge, the amount of my life that I spent in being 'educated' (as the phrase is used today: as if one was not being educated every day of one's life!) was some sixteen years. I like to think that it did me some good and indeed I am still 'square' enough to prefer the Classics which I did at school to the Economics in which I took a lowly degree at the University, but the fact remains that out of the whole long process only one or two items of instruction stand out as having sunk in at the time and been destined to remain in one's mind for life. One of these came from Mr Humphrey Grose Hodge, under whom I sat at Charterhouse and who was later to become a reforming headmaster of Bedford School. It was not, I am sure, an original observation, nor would he have claimed it as such, but it was new to me. 'Within reason,' he said, 'anyone can achieve any one thing, provided he is prepared to give up absolutely everything else in order to do so.'

The point applies doubly to Sir Aynsley Bridgland. He had two ambitions and by single-mindedness achieved them both. I wish I knew which he achieved first, because I could then make some profound observation about being worth a million helping with your golf or being good at golf helping towards becoming worth a million. However, it was a remarkable double. Whichever came first, it is undeniable that the same qualities helped towards both. 'Bridgie' knew what he wanted and in taking the direct route to it may have stepped on one or two people's toes. I don't think he would mind my writing this, if he could read it—which for all we know he can. Indeed I once had a slight up-and-downer with him myself, and in his own clubhouse at Princes at that, when he disagreed with something I had written and suggested that on account of business contacts with my then proprietor, Lord Kemsley, he would cause pressure to be brought upon me, whereupon I gave him a bouncing answer. He turned the colour of a turkey cock but the fact is that we remained on excellent terms of understanding from then onwards.

'Bridgie' was a self-made man, in the sense that his success in the property business was all his own work; and a self-made golfer, in the sense that he took it up comparatively late in life and it never came naturally to him. In all this he was remarkably akin to 'Critch', the late General Critchley, though the latter was perhaps a gayer and more colourful character. In golf, however, they were very much alike. A man might think, and indeed know, that he had a better swing and that in a match against either of them he must surely be the 'form horse'. Let him beware! They were two supreme examples of what is now the motto of the Home Park club near Kingston— '*Quomodo non quoties*'; in other words, 'It isn't how, but how many?' It was not the swing that counted: it was how many you took for the hole.

In the world of golf 'Bridgie' will be remembered for his timely rescue—I think it is not too strong a word—of Princes and Deal. The loss of Deal and the failure to rebuild Princes would have left an irreparable gap in the best of British seaside golf and it was only his zeal for golf and the fact that he had the right sort of money at the right sort of time that enabled those great courses to survive.

To restore and recreate Princes, which had been a target range of some sort during the war (P. B. Lucas, who was born in the clubhouse, his father being secretary, landed his damaged Spitfire there during the war, thus saving his life literally through 'knowing the course') 'Bridgie' chose two eminent architects, Sir Guy Campbell and John Morrison, and they divided it up, hole by hole, between them. Such things can only be a matter of opinion but I have always felt it a pity that, since Princes had been so well known to so many of the elite of golf, that they did not restore it to roughly its old layout, so that people could once again talk of such and such a hole and their friends know what they were alluding to.

Nowadays, with twenty-seven holes, they tend on special occasions, like the Curtis Cup to use a 'Special Blue Course' and so, though I can see her doing it, I cannot for the life of me tell you which hole on which course it was that Mrs Frances Smith won so gallantly, at the 18th, to make sure of the Cup. Nor, I imagine, can any but a very select few detect on which eighteen holes during the Astor Trophy last month Mlle Catherine Lacoste performed the fantastic score of 66—an achievement which seemed to escape general notice at the time. The course, so the present captain, Mr J. C. Binns, assures me, was, at 6321 yards, only ten per cent shorter than that for the Schweppes tournament last year, when in seventy-two holes only three scores were returned under 70.

Sir Aynsley Bridgland did an immense amount for international golf through gifts from his creation, the Golf Society of Great Britain—or, as some wag christened it, the Golf Society of Great Bridgland. For five guineas a year any club golfer can join and this enables him to play on about twenty of the finest courses in the country without further green fees. *Si monumentum requiris*. . . . Princes, Deal, and the Golf Society of Great Britain. No mean memorial for one man.

15 May 1969

Bobby Locke

I believe I am right in saying that Bobby Locke first came to this country for the Amateur championship at St Andrews in 1936, at which time he will have been nineteen, and that he was beaten in some round or other by Alec Hill, a Walker Cup player of that year and later captain of the Royal and Ancient. Locke at that time was pencil-slim and had already in the previous year won the South African Open. In both 1936 and 1937 he finished as leading amateur in the British Open but it was not until after the war, in which he flew with the South African Air Force, that he really blossomed forth. He was just young enough to be able to afford the six wasted golfing years.

I will not burden the reader with a lot of dates, which I do not remember anyway, but suffice to say that Locke won the Open four times between 1949 and 1957, very nearly monopolising it together with Peter Thomson. What really made him 'different', however, was that he became the first outsider successfully to beard the Americans in their own den. He won several tournaments, including the Tam O'Shanter so-called world championship, run by the late George S. May, collecting some £6000 or £7000—which today would be more like £60,000 or £70,000—and indeed was so successful in taking the bread from honest men's mouths that eventually they banned him on account of some technicality. Again I forget exactly what, but it had a rather trumped-up air about it at the time.

'The first thing you have to do if you want to succeed in America', I remember him once telling me, 'is to learn to play slowly.' This he did with a vengeance. In fact, he did everything slowly and this absolute refusal to be hurried was one of the secrets of his success. It took him about an hour to get up in the morning and an unconscionable time in the dressing room getting ready for play. When he finished, there was nearly always a gap of about three holes in front of him. Locke himself maintained that he was in fact a very quick player and in one sense, the sense in which he meant it, this was true. He formed a sort of 'drill' for every shot, especially on the green, and once all the fiddling about was over and done with—all part of the determination never to play the shot until completely composed—he did indeed set the drill in motion and the shot was immediately played. But oh, the fiddling about!

I have often written about his 'drill' on the greens, which all who saw it will remember, but for the benefit of those who did not see it I will mention it again. It consisted of two practice swings, a short step up to the ball, *one* look at the hole, and away she goes. I have not the slightest doubt that every single golfer, of whatever handicap, would enormously benefit by working out an individual drill for himself, not necessarily based on Locke's, and then sticking to it through thick and thin.

I remember so well the finish of Locke's first Open in 1949 at Sandwich, the famous year when Harry Bradshaw got his ball stuck in a broken beer bottle and the Rules were changed as a consequence. The 16th is a short hole and Locke needed the par figures of 3, 4, 4 to tie. He got on the 16th, not very near the flag, then hit the long putt lamentably short and missed the next.

What his feelings must have been as he went to the 17th anyone can imagine. At any rate he got on in two and rolled in a 12-foot putt for a three, so now, after all, it was four to tie. He did not quite get on in two and did not quite get dead in three. He was in fact about four feet away, with a curly left-hand borrow and here indeed was the golfers' nightmare. 'This to tie for the Open.' I remember watching specially to see if the drill would survive this most crucial of all tests. Surely he must allow himself just one more look at the hole? But no: the drill held and the ball rolled straight into the middle.

The finish of his win at St Andrews was also memorable, though in a different way. The 18th on the Old Course, with thousands of people lining the fairway and some even hanging onto the chimney pots, is *the* grandstand finish and Locke with a couple of shots in hand pitched his second shot up to within three feet. He then marked the ball, but a clubhead's length away to keep out of his partner's line. When the supreme moment came, he replaced the ball over the marker instead of in its original position. None of us concerned with the television behind the green noticed this nor, I honestly believe, did anyone until it came on the television in the evening. Some opposition was later raised by supporters of Peter Thomson in Australia (though I do not say by Thomson himself) but the then chairman of the championship committee, Mr N. C. Selway, wrote a fine letter to Locke assuring him that he was well and truly the Open champion.

If I may again repeat myself, if only for the benefit of those who did not know him, it has always been my opinion that Locke was the best 'bad' player of his time. Everyone, however good, has his off days. Only the other day Nicklaus, I see, took 80, which is virtually impossible. One of the differences between those who make the grade and those who do not quite is this ability to play badly well, to somehow squeeze the ball round in the sort of score which will still leave you in the hunt. Some of our younger professionals who are knocking at the door have not yet mastered this art and come up with ruinous 77s and 78s which Locke would somehow have kept down to 73 or 74. His winning score at Troon in 1950 reads 69, 72, 70, 68. No one who was there would dispute that the greatest achievement was the 72. It might have been anything.

As to technique Locke was a law unto himself, though inclined to be a little touchy if you mentioned it. The fact is that he aimed miles to the right, started the ball off to the right, then drew it round to the target. When Thomson won at Birkdale in 1954, Locke had watched his 2-iron shot from directly behind the green. It curved out to the right—I am almost prepared to swear that at one time it was actually out of bounds—and curled round like a boomerang to the green.

I wish I had space to tell of the secrets of his phenomenal putting, which he revealed to me long ago in a half hour I have never forgotten, but that must wait. One more quality I will quote. I believe he was the best judge of distance in the game. This was of course before they paced everything out and entered it in little notebooks. Alas, a few years ago he challenged a train at a level crossing and suffered an injury to one eye, and for judging the distance of the line of a putt it is essential to have two equally sound eyes. Never mind. His place in the history books is already assured.

CHAPTER SEVEN

The World of True Golf

4 February 1954

Dressed to Kill

Years ago when we were driving through some woods near Henley and I remarked upon a cock pheasant at the side of the road, my town-bred wife said, 'How do you tell the difference?'—to which I replied, and I rather like it still. 'The female, as so often, is colourless and plain. The male, however, is a fine bird.'

What a pity one cannot say the same in golf! The male it is that is colourless and plain, while the female, if she is not always a fine bird, at least has generally done her best with the material placed by Nature at her disposal.

In the old days convention had it that both sexes 'dressed up' for golf. In such case the correct garb made the movements of the golf swing so completely impossible that either the clothes or the game would have to go. Luckily, golf was spreading like wildfire over England in the 1880s and 1890s. There was no stopping it, and it was, therefore, the clothes that had to adapt themselves to the game—the women taking longer in their sartorial emancipation than the men on account of the fact, so they tell me, that the display of half an inch of ankle was enough to get the owner drummed out of the club for gross indecency.

The correct attire for women was 'sailor hat, high stiff collar, voluminous petticoats, and a wide leather skirt with leather bindings'. You also wore, for practicability and modesty, especially when playing in a wind, a 'Miss Higgins'. This was an elastic band, named after the American golfer, which you slipped round the knees before taking the shot—thus, according to my own ribald imagination, making the lady expert of the day look like three inverted onions one on top of the other.

Early Scottish pictures show the men playing in tail coats, stovepipe trousers, and top hats, but I fancy that, when the game arrived in England, the gentlemen golfer wore a tight-fitting tweed suit; knickerbockers, boots, and probably tall white spats. In these he was every inch a gentleman but not much of a golfer, and he could hardly swing the club. Advertisements in the *Golfing Annual* of half a century ago show London tailors, with Burberry's well to the fore, luring the golfer with varieties of loose-fitting coats, quite a battle being waged between the Pivot sleeve and the Gusset sleeve.

For the best part of twenty years the accepted wear for men settled at the jacket and knee breeches of Harry Vardon (the professionals for many years having worn trousers, almost as the official wear of their profession, and Vardon having been the first to break away) verging to the jacket and plus fours—never 'plus eights', in themselves a hideous memory—of Mitchell and Duncan.

Then we have the, to my mind hideous, Fair-Isle-pullover era, exemplified by the portrait of the Prince of Wales in the Big Room of the Royal and Ancient, and finally in this country at least—though I have seen men in respectable clubs in the United States playing with no shirt at all—the shirtsleeves era.

Meanwhile, the women were working steadily along the day of the Great Revolution, when a self-possessed, immaculate figure slipped out of a large yellow motorcar on to the first tee at Westward Ho! in 1934 and set the officials of the Ladies' Golf Union clucking like a flock of agitated Leghorn pullets. The figure—and what a figure!—was that of Miss Gloria Minoprio. She was attired in a neat, close-fitting little back cap or hat, a high-necked white jumper affair tucked into beautifully tailored, somewhat Edwardian, dark blue trousers. These culminated in little straps which passed under the insteps of dark blue suede shoes. My description may contain technical inaccuracies but I go on record as saying, now that all the hubbub has subsided, that Miss Minoprio was the best dressed woman golfer I ever saw. Innumerable women have copied her—though some, I dare say, would not have done so had they possessed one of those tailor's mirrors where you look in front and see behind—but none has carried it off so well.

Today the women are better turned out than the men, and among the men the professionals are better turned out than the amateurs, the most scrupulously attired being perhaps the greatest of them, Henry Cotton. My esteemed colleague, Peter Wilson, once wrote of 'women golfers with their billiard table legs, leathery faces, and clumsy great paws'. If he went to Worplesdon on a fine October morning for the mixed foursomes, he would see, in my humble opinion, some of the most attractively dressed women in any sport. And if he attended the French women's championship, he would, indeed, have to think again—though that, together with the bizarre creations to be seen in America, is beyond my present province.

No, the women, so far as I am concerned, come out of it well—except when they wear those truly appalling jockey-caps-with-earflaps, as to which my advice is, 'If it's too cold for your ears, dear, it's too cold for golf'. The women, if they do not all succeed, do at least try. Many of the men don't seem to try at all—and the main culprit is the man who is always claiming to be the backbone of the game, namely, the Average Golfer.

Perhaps it is not fair to illustrate such a charge by extreme cases, but just imagine a nice flat muddy inland course at this time of the year, with four average golfers playing their average fourball. Otherwise perfectly respectable citizens, they are attired in rather dirty, once white caps, very dirty (naturally!) black and white shoes; nondescript waterproof jackets; and grey flannel trousers *tucked into their socks*. Furthermore, they are pulling four ludicrous little perambulators. So bravo to the girls—but of the above gentlemen I can bear to write no more.

27 May 1954

Two Hundred Years On

The 200th anniversary cf the founding of the Royal and Ancient Golf Club of St Andrews is a great occasion in golf. Like all similar institutions—the MCC, for instance, and for that matter the House of Commons, which in many senses it resembles—it has had its critics and its ups and downs. How does it stand on its 200th birthday?

On the whole, excellently. Throughout the Empire it is respected as highly and as solidly as at any time in its history. Next week teams from Canada, Australia, New Zealand and South Africa will assemble at St Andrews to do battle with each other and with Britain. Most of them are youngish players who are visiting the ancient shrine for the first time. All, for a surety, will go home as ambassadors for the Royal and Ancient.

Every country in Europe respects without question the Rules and Decisions issued by the club. For a while, as golf spread across America in the early years of the century and then again after the First World War, the United States tended to go its own golfing way. Now the R and A and the United States Golf Association act as one, each determined rather to give way than to gain a point over the other.

At home I think it must honestly be admitted, certainly not in any spirit of controversy, that there was a time when certain members of the national Unions felt that they would like to supplant the R and A as the governing body. It is my impression that such feeling does not exist today and that relations between the Club and the Unions are on a sure and settled basis, each doing their own job and each helping the other.

Nevertheless there are a great many golfers at home who cheerfully accept the R and A as the governing body of golf but have little idea of what it really is. Incidentally, this may be an excellent thing, for the less 'the Government' intrudes upon the life of the citizen, the better, say I!

Many people, for instance, think that the Royal and Ancient and 'St Andrews' are the same thing. They are not. St Andrews, so far as golf is concerned, means four public golf courses crowded on the 'linksland' of sand dunes and whin bushes, so called because they form the link between the land and the sea. These courses are the Old, the New, the Jubilee and the Eden. Attached to these public courses are a number of private clubs, of which the Royal and Ancient is immeasurably the senior and most important.

Like any other club, its members, of whom there are about 800, are proposed, seconded, supported, and finally elected by the club committee. They are different only in the sense that instead of coming from one district or one city, they come from all over the world, not only from the Dominions and Europe but also from the

United States. Indeed, in 1951, the club chose one of its longest-standing American members, Francis Ouimet, as captain—not because it would be good for international relations but because they esteemed him sufficiently to do so.

On the face of it the Royal and Ancient may thus be held to be 'undemocratic'—which, when you look at some of the results of democracy might not be so bad a thing anyway. To become a 'legislator', if such be your desire, you must first be elected to the club. In effect, however, it works out as a highly democratic institution because the club's membership is so widely spread, in the four countries at home and all over the world. All you need is to know two members who think highly enough of you to propose and second you. After that, you must so impress your fellow 800 members that they put you on a committee and turn you into a legislator. If you do not know even two in the first place, it is difficult to see what qualities of golfing knowledge and experience you claim to possess as a potential legislator.

Another proof of the, for want of a better word, democratic nature of the Royal and Ancient is that it habitually seeks outside opinion before passing controversial legislation, and doubtless in the present-day world this is the proper thing—though there are some, including myself, who rather wish it wouldn't, since, if you invite popular opinion, you nearly always get the wrong answer. The best case within recent memory was the question of whether balls out of bounds, lost, or unplayable, should count one shot or two. 'One,' said the majority. The chairman and many members of the Rules of Golf committee thought otherwise, but they bowed to popular opinion and chaos reigned for two years.

As it is the bicentenary of the club which is being celebrated, and not of the Old Course, on which golf has been played for the best part of 400 years, I must resist the temptation to go into rhapsodies about a course which to me is different not only in kind but in quality from anything else in the world.

To me, to be a member of the Royal and Ancient and to play habitually on the Old Course is one of the supreme privileges of golf. To approach in the little train from Leuchars Junction, preferably with the elderly engine (which is named 'Kettledrummle') running backwards; to see the old grey city drawing nearer and nearer; to lean out of the window and wave to one's friends playing the second or

sixteenth, whose greens are one (I once waved at a fourball containing three peers and a knight and felt that I had gained a great deal of
face thereby)—all these are thrills which I know will never die.

With appropriate humility I echo the words of Bobby Jones: 'If I
had to play on one course alone for the rest of my days, I should
choose the Old Course at St Andrews.' And may the Royal and
Ancient clubhouse be presiding over it, solid, foursquare and grey,
in another 200 years' time, even if I shall not be there to enjoy it!

17 February 1955

Fit to Print!

It is a canon of all but the heaviest forms of journalism that people are
more interesting than events, and I cannot help feeling that in many
ways this is true. I think that anyone who takes an intelligent interest
in a game, while at the same time through force of circumstances
being unable to follow it in person, does like to know 'what sort of a
chap is so-and-so' about whom he reads so much. At what point
personal details merge from being interesting into being either irrelevant or impertinent or both—well, you can always choose which
paper you read! The fourpenny daily will record barely that M.
Faulkner took 74, while one of the twopenny-halfpennies will tell
you all about Maxie Waxie and his primrose-coloured trousers.

On the whole we take things fairly quietly in golf. It is not,
mercifully, a game which lends itself to 'incidents' and to the more
savage sort of criticism. I have always been sympathetic towards
those of my colleagues whose editors demand of them, on the bigger
occasions, not only an account of the play, but also a daily 'news
story' for page one. As one would have thought an editor would know
as likely as not no news story exists and the luckless correspondent is
forced to fall back on inflating some minor triviality.

For myself I do not follow county cricket very closely, but like
millions of others I do follow the Tests, and I confess that some of the
writers thereon do fill me with alarm and despondency. What they do
to the players, heaven knows. No one who has not himself been
attacked in a newspaper knows quite how unpleasant it can be.

Public figures have to pretend to be impervious to it, but unless they are by temperament an Aneurin Bevan, to whom attack is meat and drink, you may be pretty sure that they hate it underneath.

Some years ago when I was engaging in politics I found myself suddenly one morning attacked bitterly and venomously in a gossip column. A long time later I learned that the writer, whom I had never met, had engaged the local correspondent of his newspaper to hunt around the town and see if he could find something to my discredit. I am glad to say that, as he himself later confessed, he searched diligently for some weeks and was unable to find anything of which I could be ashamed. Nevertheless a savage paragraph was worked up and, if it is any satisfaction to the gossip writer, I confess that the thought that several million people were reading this stuff about me on that particular Sunday morning was most painful.

Politics is a dirty game, they always say—though I really do not see why it should be—so I suppose one must expect that sort of thing, but I do not see why we should have it in sport. After all, even at Brisbane, Hutton was doing his best. A visiting Test captain these days carries a load of national responsibility which many may think exaggerated and few would care to shoulder themselves, and it seems to me quite inexcusable for a correspondent of the stature of Mr Frank Rostron to cable back to the *Daily Express*: 'I accuse Hutton'. I am sure that in the end we should have thought more highly both of the writer and of his paper if he had said: 'With great respect, and knowing as little of cricket as I do by comparison with the great man, I am at a loss to interpret his latest decision.'

All the same I do not think that readers would like it, even in golf, if we became too subservient. All selectors, for instance, are not idiots, but some of them indisputably are sometimes, in which case, if only in justice to those who are left out, we ought occasionally to say so.

Again, if one is surprised at the selection of, say, a Walker Cup captain, I think one may with perfect propriety say so. After all, there is no need to be offensive about it! My colleague Leonard Crawley, for instance, was surprised at the selection of Alec Hill for this post and quite properly, as I thought, said so. He made the perfectly valid point that Hill would be unknown by sight to the majority of his team. I do not think he will be any the worse a captain for that—I wonder how many of the winning 1938 team knew John Beck?—but it seems a perfectly proper point for a critic to raise.

Some writers, one in particular, used to write pretty censoriously about the actual play and looking back on it—we are kinder now—I still think this was a mistake. If the Ryder Cup team, who are professionals dependent on public support, turned up on the tee with rings under their eyes due to over-conviviality the night before the match, it would be fair enough to give them the hammer, but poor Mr So-and-so, who is taking part of his holiday to play in the championship and, coming all over queer, fluffs his chip to the last green, or poor Miss Such-and-such, who is six up in the Curtis Cup match and runs into one of those agonising spells in which, the more holes there are, the more certain she is to lose them, for these luckless souls the world is a hard enough place already, without the knife being turned in the wound in tomorrow morning's paper.

23 January 1958

Maharajahs and Other Dying Races

I am afraid that I never had the honour of playing with a maharajah—and now I suppose I never shall—though I did once play with an Egyptian sheik. He was attired in a flowing nightshirt, from below which an enormous pair of brown boots protruded like skis. It was the first time he had played on grass, he said. He beat me level.

I have often seen quoted recently an expression which will probably become part of the language, namely, that we now live in a 'conforming society'. This is a climate in which the eccentric, the individualist, indeed, anyone who does not 'conform', is somewhat frowned upon, or at any rate regarded as a relic of the past and may in extreme cases be driven completely away by the herd, who do not like to see their own mediocrity shown up for what it is.

Certainly, I think this is reflected in many ways in modern games, including golf. There do not seem to be the 'characters' there used to be—the people who could fill the arena single-handed, so to speak. Perhaps this is a reflection of the changes that have come over the game itself. When standardization comes in at one door, individuality goes out at the other. In no game is this more strikingly true than in golf.

When I began to play (which is not all *that* long ago!) a set of clubs was a set of individuals, carefully and lovingly assembled one by one. You did not buy a new set: you bought a new club. And furthermore, it had a name, not a soulless number. Of course, the fact that a new club cost perhaps a pound—I do not go back to the seven and sixpenny days—whereas a set of irons alone may cost anything up to forty pounds probably had a lot do with it, but this does not alter the principle.

So, while virtually every professional was a club maker in his own right and some were supreme artists, nowadays practically none of them are. Not more than one in, say, twenty? Perhaps one in fifty. One of the finest professional's shops in America is that of Claude Harmon, at Winged Foot, NY. Yet, when one of the British Walker Cup team broke a shaft there in 1949, there was no one who could put in a new one. The club had to go back to the manufacturers. This made a deep impression on me at the time and I have never forgotten it.

This is not a criticism of factory-made clubs—and I do not say that merely to avoid offending my manufacturer friends. In the old days one used to pick up some positively frightful clubs in many a pro's shop. Nowadays, I doubt whether a single really bad club is put out at all. Only last year I toured one of the best-known factories on the occasion of a visit by Prince Philip, where they are making clubs to the very exacting standards set by Ben Hogan. No one could fail to be impressed by the care and skill which went into the making of all the clubs in this factory, nor has one any reason to doubt that the same care and skill goes into the same business in other factories. Nevertheless, the fact remains that the club maker-artist is no longer to be found in golf. The bunch of shafts in the corner, the pots of glue, the twine, the gas ring on the bench, and above all, that supremely wonderful *smell* of the club maker's shop is no longer with us to make a lifelong impression on the memory of the young golfer.

It has even been irreverently suggested to me that the kind of secretary who was able to impose his own character on a golf club to such an extent that the two were thought of as one is also disappearing—but this to me is dangerous ground, for I once incautiously wrote that perhaps the day of the highly paid club secretary was drawing to a close and that he might be replaced by the honorary variety, with a competent steward running the internal affairs of the clubhouse. Unhappily, I had forgotten that I had accepted an invitation to lunch in the immediate future with the Association of Golf Club Secretaries and at this pleasant function I was urbanely and courteously ticked off in his speech by their president, none other than Bernard Darwin—the first of the golfing CBE's.

One of the greatest delights in my own golfing life has been the company of an extraordinary miscellaneous collection of caddies, old and young, male and female, in every quarter of the globe, but in this country, alas, they seem indeed to be a dying race and only an economic depression, I dare say, would ever bring them back. It still seems possible to provide caddies for all the competitors in the bigger tournaments but the days of the 'regulars' at all but the most expensive clubs seem to be passing. I have always thought that the answer is boys, but either the boys don't know of the opportunity or else the thought of five bob no longer lures them. We all have our personal prejudices and one of mine is golf trollies. To see four grown men plodding round a muddy course in winter pulling perambulators—and as likely as not with their trousers tucked in their socks—casts a gentle melancholy over the soul and makes me think of hanging up my clubs for the last time.

Ah, well, I have no doubt that old codgers have been writing in this strain ever since golf was played. It is still a wonderful game, whatever they do to it.

28 May 1959

Golf's Highest Honour

To be elected captain of the Royal and Ancient Golf Club of St Andrews is perhaps the highest honour that can befall a man in the game of golf. His executive duties are few, his prestige great. He is elected at some time between the autumn and spring meetings by the past captains, and his first duty on presiding at the spring meeting (his first in the chair) is to announce the name of his successor.

He himself knew, therefore, sometime between September and May that this honour had come his way and from that moment until a Wednesday in the third week in September he will have been able to—and probably unable not to—continuously contemplate the playing of the single stroke by which he will drive himself into office.

At eight o'clock in the morning he will be escorted to the first tee by those past captains who may be present; his ball will be teed for him by Willie Auchterlonie, the club's professional and one of the two living professionals who are honorary members of the club—the other is J. H. Taylor and the third was James Braid; the caddies, a sadly diminishing race, will assemble in various places on the fairway, thus silently but inexorably revealing their assessment of his ability; a crowd of citizens and members will be forming a line down the left-hand side of the fairway or leaning over the rails on the right or the balcony above; and a man from the RAF station at Leuchars in plain clothes will be holding the firing cord of the ancient canon beside the tee.

He has turned out so often in the early morning to see others go through the ordeal and possibly to make merry of their misfortunes. Now he has to do it himself. Shall he ask Willie to tee it a little higher, just in case?—but then he might sky it. Shall he try and keep his left heel on the ground, which he seems to remember having read about somewhere as a tip of the first shot of the day? Shall he take his practice swings on the tee or do it surreptitiously somewhere else? Perhaps he remembers seeing Lord Brabazon practising behind the bandstand—and assuredly no good came of that!

At any rate whatever he does, being the only entry for the competition, he automatically wins the beautiful gold medal presented to the club by Queen Adelaide. It will be hung round his neck by his predecessor at the dinner in the evening and he will wear it, and his red tail coat, on all ceremonial occasions. He will hang a silver ball on the silver club, as all past captains have done since 1754, except Princes of the Blood Royal who have hung golf ones.

The ceremonial occasions, if he has time, will be quite numerous. Clubs and golfing associations all over the country feel honoured by the presence at their own dinner of the captain of the R and A. He will be expected, of course, to make a speech and, though his remarks may be light, anything serious he may have to say will be taken, rightly or wrongly, to reflect the feeling and policy of the ruling body. He will be expected to be present at any championship or international match that may take place at St Andrews and to present the trophy and to welcome visiting teams from the Commonwealth and such like.

He will preside at the spring and autumn business meetings, the latter on the eve of his successor driving himself into office. He may strike a year free of controversial topics. On the other hand he is presiding, as Mr Speaker, over what is virtually the Parliament of Golf and must be prepared to conduct a controversial meeting with a firm and understanding hand.

His executive duties are strangely light. He is automatically a member of the principal committees but in practice—or so I am told—he rarely attends. He will in any case have done his stint in serving on many of them before. This is certainly true of Mr Henry Turcan, who has recently been announced as the captain-elect and must in his time have served on almost every committee in the club.

Though he lives not far from St Andrews, Mr Turcan is a much travelled man and in no sense a 'local' member. He is one of the club's two representatives who went to the United States to fix up the first tournament for the Eisenhower Trophy or 'World Cup' which was played at St Andrews and has throughout been a member of the championship committee which has done so much to enhance the prestige of the Royal and Ancient. He will prove, I am sure, a most worthy successor to the 200-odd gentlemen, including two past kings and the late Duke of Kent, who have driven themselves in as captains of the club.

17 September 1959

The Arrival of the Golf Buggy

I think American golfers are more likely to lose the use of their legs than we are, or at any rate to lose them first. It is an absolute fact that great numbers of them have already lost the use of their legs so far as golf is concerned and would no more *walk* round a course than fly.

In the early days it was the custom of the gentleman-golfer to have a caddie. The caddies seem to have varied from bottle-nosed old characters of uncertain temper—particularly, I think it may be suggested without offence, in Scotland—to eager little boys at 6d a round, like J. H. Taylor eighty years ago.

Many of these golfers would not think of playing without a caddie. They would rather not play at all. As golf bags and sets of clubs got bigger and bigger and caddies got fewer and fewer and more and more expensive, golfers who were either unwilling, or in so many cases unable, to lug round this vast mass of mainly unnecessary equipment were faced with two alternatives. They could either limit themselves to the number of clubs they were capable of using— anything from five to ten—and carry them round in a drainpipe bag, or haul them round on a special perambulator.

For myself I have chosen the former alternative. I carry nine clubs and am in the process of designing for them what I hope will prove to be the perfect drainpipe container. Frankly I never thought to see the trolley 'catch on' but it certainly has done and I do not look down my nose at this form of transport, though nothing would induce me to use it myself—quite apart from its tendency to slow down a round of golf by anything from twenty minutes to half an hour.

In America this perfectly logical process has gone further. I thought that the next step would be a trolley-and-battery like the milk delivery carts, with the trolley supplying its own power and the player walking along beside, but though experiments have, I believe been made, this step has been left out. The Americans went the whole hog and designed the trolley to carry not only the clubs but the man. Experience shows that within a few years American tendencies in golf find their way across the Atlantic and the electric buggy is no exception.

The pioneers in this country are the Sprite Company, who recently put on their first tournament at Selsdon Park. They make caravans and boats and their factory at Newmarket, which I had the pleasure of visiting the other day, is the second largest of its kind in Europe. Electric buggies are, in their present stage of course, by way of a sideline.

At first I confess that I rather pooh-poohed the idea that they would catch on in this country, at any rate for golf. In America golf is a hotter and on the whole I think hillier game than here—hotter certainly since in the north and middle-west they play only in summer and in the south it is a warm business all the time. The idea of having the weight taken off your feet between the longer shots becomes extremely attractive to those of middle age and over.

After writing about the electric buggies at Selsdon Park, however, I was astonished at the number of people who wrote to me to ask how they could get one. From these letters I judge that over the whole of the country there must be many thousands of people to whom the use of a buggy would mean almost a new life, and not merely golfing life at that. Everyone, for instance, afflicted with that maddening malady, arthritis of the hips, could at once become mobile again. So could anyone who has had the first warnings of a 'fluttering' heart. He could watch golf, drive round to the club of a morning and see his friends or, if it comes to that, drive down to the shops without feeling that he had come down to an 'invalid carriage'. What is good enough for President Eisenhower, for whom the Sprite people sent a buggy to Turnberry, is good enough for him.

I adhere to my original belief that it is really rather ridiculous for any youngish able-bodied man to play golf for fresh air and exercise and then deliberately do away with the exercise by riding round the course in a buggy. In the past month, however, I have come very much round to the point of view that these little carts may prove a real blessing to many hundreds of people.

10 November 1960

'Ex-Cambridge Triple Blue'

Of course, there are fewer all-rounders—in life itself as well as in sport—and the more's the pity; but before we condemn the young men of today for not being the all-rounders that many of their fathers were, let us remember the different world in which they are brought up. I was brought up on the principle that you ought to save something of what you earned and try to preserve the family fortunes in order to hand them on, intact or if possible increased, to your children. Now more than half what a successful man earns is confiscated in tax and his main object is not to be caught with anything on him when he dies.

This is not a climate in which the amateur, to use the word in its true sense, can flourish. The gifted amateur, whether in the arts, in politics or in sport, is always more to be desired than the professional. Now he is almost an extinct species. The specialist of today is neither fish nor fowl, neither a good amateur nor a good professional. For whom have you the greater personal respect—Dan Maskell or the annual winner of the amateur singles at Wimbledon?

Let me quote a case of the total amateur of earlier days, which I am sure will cause the specialist of today to stop and think. I refer to Roger Wethered, whom Bobby Jones played in the final of the Amateur championship at St Andrews, the first 'leg' of his historic Grand Slam in 1930. After saying, in his new book not yet published here, that he honestly thought Roger had himself little hope of winning, being a 'completely charming person without any semblance of aggressiveness on the golf course', Jones goes on to say:

'I recall so well the evening in 1921 when he, an amateur, had surprised everyone by finishing in a tie for the Open championship with Jock Hutchison. I had stood in a group of Roger's friends near the 18th green below the cement steps going up to the clubhouse and had joined in an effort to persuade him that it was more important for him to remain over to participate in a play-off for the Open championship than to return home for a neighbourhood amateur cricket match in which he had agreed to play the next day. Our arguments finally prevailed . . .'!

Another tremendous all-rounder of the time was my very old friend and sparring partner 'J. S. F. Morrison, the ex-Cambridge triple blue', as he was always styled by the newspapers. He played cricket and soccer for Cambridge before the First World War and, after a spell of flying elementary bombers from the heel of Italy, golf after it. He went on to play full back for the Corinthians in the golden days and also for Sunderland under the captaincy of the late Charles Buchan, among whose many tales about him was that he was allowed a special ration of a quart of beer before the kick-off and a quart at half-time!

In the winning Carthusian Halford Hewitt team just before the last war, of which John was so distinguished a member, we had two other 'gifted amateurs' of the kind that cannot flourish today. Jack Thompson, one of the finest shots in England, amateur pilot and pretty well scratch at skiing when well into the forties, would turn up at Deal without having played a round of golf for several months and, after a few prodigious 'tops', would settle down to play to plus one. Lionel Burdon Sanderson, not heard of since the previous year, had generally just returned from shooting lions or some such. He settled down to play impeccable golf in the top foursome, much to the surprise of opponents who had never heard of him; attended the winning celebrations, and departed till required again next year.

My esteemed colleague, Leonard Crawley, reached great eminence in golf, yet in a way I wish he had stuck to cricket! This is not to be taken as a back-handed compliment. Leonard, for Essex and for the Gentlemen, was a mighty and fearsome hitter, respected by all, even in the days of Hobbs and Sutcliffe. He adorned golf, but cricket could have done with him even more.

On the other hand we have his parallel today and this time cricket, I am glad to say, has won, in the person of Ted Dexter. If ever there was a Walker Cup certainty, it was Dexter. I remember him particularly for two shots, a 3-iron and a 4-iron, into a tremendous wind at the 15th and 16th holes at Rye during the University match of 1955 when he captained Cambridge. No one else, I fancy, reached either green with any club.

Dexter chose cricket and has just proved himself one of the most successful captains of my home county, Sussex, in recent times. He draws the crowds because at any moment he may knock a couple running straight out of the ground. There is yet time for him to captain England against the Australians and then after a few months' practice turn out against the Americans at golf. If only there were more like him!

18 January 1962

The Case for Female Caddies

I have always felt that caddying was a job for the young—possibly because the first caddies I ever saw were boys and because I envied them so much. These were to be seen on the skyline, plodding along behind their plus-foured and knickerbockered employers on the first hole at Royal Eastbourne, while my own attention was constantly redirected by the headmaster to the Greek unseen. Later I realised that these boys were submitted to the most stringent rules, laid down by the club and administered by Mr Holly, who was the caddie master at 'The Royal' for fifty years.

One offence, I remember, was 'caught without sponge', for which a fine of 3d was exacted. From time to time they were caught looking for balls on the bank beside our playing field, in which case they were either shot at with a .22 rifle by the school sergeant from the armoury window or beaten by the headmaster. What a commotion either of these salutary forms of discipline would cause today!

If boys, why not girls? There have always been girl caddies on the Continent. The first I came across were at St Germain, outside Paris, to which my old friend Eric Martin Smith and I repaired when we were at Cambridge. In the following year he won the Amateur at Westward Ho! and I always maintain, to him, that he would have won the French championship if his girl caddie had not been so devastatingly good looking.

Later on, when I had the good fortune to win the German championship, I was attended by a blonde young Amazon called Gertrude, whom I naturally remember with affection. Her hair hung down in a pony-tail at the back and she carried a little wooden rake attached to the bag with which to smooth out the marks I made in the bunkers. Professionally speaking she was as efficient a caddie as I have ever had.

In France, of course, grandmothers carry clubs as well as girls but I have never been easy in mind at seeing a woman older and, apparently, though not in fact, frailer than my own mother shouldering one of those ridiculously vast bags in which the experts find it necessary to carry, or cause to be carried, a set of clubs which in themselves do not weigh 14 lb. Still, they do it, so it is not for me to complain.

If you *must* take this enormous paraphernalia with you, however, and cannot get, or afford, an adult man, the answer has always seemed to me to be trolley-and-boy, but, when one comes to think of it, there is no reason why it should not be trolley-and-girl. Every instinct tells me that girls might well be the better bet, as being less susceptible to fidgeting, wandering off in search of larks' nests, and hiccoughs.

In England there is a precedent for girl caddies, as I remember being shown pictures of them in Edwardian, or it may have been Victorian, times at Huntercombe. When I lived in that delightful part of the world, up to eight years ago, I often had the pleasure of being 'caddied for' by Mrs Streak, the wife of the greenkeeper, a stern and lively critic of the game in general and one's own play in particular.

However, if you want to see the girl caddie at her finest, you must go to Japan. When they played the Canada Cup at Tokyo, there was tremendous competition among the girls for the privilege of caddying, and those selected wore uniform blue blouses and trousers and white 'sneakers' and each had the name of her player emblazoned on her smock.

How they carried the huge bags I hardly know to this day. It is no exaggeration to say that without too much of a squeeze many of them could have got into the bags themselves. Snead threatened to leave his clubs behind and take his home with him. I did not blame him!

31 May 1962

Carry Your Bag, Sir?

A good caddie is more than a mere assistant: he is a guide, philosopher and friend. The bond between a golfer and caddie, to me, is one of the most enjoyable relationships that can exist between employer and employed. Looking back over the years, forty of them alas!, I can see that this feeling began to grow in my mind in the first open competition in which I ever played. This was on the short course at North Foreland and I can safely say, even after this period of time, that I should not have won it had I not been bolstered up, as the pressure grew and I began to falter, by my caddie.

He was a boy of about the same age and his parents were on holiday at Margate. We became close friends and the late Endersby Howard wrote an article about us in the *Daily Mail*—my first experience of the heady wine of publicity. My caddie, whose name was Frank Honour, admired a handsome pair of white shoes I was wearing and in a burst of fellow feeling I said that I would give them to him if we won. I know that I said 'we', not 'I', and I have thought in terms of 'we', just as every good caddie does, ever since. In due course I sent him the shoes and he wrote to thank me. I have his letter still. When I came across it about twenty years later, I saw that the address was in Acton, for which constituency I was at that time Member of Parliament. I looked in the register and to my delight found that there was still a whole family of Honours living at the same address. I called on them, hoping to renew an association which had proved so agreeable in the past, but unfortunately my friend had gone to seek his fortune in other parts of the world.

I can remember as though it were yesterday three of the caddies who carried my clubs in my four University matches. At Princes I was assisted by a member of the Gisby family, well known in Sandwich, who was a good deal older than I and knew every fold and undulation round the greens like the back of his hand. I was never much of a player through the green but, perhaps through so often being left with a pitch instead of a putt, I did become a very accurate short game player. Gisby would point to the exact spot on which the ball should pitch— 'About a foot to the left of that match stick', I remember, was one of his instructions—and I would duly pitch it there. Time and again it was not the place I should have chosen myself, but I soon developed a blind faith in Gisby's judgment and it was inevitably correct. I won by 8 and 7. Alone, I might have gone to the last green.

In the following year at Rye, I took with me a caddie who had attached himself to me at Walton Heath. Not only was he a first-class caddie but he committed on my behalf a really splendid piece of gamesmanship over which my Oxford opponent, Pat Jackson, and I have often laughed since. I was just off the 15th green in three, whereas Jackson was only five or six feet from the pin. At this point I holed the chip. 'Yes,' said the caddie, as he picked it out, 'I thought we should get one of them, sooner or later.' Having been four years together in the same house at school, Jackson knew me well enough merely to remark, with some feeling, 'You bloody little worm!' He missed the putt, of course, but in the circumstances I doubt whether many would have holed it.

Two years later I took the same caddie to Sandwich, but unfortunately he had so much to drink that twice he actually fell down on the course—he attributed it to having been gassed in the First World War!—and there was nothing for it but to replace him. I forget the new caddie's name, but I should recognise him instantly if I saw him. He was absolutely wonderful and coaxed me into playing the best game of my life.

Many professionals have been accompanied by the same travelling caddies for years on end—Cotton, Padgham and Rees come at once to mind—and there is not the slightest doubt that this special relationship does produce dividends. When the pressure begins to mount up, a trusted caddie-cum-friend can be a tremendous help, not only in sustaining one's moral fibre, but also preventing acts of obvious indiscretion that one tends to commit when the tension distorts one's judgment.

I have had innumerable caddies, from blonde Gertrude, who helped me win a championship in Berlin, to a huge black convict from an African gaol with the blue diamond sewn on his nightshirt. It is only as I have been writing about them that I realise how vastly they have added to the enjoyment of my golfing life and I only wish I could thank them all once again.

13 September 1962

In Loco Parentis

Quoting from my own experience, both on the receiving end and the giving out, I am regretfully inclined to think that children will not in any circumstances take direct advice from their parents. It is only rarely that they will even communicate freely with their parents, either by letter or in person. All must be done with a subtle indirectness. Thus, if you want to know how little Tommy is getting on at school, it is no use taking him out alone for half term and asking him. You will get the answer, 'Oh, alright'. You must make him bring one, or two, or even three friends with him, get yourself settled down with a drink, order them each a huge concoction which the Cavendish Hotel, Eastbourne, in my day both as boy and parent used to call a 'Half-term Special'. and wait for the moment—it won't be long—when they are all chattering away like monkeys about school 'shop'.

Similarly, I do not think that, in golf, children will 'take it' from father. What does he know about it anyway? Fashions change in golf like anything else. He was brought up on the waltz. Now it's the twist. My father was a model of the 'backbone of the game', the

16-handicap club golfer, and I used to play a great deal with him, but I was always sure that I knew more than he did. I would have taken anything as gospel from the late Jack Seager, professional at my home club at Bedford, and later from his successor, Bill Moore, who has now been there forty-one years—but from poor old father, no! It reminds me of Mark Twain's comment about his father—I hope I have it verbatim—'when I was fourteen, my father was so ignorant that we could hardly bear to have him about the house. When I was twenty-one, I was astonished at how much the old man had learnt in the last seven years.'

I got 'bitten' by golf instantly and completely when I first took up a club with two other boys to play on three makeshift holes, without flags of course, on the common at Yelverton, where my parents were on holiday. Even at this vast distance of time I can feel again the thrill of waiting to get up and go out before breakfast. Here was love at first sight indeed—equalled only by one's feelings towards one's first new bicycle.

Neither of my children have been thus 'bitten', possibly because not much opportunity has come their way. If they had been, I should look back with gratitude on what my parents did for me and do the same for them. It would cost a bit more today, of course, but never mind. The dividends in later life are priceless. In a way it is easier today. Golf is 'respectable' for the young. In my day it wasn't. 'Not a team game,' they said. I always thought this was nonsense and now I think that most people realise that, with the best will in the world towards team games, it was. How in the world, I used to wonder, can they expect you, if you live in a village in darkest Bedfordshire, to find twenty-one other boys of the same age, and a pitch on which to play?

I did, it is true, turn out in goal for the village when I had reached the age of about sixteen and rather fancied myself, but we were beaten by 11–2, and I shall go to my grave declaring that at least nine of the goals were the fault of a pair of idiot full backs. From the age of about eleven, however, golf was my real love, and almost every day I used to ride down to the club (not allowed in the clubhouse, of course) and either have a lesson with Jack Seager, or play round with other young people—almost running along in case we got in the way of peppery Indian Army colonels, of which the entire membership appeared at that time to be comprised—or just hanging about Jack's shop, inhaling into the memory for ever that unique and indescribable aroma of shavings, leather, twine and glue. Sometimes he would actually be engaged in making me a new club, a driver for Christmas perhaps, and then one's happiness was complete.

I should always start children off with the pro—or, if the club is rather a 'grand' one—then with a young assistant of whom they could make a personal friend. There are so many short cuts to golf. Individual styles vary, but there are certain principles—how you hold the club, how you stand, how you start the swing—which trial and error over forty or fifty years have turned into an acceptable 'standard' method. If he learns these when he is young and pliable and adaptable, a boy can start working on his own patent 'improvements' later.

All boys should be encouraged to be able, when asked later 'Do you play golf?', to answer 'Yes'. Golf, as I am conscious of having remarked before, is the universal letter of introduction, the Esperanto of sport. You can take your handicap with you to any part of the world—and borrow some clubs when you get there.

17 January 1963

Winter of Discontent

At the moment of writing the President's Putter is being played at Littlestone instead of Rye, and I myself am still cut off by vast drifts of snow from the windmills which I normally inhabit. The whole scene is one which we in Sussex expect sympathetically to see portrayed in Derbyshire or Beattock in Scotland, but do not expect to have to endure ourselves. Perhaps it is good for us to know what others suffer. For myself I have had enough of it. Nor am I encouraged by hearing on the radio that some American forecaster who has been particularly successful in predicting weather in Britain says that we are to have it for the rest of January.

When I was a boy you reckoned to be given, quite early in life, a pair of skates for your birthday and it was a poor year indeed when you had no chance of using them. Even when I was at the University, which alas is thirty years ago, hardly a year passed when lean fenmen did not emerge in long black tights and woollen hats with bobbles on top, and, with their hands behind them, skate from Cambridge to Ely.

At least, it seemed, we knew where we were. You had winter in winter and summer in summer. One of my first golfing impressions was of the great drought in the summer of, I believe, 1921, when the fairways of the Bedfordshire Club opened in great cracks and a ball rolling merrily along would vanish suddenly from sight. All over the course people would be seen lying on their stomachs, fishing for balls with a fully extended arm and niblick. I remember vividly doing this myself, perhaps for a much prized black dot Silver King, and the agonies of hauling it almost within reach, only to see it slither from the club-head and disappear, this time for ever.

In some cases members were even known to lose not only the ball but the club with which they were fishing for it. Maybe in some remote future these clubs and balls—some of the latter 10 or 12 feet below the surface—will be recovered, and I often wonder at what conclusions the geologists of 1000 years hence will arrive. Perhaps they will conclude that the people of Bedford still engaged in some strange and curious burial rites.

Nowadays the seasons seem to be neither one thing nor the other. The winter is generally just messy, August is generally a washout, and, if I were taking a golfing holiday, I should be inclined to take it in October or November. Our climate does sometimes turn the country into such an earthly paradise that one feels guilty at having ever contemplated chucking one's hand in and departing for a place in the sun—but no one could call it predictable. People who live in predictable climates with day after day of blue skies and sunshine often sit dreaming of a nice grey mist over the countryside at home—and indeed I have spent long enough in such places to begin to get the feeling myself—but what a wonderful country this would be if we could know what was coming!

I have not the slightest doubt that one of the reasons, though not the only one, why the best British golfers, especially the professionals, are not the equal of the Americans is that, even if they continue playing in the winter, their muscles stiffen up and they lose the competitive 'edge'. It takes them some time to recapture their form in the spring and even then they may have to face a comparatively miserable summer, with a complete day's play in the Open washed out two years runnning in the first week of July.

What a difference it would make if they could rely on the climate. They could reach their peak in the summer, and, as to the winter, push off and forget it. Take one job for the summer and another for the winter, as do their opposite numbers in the northern parts of the United States. Some are beginning to get wise to this already. Jimmy Hitchcock and Guy Wolstenholme, I see, are to tour India, while others, including David Thomas, are to play in the five-week circuit of tournaments in the Far East.

Senior players, when I was young, often told me that they reckoned to put their clubs away in the winter and again in the summer. Many would shoot grouse in August and resume their golf for the September 'season' that used to be so fashionable at North Berwick. In 1901 the editor of *Golf Illustrated* wrote that he trusted that the American habit of playing in shirtsleeves would not spread to this country. 'If it is too hot to play in a jacket,' he said, 'it is too hot to play at all.' Those were the days.

For myself, I have a feeling the ice age is coming.

14 April 1966

Four-footed Friends

The finding of golf balls by dogs appeals strongly to the 'something for nothing' instinct in us all, like finding mushrooms, and indeed one of my more pleasant dreams, when I am not stuck on top of a tall chimney or falling from some great height, is of being on a pebble beach and detecting a golf ball, and then another, and another, till I have crammed my pockets full of them. I do not know what the psychiatrists would give as an explanation of this, but my own is quite simple. It is a relic of playing so many foursomes with John Morrison in the Halford Hewitt at Deal before the war and so often searching for our ball on the pebble ridge behind the sixth green!

The first dog I ever watched finding balls belonged to my very old friend, Bill Moore, who retired a year or two ago after forty years as professional to the Bedfordshire club. This dog was a spaniel and I could walk straight to within a yard or two of the spot in which he suddenly began furiously digging at the leaf mould underneath the hedge on the left of what was then the 11th and is now the 14th. He eventually came up with an incredibly ancient 'Chemico Bob', a ball which had not been manufactured for I do not know how many years. It must have been buried six or eight inches deep.

How could the dog have possibly known it was there unless it was by scent? Yet the experts say that dogs find balls in ways which absolutely preclude their having been able to scent them. It is also said that, even though we ourselves can smell a new ball, dogs cannot and can only find one when it has been lost for a day or two and is beginning to 'mature'. Does anyone know whether this is true either?

At the Pyecombe club, just beside where I live on the Sussex Downs, I remember some years ago watching the then professional training a small spaniel puppy to retrieve balls and so far as I know it only took about a fortnight. The dog is now middle-aged but none the less keen for that. The other evening, for the purpose of this article, I asked Mr Goldsmith, the present steward, whether the dog was still active as ball-hound. He had just come in off the course after playing a round accompanied by the dog, 'Buster', and his answer was to turn out one of the pockets of his golf bag. Out of it came 20 balls which the dog had picked up in that round alone. Altogether in the last two years he has found more than 4000—some of them, I dare say, quite a number of times.

There is not the slightest doubt that Buster is better when the ground is damp and this lends force to the scent theory. A veterinary friend of mine would only go so far as to say that scent was 'a curious thing' and went on to advance the theory that it might go in layers. He had often, he said, when out hunting, been able to smell a fox from the lofty eminence of his horse, whereas the hounds were unable to trace anything at all. I touched on this point about how dogs detect balls some time ago elsewhere and have been looking up some of the interesting correspondence it aroused at the time.

A Worthing golfer, for instance, quoted the case of his Jack Russell terrier which had been finding an average of 18 balls per round for several years and had established a 'record' of 32. 'I cannot,' he wrote, 'throw any light on how they do it but I can perhaps add to the confusion . . . The dog normally appears to detect by scent but there are some things that cannot be explained. More than once I have seen him jump into a ditch containing a foot or so of dirty water and emerge immediately with a ball which, from the state of his nose, has clearly been dug out of the muddy bottom . . . Several times he has been seen to drop a ball which he has been bringing to me, dive several yards into thick bushes or gorse and to come out with another ball. In every case the position of the second ball has been such that it would seem impossible for him to have detected it by smell or sight from where the first ball was dropped.'

This dog would find, sniff at, and leave alone, any ball belonging either to his master or to any of the other three players with whom he was playing, but would pick up any other ball, even if it was in play and at the moment being searched for by other players—all of which again seems to add force to the theory of scent.

Huntercombe, where I spent many happy years, was a great place for ball-hounds, each with its own accepted territory, and nothing was more exasperating than to see Mrs Wilkins and her pack of two (or should it be one couple?) stationed at precisely the point where a high slice would pitch in the bushes and then to pitch it there. Long experience had taught her, of course, exactly where to position herself and sometimes the dogs had only to burrow into the bushes for a yard or two in order to retrieve one's ball.

P.S. Since writing the above, I have been down to Pyecombe again. Mr Goldsmith had just spent half-an-hour with Buster in a patch of rough on the right of the sixth hole measuring, he thought, about 100 yards by 20. The dog scrabbled incessantly in the long grass and came up with what must almost be the world half-hour record—50 balls.

25 August 1966

An 'umbling Game

It seems somewhat naive to suggest that golfers are conceited—just like that. You might just as well say that golfers are unconceited. In many instances, you would be right in each case, but taking the *genus* golfer as a whole, in each case wrong.

As to the younger generation I cannot help feeling that my own vintage, of the late twenties and early thirties, were more conceited than our opposite numbers of today, certainly in the way of clothes.

We tended to wear over-long plus-fours, often of light grey flannel, together with (ghastly thought!) black and white shoes. We were also liable to affect caps, probably of some pronounced chequered material, worn at an angle on the side of the head. On the other hand perhaps we were not to be blamed, for after all this was the fashion. It was the time of the *Boy Friend* and women's fashions also were more hideous surely than at any time since, with the possible exception of the mini-skirt.

Again, we naturally copied our elders and betters and they too paid a great deal of attention to their clothes. The immortal Hagen thought nothing of changing his attire at lunch time and emerging with an entirely different outfit for the afternoon's play. Everyone knew that Johnny Farrell, who is still at the Baltusrol club, in Pennsylvania, was the 'best dressed golfer of the year'. He used to wear white plus-fours, and extremely elegant they were. Such clothes, and Hagen's, were not to be confused with the many-coloured raiment which Jimmy Demaret later used as a sort of personal gimmick, though, I should add that both he and Max Faulkner, who has worked the same gimmick over here, have always been immaculately turned out.

Perhaps, after all, to be gaily turned out in the fashion of the day, however bizarre it might look twenty or thirty years later, is not a matter of 'conceit'.

To find out, I have just looked the word up in the dictionary and it says: 'Over-estimate of oneself; too favourable an opinion of one's own good qualities.' I have never 'defended' golf, or sought to influence anyone to take it up, but I will certainly go on record as saying in its defence that it is not a game which makes people, in the dictionary sense of the word, conceited. Indeed, precisely the opposite. Golf is just about the greatest knocker-down of conceit, the surest deflater of the human balloon, that exists in this world.

I trust that it will not be considered a 'religious' belief, and therefore to have no place in these columns, when I say that, if there is one thing that I do believe in, it is the 'Little Man in the Tree', as Francis Ouimet termed it in a memorable discussion we once had at the Country Club at Brookline, Mass.

The Little Man in the Tree is akin to the P. G. Wodehouse character (I wish I could find the exact quotation) who, as you pass through the doorway whistling and rejoicing that all is right with the world and what a good fellow you are, is standing behind the door with a sock loaded with a lump of lead. The Little Man in the Tree not only hears everything you say but knows every thought that passes through your head—but, of course, however quickly you whip round, you are never quite in time to see him.

'Level fours and five to play' you think to yourself. 'Even if I take five at the 16th *and* the 17th and don't get a three at the short 15th, it can't be worse than 74. On the other hand, playing like this, it could well be 71, or even 70, or even, it wouldn't surprise me, 69. There should be quite a bit of applause for that. I suppose I should have to make a short speech . . .' You never said a word, but the Little Man heard you. Three putts at the 14th, five at the short 15th, out of bounds at the 16th and a five with the second ball, making seven. If you carry on trying, he may let you off with a couple of pars for the last two, making 77. If you 'bellyache' or give in, he will give you a five and a six for an 80, and you will hardly remember how it happened.

No. A golfer may be conceited but, believe me, he won't be conceited for long. Not for nothing has golf for a hundred years been known as 'an 'umbling game'—though, of course, it isn't really the game that 'umbles us. It is the Little Man in the Tree.

14 September 1967

Money Talks

When I came into golf, playing for Cambridge against senior London clubs and the notabilities of the day, the emphasis was distinctly on the amateur rather than the professional. The Open championship, of course, attracted enormous interest, and the Ryder Cup, and the 'emergence' of Henry Cotton, but there were only about half a dozen professional tournaments and the American 'circuit'—ghastly word!—did not exist in its present rather ludicrously affluent form, so that players become so wealthy that they can afford not to trouble to attend a tournament in which the first prize is $35,000 or roughly £12,500.

I began in the late twenties when only the 'heavier' newspapers really dealt with golf and it had not yet become a 'popular' game. It was almost universally frowned upon at school and, although it turned out to have been absolutely the game to have played for the University, because of the travel and the experience and the contacts which were so useful and so agreeable in later life, it was quite a poor relation at the University itself.

With the smaller numbers of players the higher grades of golfers—higher in the sense of skill rather than social standing, though that came into it a bit as well—tended to form a smaller coterie and this was in many ways more fun. You tended to assume that, if you said you had got a two at the Maiden at Sandwich or the Dowie at Hoylake, the other fellows would know what you meant and be familiar with it all. *The Times*, *Telegraph* and *Morning Post* all reported this sort of golf at great length and even for our Saturday matches against London clubs we would get a whole column, and almost everybody's name would be mentioned so that they did not feel left out. *The Times*, of course, kept their correspondents anonymous and have only just given up doing so, perhaps 20 years late, but anyone who did not know that Our Golf Correspondent was Bernard Darwin and anyone who could not quote from his Saturday article on Sunday morning was beyond the pale.

In this sort of climate it was only natural that an event like the President's Putter of the Oxford and Cambridge Society should claim national interest. I seem to remember that in a friendly match before the Walker Cup the Society beat the American team and I am sure that their best team could at any time have beaten England, Scotland, Ireland or Wales, so that a large proportion of the leading talent in the country would be assembled at Rye for the Putter. The event is still reported, but largely because it is the first of the year and there is nothing else to write about. It can hardly be expected that nose-to-the-grindstone, state-aided students possess the same appeal, or the same skill, as a Tolley or a Wethered. If this sounds snobbish it is not intended as such. I am merely quoting realities.

Many influences have contributed to the decline of interest in amateur golfers, coinciding, strangely enough, with the tremendous upsurge in the numbers of those who play, all of whom after all are amateurs. The first, of course, is money; the second that it is now both easy and respectable for an amateur to turn professional, whereas previously the professionals' trade union was able to maintain a comparatively closed shop.

It costs a lot of money to play competitive golf as an amateur, especially in these days when selectors seem to expect a young chap to take about eight weeks off a year playing in tournaments, quite apart from every weekend. Not many these days have that sort of money nor are their employers willing to grant them that sort of time. It is only natural, therefore, that they try to wheedle a free year or two out of Father, or some unrelated sugar daddy, to see if they are good enough to turn professional. The best of them do so and take their public image with them, leaving others trying to rise from obscurity as amateurs. If they succeed at golf the money they earn almost at once is fabulous by comparison with what they would have earned at that age in any other way.

Clive Clark, for instance, was going to be an architect, probably stuck in this country and taxed to the hilt for life. Instead he has been touring all over the world at the expense of an equipment company (and rightly enough at that) and has not only picked up several hundred pounds and an enhanced reputation, and therefore value, in the Open, but has already played in one of the BBC's television matches (I won't reveal the result) in which you get $4000 if you win and $3000—more than £1000—if you lose. Furthermore Peter Townsend and Bobby Cole, under the same management, are also due to get a turn in these matches. £1000 for losing: that really is nice work if you can get it!

It is a newspaper axiom that nothing interests people so much as other people's money, and I think this is probably true. I am often accused of neglecting amateur golf, but although I detect a certain boredom with the everlasting business of who has won most money, people are still inclined to emit a low whistle at the thought that Nicklaus has so far won $156,000 this year in prize money alone and now, long before his 30th birthday, is assured of being a multi-millionaire for life. I find it difficult to work up the enthusiasm that we used to feel 'when I came in' for the young amateur of today who one feels certain is going to turn professional directly he reckons it is worth taking the plunge. If you feel that I am wrong in interpreting public interest in this way, just tell me this: who is the amateur champion of Great Britain; where did he win; and who did he beat in the final?

4 April 1968

The Race is to the Longest

It seems to me, and I may be talking nonsense, and not for the first time at that, that the so-called 'power golf' is the natural result of the increasing intensity of competition for a share of the fantastic riches now available to those who reach the top of the tree. The fact that there are so few of them and that only 70-odd tournament professionals in the whole of the United States make enough to cover their expenses does not in any way deter the rest.

It was always said that Bobby Jones, and come to that, our own Henry Cotton, had an extra 20 yards in hand, to be pulled out when necessary. For the rest of the time the chief thing was to drive straight—a long way farther than the rest of us, certainly, but still not flat out. In these days I simply do not believe that is true. I believe that Nicklaus and Palmer are 95 per cent flat out all the time and that the other 5 per cent is only worth pulling out as a considerable and calculated risk.

This means that in the highest quarters the day of the golfing artist is over. If the good big 'un is equally talented and reliable, then there is nothing that the good little 'un can do about it. He may finish ahead of him occasionally but not when it really matters, not on the sort of courses on which the really big events are played. This is a pity and in many ways unfair, but there it is. Life *is* unfair.

Gary Player, not too well endowed to start with, had the sort of physique which, with considerable willpower on his part, was capable of being built up so that he could keep up with the big 'uns. For myself, nothing on earth could have built me up, in my twenties, to compete with Nicklaus and I therefore, despite all my well-known devotion to physical fitness, could never in any circumstances have played in that class.

As good an example as you can find is the Augusta National course, where in a week or two I hope to be watching the Masters. Here the 13th and 15th holes are very similar. Both greens are guarded by a deep creek in front of the green and both, for most of the players, are true par fives, in that, although they might conceivably have got up in two in the ordinary way, they cannot hit far enough to carry the creek and pitch on the green. They therefore have to play their seconds not as far as they can possibly cover in two shots but well short of the creek, and this may cost them perhaps 30 yards that they were otherwise capable of covering. Just a few of them, however, *can* reach the green full pitch with their seconds and this is a risk well worth taking. If they go in the creek, they drop just behind and have a good chance of getting down in two more to save their par five. If they carry it, even if they finish in a trap, they will more likely than not come out with a birdie four. When this happens eight times in the tournament, what chance have the others got?

It is my strong impression that the race as a whole, at any rate the top-class American golfers, are getting bigger and stronger. Without going into the old arguments of merit and skill, could Harry Vardon or J. H. Taylor or even Walter Hagen, have stood against Nicklaus and the huge power that he seems to generate? Your guess is as good as mine but I should have thought the answer to be no. They could stand against the mighty hitters of their day simply because the latter had not yet harnessed their length as the best of them have today.

Is it the club you have to take or is it the distance you have to hit the ball that makes the difference betwen the big 'un and the little 'un, I often wonder? Perhaps a bit of both, and once again an unfair advantage to the big battalions. What I mean is that, if both players have 160 yards to go, they theoretically have the same problem. Is it really an advantage to be able to hit it that distance with a 6-iron as against a 4-iron? After all, it is the same distance for both. Yet somehow I think it is an advantage—but when the big fellow hits it 260 yards off the tee (the average drive in the US Open) and can reach the green with, say a 6-iron, what hope has the man who drives 230 and now has to take a 4-wood? Day in and day out, the answer is 'None at all'.

On the other hand, in the world of true golf, the variety played by the other few millions of us and the only one that really matters, I have not the slightest doubt that there is still ample opportunity for the crafty player, or even the player who will trouble to bring to his golf just one-quarter of the commonsense that he likes to think he brings to his business. The number of what I think of as 'BF' shots played by the average club golfer is quite unbelievable. Add to this the fact that the club's mighty hitter can generally be relied upon to be in the bushes two or three times a round and there is hope for all of us. And if you don't believe it, see Admiral Benson, who at the age of eighty-one had his handicap reduced from 17 to 16 on account of his performance in the autumn meeting of the R and A, playing from the medal tees on the Old Course in quite a high wind. This remarkable feat was achieved by playing straight, though not far, down the exact centre, holing out from five feet and under—and never by any chance playing a 'BF' shot.

18 April 1968

Seasonal Golf

When I was a boy, the gentlemen golfers, though I cannot claim to have known this, or them, until later, would put aside their clubs for the winter altogether. They would mostly do the same in the summer too, on the ground that the ball ran too far and it was liable to be too hot and 'everyone was away' and the rest of it. This left the spring, at such times as you were not fishing, and the autumn, at such times as you were not shooting—and, my word, what a life it must have been at that! Though I have always regarded myself as basically a common fellow, perhaps I have some gentlemanly instincts in me after all, for I have never been much of a one for winter golf, though of course the march of time may have something to do with it. Nor, though, did I ever really like mid-summer golf, having also an unsuspected strain of honesty in my make-up which declines to afford me any great satisfaction from seeing the ball go about 40 yards farther than in winter when I know I have not hit it any better.

If ever a game called for two kinds of ball, it is golf. We could call them the summer ball and the winter ball, but of course we could use them all the year round. What they would really be would be a shorter ball for 'them' and a longer one for 'us', and this would add tremendously to the sum total of pleasure, always allowing that the two balls were equally enjoyable to hit. The really fine players of golf never really get a game—not, at any rate, as the architect designed it to be played. The aristocracy, as in so many other walks of life, are brought down to the common level, so that fine hitters of the ball like, say, Thomas or Alliss are often reduced to taking irons or a 4-wood off the tee and the same sort of clubs for their second shots as I should take on a course of 5000 yards.

Every course ought surely to have two genuine long holes, the kind where if you mis-hit your first or second you are hard put to it to get on in three. A 500-yarder effects this easily enough for most of us, but for the aristocracy we should need to make them walk about 750 yards.

During the US Open last year at Baltusrol I spent a lot of time at the 17th, which was more than 600 yards—620, if memory serves aright—and the only reason that some of them did not get on in two was that there was a desert of sand just short of the green. If 'we' had the present ball and 'they' had one which they could hit about 220 yards, what fun the game would be, especially for 'them', able at last to open their shoulders and hit out with a brassie instead of creeping round with a series of wedges and 9-irons.

I have digressed from the point, perhaps, and not for the first time, and I return to the subject of foul weather golf, in which I marvel at how well some people, and those not necessarily the youngest, manage to perform. We see many examples of it in the President's Putter at Rye, which is 'made' by the fact that, come what may it is played in January. I do not myself play in it any more but I certainly recall every conceivable kind of conditions, including playing in shirtsleeves. Often, however, the ground has been frozen bone hard, with the ball bouncing in every direction, complete with icy blizzards from the east. Yet many a time you will find some hero, dressed as though about to go out in the lifeboat and reduced to a quarter-swing, coming in with a perfectly genuine score of level fours.

I once won what was for me an important competition in such rain that the whole event was on the point of being cancelled. I should like it to be thought that this was on account of my superior skill and determination, but in fact it was due almost solely to the fact that I had made the discovery, all on my own, that the only way in which to hold golf clubs in real rain was to go to the ironmongers and buy, for about 18d, a pair of those ordinary cotton gloves in which women used to clean the grates in the days when women cleaned grates. This, I thought, was very crafty of me—till only ten minutes ago, looking idly through a copy with which a friend had just presented me of *Advanced Golf* by James Braid (1908), I found that the only way to hold your clubs in wet weather was to use cotton gloves. Perhaps, however, I may pass on to those who play in glasses a wet weather tip which may be more original—and I would give credit to the inventor if I could remember who it was. At any rate, this character's wife told me that after much trial and error he had found the perfect solution, and this was an ordinary sou-wester worn back to front.

For the professionals a start in early April has always been 'dicey' and one remembers a number of occasions on which the opening tournament of the year, their close championship, has been made a complete toss-up by freezing conditions and immature greens. Whether the records confirm it or not I do not know, but it is my impression that during my lifetime spring has tended to come later and autumn to go on longer, and nowadays, if I had the choice, I would settle for the third week in November rather than the second in April. That is, if I could not be either shooting or fishing!

CHAPTER EIGHT

Committee Man

The British Way of Handicapping

I doubt whether one club member in twenty habitually plays to his handicap. This would make a total of 20 in a membership of 400, and when have even half this number equalled the bogey in a score competition?

There are many reasons for this. One is that your handicap is meant to represent something like your best golf, ignoring the occasional freak round which you are not likely to repeat. I am reminded of the old story of the golfer sitting in the club room bemoaning the fact that he was off his game. In a sudden burst of honesty he added, 'Come to think of it, I have never really been *on* my game!' Your handicap should reflect your ability when you are 'on' your game— and the fewer times that you are on what you are pleased to call your game, the less will you play to your handicap.

Furthermore, if you are rash enough or lucky enough to play slightly above your form, you will at once be deprived of your handicap, for in no branch of golfing activity is a man so conscientious as when he gets on the handicapping committee and is empowered to cut the handicaps of his fellow members. It is rather like the trains, about which complaints are also made from time to time. After all, the wretched things can only be either exactly on time or late. They cannot be early, or people would not catch them. So it is with your handicap. You can either just play to it or, as it were, be late. The moment you get ahead of it, you haven't got it—if you see what I mean.

Another point is that in Britain at any rate only an infinitesimal percentage of club members ever play their own course in the conditions under which it is laid down that the bogey (on which their handicaps are based) should be assessed. How often for instance have you, gentle reader, played your own course from points within six feet of the back of the back tees, all holed out and marked on a card, in fair conditions of spring or autumn?

If you played half a dozen rounds on this basis and took the average of the best three, the difference between this and the bogey as marked on the card (or standard scratch score, if you care to use the Union jargon) would represent your true handicap. I should like to bet a sovereign with every reader of *Golf Illustrated* that this figure would be higher than their present handicap.

Of course I assume, in the superior way that men have, that we are talking about men. The women have a system all of their own which I regard with wonderment and awe but do not profess to understand. They are, I believe, strongly disciplined by the Ladies' Golf Union, and quite right too. If you do not put in three cards every time there is an R in the month you go back to scratch—or something like that. Whatever it is, I am prepared to believe that it works better than the men's.

The men's system, as laid down by the golf Unions, is worked out to the last detail and is perfect except for one flaw, namely that, broadly speaking, nobody pays the slightest attention to it. I remember when they altered all the bogeys a year or two ago—a point on which I resigned, with goodwill I trust, from the committee of the English Golf Union—'Tiny' Lavarack, who was then secretary and is now, we are all glad to see, president, was offering to club secretaries for 15s 11d extra, the Large Outfit, containing 650 scores register sheets, the alphabetical index and, mercifully, the sheet of instructions.

How many, I wonder, applied for it, and of those who did, how many have kept it up? The answer is that they cannot keep it up, even if they are willing to do so, because the English simply do not play medal golf. The Americans on the other hand do play medal golf, and in this lies the whole deep difference of approach to the game in the two countries, however much goodwill there may exist between the Royal and Ancient and the United States Golf Association. The British, as a generality, look on golf as a game wherein you play with another fellow and see if you can beat him. The Americans basically regard golf as a matter of seeing how many you can go round in.

Though I prefer our own approach, the above is not written in a spirit in any way critical of that of the Americans. Every man to his own taste, and anyway there is much logic in the American way. If you are going to play a fourball, as most people do on both sides of the Atlantic, why in heavens name pick your own ball up just because your partner has got a four? So everyone holes out at every hole, cheerfully taking four and a quarter hours about it, and it is the caddie's job to see that the score is marked on his employer's card. Indeed at Los Angeles, so Johnny Dawson told me, he gets the sack if he doesn't.

So the Americans, having a vast wealth of information to work on, run a highly complicated but efficient system of 'basic' handicaps and 'current' handicaps, one based on the last fifty scores and the other on the last fifteen.

One final comment. It is true that over here we pay little attention, really, to the official system and therefore judged on that basis our handicaps are all haywire, but here is a splendid example of the maddening British habit of muddling through. Our handicaps are all wrong by official standards, but perfectly correct when judged in relation to each other. You can't play to 12, he can't play to scratch, and I can't play to 5, but so long as we don't start mucking about with them these handicaps keep us just right in relation to each other. Typical!

9 December 1954

Utilize the Plant

Such experience as I have had of this life, including a two-year incursion into politics, a field in which the problem of economics is earnestly discussed on a national basis, has brought me to the conclusion that in the long, long run there is nothing to beat the old law of supply and demand. In matters of government you can pass laws compelling people to pay this much for this and that much for that, and other laws saying that they may not charge more than this much for this or that much for that, but in the long run, if these laws do not represent something approaching the ebb and flow of supply and demand, the people will beat you to it—and an excellent thing too, say I!

If this happens when people can for a while be coerced by the force of law, how much more will the law of supply and demand operate in spheres where no law can touch them at all? One such sphere, thank heaven, is golf. They can get at us, of course, with increased rates on buildings and land, discriminatory taxes which do not apply to games whose followers have a more massive and easily provoked voting power, but no one, so far, has suggested forcing people to belong to a golf club of their own or to take a day off at someone else's.

As to the question, how much to charge a visiting society—my own answer is simple and, if you like, cynical, though I do not really mean it that way. It is: 'As much as the traffic will bear.' If they willingly pay 25s for their food and green fee, which seems to me not unreasonable considering the excellent meals you get at a good London club these days (and it is this sort of club in which visiting societies are mainly interested), I would not in the least mind sounding them on the question of 30s next year. If, on the other hand, 25s was known to produce one or two dark hints about paying it this time but next year, etc., etc., I should be the first to suggest making it an even sovereign next year—or split the difference and say a guinea!

These are difficult days for club management. A few have gone under. A few struggle on. Others have become mighty prosperous. Partly it depends on geography, but largely it depends on how soon the management recognise the cardinal principle on which clubs succeed or fail today, namely '*Utilize the plant*'. The first person to crystallize the problem in these words in my hearing was General Critchley, so to him be the credit. This is probably not unfair since he had a large hand in the classic failure-to-success story in post-war golf, that of Sunningdale.

To some people when a club is in trouble the only remedy is to increase the subscription. The real answer, if you have vacancies for further membership, is to put them down. Be that as it may, the principle remains: 'Utilize the plant'. It is like the parable. If necessary, go out into the highways and byways, but bring them in somehow. Keep the staff occupied. Keep the bar going. Keep the kitchen going. When Sunningdale was nearly on the rocks, the place was empty throughout the week; at weekends those whom you might have expected to be playing there were now spending their money elsewhere—and no women were allowed into any part of the clubhouse.

They altered all that and I remember calling in one Sunday evening some months ago and thinking what a wonderful company it was that I found there. The original bar was filled with men. The old lounge on the left, always empty, was filled with mixed company. The people there that evening varied from elderly gentlemen whom I had played against, for Cambridge, twenty years previously, and ex-undergraduates against whom I had been playing that year as an equally elderly club member. As a result of all this—and the figure has been quoted to me so often that I think it can hardly be confidential—Sunningdale last year served 18,000 lunches and took £19,000 through the bar. Work that one out!

None of this comes the easy way. It does not just happen. It means that even so eminent a club as Sunningdale has to realise that there is no reason for people to go there, or be a member there, if they don't want to. It is a buyer's market and you have to 'sell' a golf club these days. By very hard work on the part of a small number of people Sunningdale was turned from near ruin to great prosperity. At nearly every other club which is 'doing well' you will find the answer to be the same. They utilize the plant.

17 May 1956

A Wembley of Golf?

It has been a lifelong ambition of mine to see the Cup Final. This has been due partly to the fact that I always played soccer, except in the Easter term at my preparatory school when we were compelled to play rugger—an experience which left me with a profound distaste for that abominable game—and partly because I have gone through life on the principle that you should always do anything or see anything once if you have not done it or seen it before.

This principle has paid handsome dividends so far and it certainly paid this year at Wembley. Cup Final Saturday was the first of those supremely wonderful days that we eventually get each year in England, even if every year we seem to have to wait longer for them. The London that we were able to present to the thousands of folk that spent the morning 'doing the sights', having spent half the night in coaches and trains on the way from Manchester and Birmingham, was the sort of London that exiles dream about in the far quarters of the globe. The guardsmen's tunics glittered in the spring sunshine, the parks were radiant in new green leaf, the girls seemed to have taken a little more trouble than usual, and altogether life had a wonderfully mellow glow.

The English are a curious people. The part of this great annual jamboree by which they are most moved is when they sing what is perhaps the most doleful hymn in the book, 'Abide with me'—'change and decay in all around I see,' . . . etc. The occasion also brings out an incredible urge to reform the other fellow by means of admonitory placards. I could not help wondering what the caddie-fee is for trailing round the outskirts of Wembley reminding us what sinners we are. A pound a day, I suppose. I also could not help thinking what might be the reaction of some luckless fellow as he tees up on the 18th, needing a four to win the Open, only to be confronted by an elderly bearded gent with a placard saying 'Prepare to meet thy doom'!

It is inevitable that a person like myself should find himself making comparisons between the Cup Final and the great occasions of golf. There were many of these comparisons, but one is outstanding. It is controversial in the extreme and I cheerfully confess that if I were a member of the championship committee I should run away from it. It is that the Cup Final simply would not *be* the Cup Final if it were not played every year at Wembley.

The logical conclusion is that we ought to have a Wembley of golf, and the answer is, of course, that we have, and that people were playing golf there, and 'futeball' too, 400 years before Wembley was thought of. I have thought for years, and still think, that the Open championship should be played for evermore on the Old Course at St Andrews. I am sure that Cardiff and Bolton and Everton and Sunderland, to say nothing of our old friends Tranmere Rovers, have beautiful football grounds, though I have never seen them— but imagine the Cup Final going from one to the other in turn. What a come-down from Wembley!

I go further. I think that not only the Open but also the Walker Cup, so long as it survives, and the Commonwealth tournament when it comes our way every twenty years, should be played on the Old Course at headquarters. For the other clubs this still leaves the Amateur, the internationals, the national championships, the Curtis and Ryder Cups, and all the professional tournaments.

For the student of the psychology of sport the Cup Final is a fertile field. I can well believe that these young fellows, many of whom are in their early twenties and in any case have not seen much of the world, become unbelievably 'het up' before emerging in front of Her Majesty and a hundred thousand of her subjects. Also, unlike the golfer, they know for six weeks that they are going, as it were, to be either the winner or the runner-up in the Open—but they have to wait these six weeks, all square with 18 to play, before they can go out for the final round.

As against that, I cannot believe that the strain is anything approaching that which is suffered by a reasonably imaginative player who knows that if he can only keep his head for the last six holes he will win the Open. To play these last six will take him substantially longer than a whole half of the Cup Final, and if he wants he can take longer still. No one is hurrying him, no one is trying to put him off, but there he is, all alone, with the opportunity of a lifetime staring him in the face and no one in the world who can help. The only comparison in this awful loneliness is the poor devil who has to take a penalty to decide the match in the last minute or two or, perhaps, the goalkeeper at all times. Having played in goal since the age of eight, and in no other position ever, I have a fellow feeling towards goalkeepers. Theirs, like putting in golf, is a game within a game. The goalkeeper is, as Sir Winston wrote of Jellicoe at Jutland, 'the only man who could have lost the war in an afternoon'. The thought of letting the ball slide very quietly and slowly between your legs and over the line in a Cup Final, as one miserable fellow indeed did, is enough to make any goalkeeper wake screaming in the night.

In soccer, people do not mind exhibiting a healthy partisanship. You can tell which side they are on. They wear their colours. And lest this seem *infra dig*, let us remember that they do the same at the boat race. This clearly should be extended to the University golf match. The sight of Messrs Darwin and Oppenheimer with light and dark blue top hats and vast rosettes, waving their rattles, is one for which I cannot wait.

9 August 1956

Flag In or Flag Out?

I am sure there is no body of professional games players who so cheerfully know so little of the rules of their game as do professional golfers, which in a way is a back-handed compliment both to themselves and the game. In contrast to which, all club members of course know all the rules all the time. In case there remains anyone who is 'not quite sure', as one always used to say at school when one had not the faintest idea what the man was talking about, here is the essence of the flagstick rule:

In match-play and stroke-play the responsibility for its treatment, and for all penalties, placed upon the person about to play. In match-play and stroke-play the unattended flagstick may remain in the hole and be struck without penalty at all times and from all distances. Penalty in match-play and stroke-play is always on player for striking unattended flag.†

The rule itself is easy enough but how to interpret it to the best advantage is still a matter of debate. Everybody at first quotes the 11th on the Old Course at St Andrews and this of course is a 'natural' for leaving the flagstick in when you putt. The green runs sharply down from the banks of the Eden Estuary and there are times in summer, especially with a following wind, when, if you get past the flag, you have only to set the ball in motion for it to run completely off the green. Newcomers naturally say this is crazy but once you know the Old Course it adds greatly to the zest of the thing. Anyway, in these highly exceptional circumstances you clearly leave the flag in—only to miss it by a hair's breadth and still run off the green.

The first experiments I made were at a small and not very affluent club near my home where we only run to cheap hollow bamboo for flagsticks. These ancient, cracked affairs I found were ideal for putting. However hard the ball hit them it dropped lifeless into the hole. Here at last was the answer to the short putt and I went on my

† The flagstick rule has now, of course, been altered—Ed.

way rejoicing. After all, any fool can hit the stick from three or four feet if it doesn't matter hitting it hard.

Alas, however, the more wealthy clubs run to what seem to be flagsticks of teak, and the ball bounces off them with a merry clatter. Some of them are so thick at the bottom that the ball will not even drop into the hole but will only lie against the stick—and then only if it hit it with its last legs, so to speak. In this case I cannot help thinking that it is worth having the flag attended for any putt under 10 yards.

The ideal to which every club should aim and which is encouraged by the authorities is the good solid flag with a thinner iron bit at the bottom, so that there is room for a ball to drop into the hole. If memory serves me right, they had this kind of flag at Hoylake for the Open, when there occurred to the runner-up, Van Donck, two occasions when he hit the flag with putts which he and all neutral observers declared must assuredly have gone in the hole if the flag had not stopped them.

In the long run the player probably knows best but here on his own admission was a clear case of misjudgment by Van Donck. For a player of this calibre I should have said that he must on balance lose a shot through having the flag in more times than he gains one. After all, you don't actually *gain* a shot unless you hit the stick and stay dead and *would have missed the one back* if the first had not been stopped by the flag. You lose a shot *every* time it hits the stick and stays out when it would otherwise have gone in.

Of course all this assumes that the flag is straight and upright. Playing with a friend at Brighton and Hove the other day with the wind sweeping across the Downs, working itself up for the great gale on the morrow, I found that the flags naturally enough were lying across one side of the hole. They inevitably lay away from my opponent who several times was able to bang the ball in, with the flag, as it were, acting as longstop. When I came to putt myself, the flag was invariably leaning towards me. There was a ruling about this the other day from St Andrews. It said, I seem to remember, that you could have the flag fairly in the middle (I had forgotten this) but I do not recall whether it said you could straighten it out before your opponent played. Logically, you ought to be able to.

I have read in American magazines and news clippings of many instances of professionals leaving the flag in for all the holing-out putts. This was not in the Open championship but in the run-of-the-mill tournaments where, for all I know, the promoters had put in patent flags calculated to help the players produce 'record' scores. It seems strange that in normal circumstances anyone would putt the short ones with the flag in.

One thing I am quite sure of in my own mind is that this is a really splendid rule and I think the people responsible, both from Britain and USA, are to be congratulated on daring such a revolutionary move. The golf that matters is the golf played every day by club members, and the greatest danger to it at the moment is slow play. Anything which helps to speed it up has the blessing of us all.

21 February 1957

Leaders out Last

The championship committee of the Royal and Ancient, under the chairmanship of Mr N. C. Selway, are nothing if not progressive. Whether you regard their progress as being in a forward or backward direction, you certainly cannot accuse them of standing still. They break cheerfully with tradition—and, it is said in one case, with the Rules of Golf! If you agree with them, you use the time-honoured expression, 'hidebound tradition'. If you don't, you just call it tradition and declare yourself to be deeply shocked.

The most complete departure from established precedent is, however, the arrangement of sending the field out in reverse order of merit for the final day's play in the Open—in other words pairing the overnight leaders together and sending them out last, and so on throughout the field.

This has for many years been the practice in sponsored tournaments in the States and recently has been tried in similar events here—personally I think with complete success but I know that opinions differ. At any rate no one seems to deny that the promoters of these tournaments, who pay the piper—and very handsomely too—are entitled to call the tune to the extent of putting on as good a 'show' as possible and I think it is indisputable that a guaranteed 'grandstand finish', at the end of the day and at a known hour, does make a better show than a 'finish', as it were, an hour or more before the finish, which can easily happen by the luck of the draw. Nothing is more boring than a whole hour, with the winner already established, waiting for the smaller fry to come in.

So the question, as I see it, boils down to: 'Are the championship committee entitled to regard the Open as a "show" and to act accordingly, overriding precedent and tradition in the process?' This must, surely, be a matter of opinion—except in so far as they can be shown to be 'breaking the law'. This is a point which I confess I should never have thought of if it had not been brought to public notice by what I hope I may call, with neither malice nor offence, the junior golf correspondent of the *Daily Telegraph* Mr J. G. Campbell.

Weighing in immediately after the announcement with a report of its 'hostile reception in Scotland', Mr Campbell adroitly quoted against the committee Rule 36(2) which states: 'The committee shall arrange the order and times of starting, which when possible shall be decided by lot.' What, he would like to know, made it impossible on this occasion? Mr Selway, I suspect, had not faced one like this since they abolished the stymie! I fancy he will have to put the putter back in the bag and call for the niblick. He may take courage, however, from the thought that many a worse one than this was 'lofted' in the old days.

The senior correspondent of the *Daily Telegraph*, Mr Leonard Crawley, weighed in, a day late, like a battleship caught at anchor by a destroyer, and let off some powerful broadsides on what I personally hold to be the correct side—namely that the Open *is*, in its way, a 'show' just like Wimbledon, the Test matches, Twickenham and the rest, and that so long as it has got to pay its way from year to year or face extinction, then the committee are justified in taking what steps they feel right to make it as fine a show as possible.

The fact is, they depend on the 10s-a-head gate receipts of the last day, and two bad 'last days' in succession could ruin them. They have a certain amount in the kitty, but no means—until the finances of golf are organised on a proper basis, and the sooner the better—whereby they can augment it except from the proceeds of the Open. On this day they have to pay entertainment tax, even if they make a loss, and income tax, should they make a profit. First prize before the war was £100. Now it is £1000. To risk being forced to reduce this below the level of commercial tournaments might involve not only a tremendous loss of face but in their opinion, and, for what it's worth, in mine, a breach of their own trust.

That the Open will be more exciting under the new conditions is hardly open to challenge. The suspense of the final half-hour, for thousands who are there and for millions who are not, will be terrific. I refer, of course, to the television, for which I have so far had the honour to do a number of commentaries and to which, in company with BBC producers, I have naturally given a lot of thought.

There is no doubt that golf can be extremely dull on television. If by mischance nothing much is occurring within view, nothing that producer, cameraman or commentator can do will make it exciting. On the other hand to show the winner winning, as we were able to do in the Swallow-Penfold tournament—and with the last putt of the day—makes a climax of which complete non-golfers are able to catch the thrill. This, it seems, can now be pretty well guaranteed and almost for this reason alone I am grateful to the championship committee. To the devil with Rule 36(2)!

20 March 1958

Owning a Golf Course

I feel uneasy at writing about the very thought of owning a golf course—in case somebody left me one! Fancy, for instance, finding that a rich uncle had died and left you the Royal Liverpool Golf Club at Hoylake—which, says Guy Farrar, cost £94 to run in 1870-something, and made a profit of £6 and costs £15,000 a year today. It must be a headache enough to be on the committee of such a club, let alone owning it.

Nevertheless, I have always thought that in many ways the 'benevolent dictator' was the best form of government for a golf club. Today, such a person is almost non-existent and, even though a man may virtually own a club, the running of it is inevitably left to a committee elected by the members. A case in point is Huntercombe, surely one of the simplest and loveliest golf courses in the world and one on which I would cheerfully settle to play golf for the rest of my days.

Here the owner is Lord Nuffield. So far as I know, his only privilege as such is to put his hand in his pocket to the tune of a few thousand pounds a year to pay the losses incurred in maintaining the vast inconguous clubhouse on the wrong side of the road from Henley to Oxford. One day I shall reveal also the various trials endorsed by his lordship in connection with the local Borstal boys— but that will be another story!

Among the outstanding 'benevolent dictators'—and there were times when not everyone would have subscribed to the 'benevolent'—was J. F. Abercromby, who created the two wonderful courses at Addington, of which the New, alas, was grabbed for a council estate after the war. When I knew him in his later years he was a gaunt, lean, faintly sinister figure (at any rate to the young) attired always in a green velour pork-pie hat.

There were no flies on 'Aber'. One day a man came in and said incautiously, 'Where's the suggestion book?' He did not know that Aber was beside him. Aber turned round and, prodding him with a bony finger, said 'I'm the suggestion book!' Some of us younger members derived a childish delight from baiting the old man. Standing casually behind him in the bar we would remark, *sotto voce*, but just loud enough for him partially to hear, that it was 'a pity about the greens' or that we understood that 'another six members had gone over to Addington Palace in the last month'. One could see the back of his neck stiffening, until at last he 'rose' in tremendous style. 'Ach!' he would say, 'it's you again!'

One of the oldest golfing chestnuts was always being told of Aber—of how some ostentatiously well-to-do visitors drove up and asked him if he were the caddie-master and how he replied: 'No, but I happen to know that he does not require any more caddies today.' Lots of people have told me they were there when it happened—and not only to Aber at that. The essence was, though, that Aber unquestionably knew his job, and everyone knew he did, even if they did not agree with him all along the line. It made life very simple. If you didn't like it, you knew what you could do about it.

To own a golf club today must be murder. Rising costs; rising wages; can't get a greenkeeper; can't get a steward; why don't they paint the clubhouse? if they put the subscription up again I shall resign; someone has pinched the nail brush again from the locker room; why don't they put on a cheap lunch? why do they allow visiting societies at the weekend?—the headache list must be in the writing rather than the receiving end of a golf-club suggestion book.

On the other hand the advertiser in *Golf Illustrated* who inspired all this did say 'golf course or land suitable for same'—and to design and create a golf course does indeed seem a laudable thing. What enduring monuments men like Aber, and say, Harry Colt, have left behind them, giving constant challenge and enjoyment to generations who perhaps have never heard their names. And what a deep satisfaction it must be to others like Tom Simpson, Sir Guy Campbell, John Morrison, C. K. Cotton and our revered old friend, J. H. Taylor, to think that at this moment thousands of people are enjoying the fruits of their creative labours all over the world.

It even occurs to me that their contribution may exceed that of those who merely write about the game!

17 April 1958

Honorary Membership for Captains

Clubs vary so much, from the ultra-sophisticated in the London area to the humble little affair on the local common, that it would hardly be possible to generalize upon whether their structure is out of date or not. I am expressing only a personal opinion when I say that in a good many clubs in the south of England the whole business has become unduly lush and luxurious and that this is why we hear so much about the 'cost of golf' and its being a rich man's game and so forth.

If you require a four-course lunch with a choice of half-a-dozen dishes, locker room attendants, caddies at twenty-five bob a day and the rest of it, then, of course, it can become a very expensive game and a day's golf can easily lead to the expenditure of a fiver. Analysis might show, however, that only a minor proportion of this was expended 'wholly and necessarily', as the income tax people have it, on the golf. At least half might be found to be attributable to the tax on spirits! I am not saying that such a day's golf is anything but enjoyable, or that it is morally to be condemned or any such nonsense: merely that it does leave a considerable margin of what I call the fleshpots of golf to be trimmed before you need find yourself priced out of the game altogether.

As the overheads involved in running a golf club seem to rise in inverse ratio to the private incomes of the members, it seems to me that the captain will become more and more important to smaller clubs and will be called upon to shoulder more and more responsibility. I will not make the mistake of saying, as I did once in *Golf Illustrated*, that 'the day of the highly paid secretary is drawing to a close'—partly because I should not wish to risk being admonished again by the Secretaries' Association and partly because, so long as the 'lush' clubs continue to exist, I do not think it is.

On the other hand, as costs go up, an energetic, enterprising and imaginative captain can do much towards offsetting them in the only way by which, so far as I know, this can be done—namely getting the members to use the club. Broadly speaking, his aim should be to cultivate such an atmosphere that people would rather 'go up to the club' than anywhere else in the neighbourhood. Nearly all of us are the same in this respect. However good the food and the service may be, who wants to dine in an empty restaurant?

It is the captain's job, as I see it, to foster the extra-curricular activities which make a club pay. Perhaps I may give a personal example—in the shape of a film show which I myself have presented at many golf clubs. This is the sort of evening a club captain should encourage. The secretary—since golf club secretaries are, I am able to reveal, human after all!—see such an evening as 'a hundred chairs, notices all over the place, someone to collect the money at the door, extra bar service', and all the rest of it. The captain sees it, or should do, as 'getting a hundred members together, selling four hundred drinks and making a nice profit on the bar, and giving the members something in common to talk about'. In other words, if the captain does not do it, nobody will.

This means extra work, **extra** responsibility and, since he must himself be the fountain **head** of all this, extra cost for the captain. It seems to me that two things could be done to make this worth while, one of which I believe myself to have invented in the last five minutes. The first is that the *office* of captain, irrespective of the current incumbent, should be 'made a fuss of'. This is, of course, done to a large extent in some clubs, not at all in others. I think, for instance, that a tradition should be worked up whereby he not only has the right to go off the first tee at any time but should be automatically invited to do so by those members present. He should have his own place in the car park and in the dining room, and the steward should be instructed to serve him 'out of turn' if the bar is crowded. He in turn should make a point of being present on all crowded occasions as a kind of social focal point for his fellow members, having a drink with all and sundry rather than merely the members of his own four-ball.

In return for his efforts on the common behalf and the expense which they will involve, I make the, I believe, original suggestion that, as a gesture by the club and not in any way as a reflection on his willingness or ability to pay, he be made an honorary member for his year of office.

15 May 1958

Selectors Courageous

I often think that selectors of golf teams must have a more difficult job than those at any other game. An obvious comparison is cricket. In this, as in most international games, all the players from among whom teams must clearly be chosen play regularly, competitively and in public. Their form may vary, but it is known. Few—I imagine none—'haven't been able to play for some months but will be getting into form later'. None have been 'playing regularly but have not been able to get away for most of the tournaments'. In most games, in other words, the players parade before the selectors. In golf very often the selectors have to go to the players. Their inability to do so in the past led many a golfing flower to blush unseen and waste its sweetness in the desert air of some remote club.

The Royal and Ancient selectors, under the chairmanship of Raymond Oppenheimer—who select our British amateur teams, not merely the Walker Cup team—were appointed for a period of four years and have served nearly three. Their energy and zeal and obvious knowledge of golf and golfers have earned them a distinction which, so far as I know, is unique in games, namely that chey are assured of a good Press in advance because it is evident to one and all that they know more about it than any member of the Press—including, most emphatically, myself.

It is essential, of course, for the golf selector to have liberty of movement, both in time and wherewithal, and this a number of the present body have. They have turned up in places, especially in Scotland, where no selector has ever trod before, thus enabling justice not only to be done but to be seen to be done. I cannot help it if Scottish readers take this amiss but the fact is that many Walker Cup teams in the past were bewildered by what one can only call Scottish nationalism. In the end the teams have to be chosen, like the selectors themselves, on a regional basis, and the Scottish selectors seemed to fear that they must never show their faces in their native land again if they did not get at least three of their men in. It was therefore impossible to choose a team strictly on merit, though the fact is, of course, that with the see-saw of international golf, there are some years when half a dozen Scotsmen are well worth a place and other periods when none are. In England nobody cares what are the individual nationalities of a Walker Cup team. It is a tribute to the present selectors that the Scotsmen among them would almost certainly have the nerve to select an entirely non-Scottish team if they thought it the best possible and that, if they did—which is highly unlikely in any case—Scotsmen as a whole, and even the Scottish Press, would probably accept it.

The present selectors have gone on the basis of 'let 'em all come'. When some bright spark is hailed as an infant prodigy in some obscure locality they will make a point of giving him every chance. They do not peer furtively round the sandhills to catch a fellow missing a short putt. They merely ask whether, given encouragement and perhaps a little professional tuition, he might make the grade. Sometimes they have themselves detected a fellow in comparative obscurity and raised him to the highlights. A case in point, as I am sure he himself would agree, was Max McCready, whom Raymond Oppenheimer detected in the RAF soon after the war.

Only constant watching makes a good selector. No one can do it from the book of form. A man may be seen in the paper to have won a tournament. He may therefore be assumed to be superior to those who didn't. Those who know golf know that this may be far from true—but they can only know if they were there to see.

Few people, I think, would deny that the present selectors are the most *constructive* that we have ever had. Their goal all along has been the Walker Cup match of 1959—though heaven knows they came within measurable distance last year in winning what would have been the only international golf match, amateur, professional or women's, to be won in America. For this reason they have set themselves not merely to select but to encourage.

They have taken innumerable young players and drawn them out of their shell, insisted they play in communal weekends and generally jollied them along to give them a better conceit of themselves. It is a process which has been a great pleasure to watch as well as for the young fellows concerned to enjoy. Nothing quite like it has happened, in my experience at any rate, before.

For myself, I leave everything in their hands with the utmost confidence. I admire the work they have done, the time and enthusiasm they have given to it, and the chances they have given to so many players, even though in the end they may not make the team. To be a member of a selection committee is usually reckoned a thankless task. In case they should fear it should prove so in the present instance I hereby thank the Royal and Ancient selectors in advance.

I am also grateful for the thought that there is no fear of their asking me to join them.

12 June 1958

Drink up, Gentlemen

I do not know what would happen to British golf if clubs in this country were to go dry, but I do know what would happen to the clubs themselves. They would go bust! Every one of them.

I am myself, as many readers will be aware, a virtual teetotaller, but I always lift my hat to those who lift the elbow, since without them the rest of us would have to pay about double our present subscription in order to keep the club going.

Perhaps there is more cant and hypocrisy talked about drink than any subject other than sex. The truth is, that those who drink—and smoke—pretty well keep the country going, never mind the golf club. We contribute, I believe, about twelve hundred million pounds a year in taxes—after paying the same income tax as the tea drinkers. It is rather a pathetic commentary on our super-civilization that, whereas a bus strike in our biggest city hardly affects life at all, a one-month strike by drinkers and smokers would bring the country to its knees and the Chancellor to his senses. And pious people talk about us as though we were not benefactors but sinners!

Golf, and what the law smugly calls 'intoxicating liquor'—you might just as well call a motor car a 'killing car' on the ground that so it is, if you misuse it—have always gone together. In the old days they were always playing for 'tappit hens' or magnums of this or that. Dozens of entertaining examples could be quoted from the records of the older clubs, especially, of course, in Scotland.

Nowadays, man for man, I dare say the golfer drinks less than he did, if only because he can't afford it. Modern beer is not much good to anyone above undergraduate age—at any rate when you come in after a round of golf and feel like a reviver—and to buy an 8-shilling bottle of spirits you have to pay a 26-shilling fine to the government. What a change from the days when at Formby, well within the lifetime of older members to-day, the bottle was left out with the notice, 'Twopence the small go!'

Even I am old enough to remember a golf club which was totally dry, and that was Leighton Buzzard in Bedfordshire. How many years ago was that, I wonder? Twenty-five perhaps. Nowadays, as I say, most clubs keep their heads above water only by inducing their members not to drink it.

All the same I am constantly surprised at the lack of enterprise in so many clubs in making it easy for members, at crowded periods, to get a drink when they want one. The pleasantest and most luxurious way, of course, is to ring the bell and have it brought on a silver tray—shades of old Owen at Sandwich!—and the next best is to have a tiny hatch through which the drinks are passed, thus enabling the members to mingle together in their clubroom without the feeling of being in a saloon bar. This being to put the drinks out on a table and let the members help themselves—their honesty being at least equal to that of people who leave the money for absent newspaper vendors. I cannot think why this is not more often done.

Whether the golf would improve if the game became dry, I cannot say, but the thought is really so disturbing that I will not pursue it. I have endured a voyage to Cairo on a dry troopship and on luxurious trains in America when suddenly the bar closes because we have crossed the boundary of some dry State, in which we do not in any case propose to stop, and both were experiences which remain in the mind.

I have also seen the consequences when a small part of the community who don't want a drink try to impose their will on those who do—in America in prohibition days and in so-called dry States now (they are, of course, the 'wettest'!)—in Australia, where they kept the pubs open all day and then closed them at exactly the hour when people wanted a drink; and in Scotland, where on the Sabbath '*bona fide* travellers' flash to and fro from town to town in order legally to sample their native brew. It all ranges from the ludicrous to the abhorrent and I wish none of it. Live and let live is the motto—so drink up, gentlemen, and keep the country going!

16 October 1958

Running a Dinner

No-one who has attended so many golfing dinners as your humble servant could possibly fail to acquire some fairly strong ideas as to how they should and should not be run. My first thought is that there is quite an art in running a dinner and that so few people have ever been put in the position of having to run one that they may well be excused if they fall into one or two unsuspected errors.

The quality of the fare is in my opinion only one of many items which determine whether people, on being asked next day whether it was a good dinner, will reply yes or no. For myself I would always go for quality rather than quantity—in other words give them three excellent courses rather than eke out four on the same budget. In no circumstances should there be more than four. There isn't time.

As to the 'refreshment', let him who runs a dinner beware of two things. The first is the tray of made-up drinks in microscopic stemmed glasses. 'Dry martini, Sir? Sherry?' Dry martini, my foot! This miserable little thing I have in my hand is a sickly yellow mixture of one part gin and four parts lukewarm vermouth—an insult to the intelligence as well as to the palate. There is *no* excuse for this. The second is our old friend, 'I ask you to charge your glasses and rise etc. . . .' But, my dear sir, their glasses are probably empty—though yours, since you are at the top table, is doubtless full. If only you knew the fury in their hearts. 'Charge your glasses,' indeed. If only they could!

A dinner is made or marred by the speeches. Now it is an inescapable fact of nature that there will be those who at the end of dinner wish to retire for a minute or two. One or two of the speakers themselves may be among them. If you, as chairman, do not let them, many of the company will be physically unable to enjoy the speeches, however entertaining they may be. A quarter of an hour devoted to an interval will pay handsome dividends.

As to the speeches, a heavy responsibility lies on the chairman. Not only does he select the speakers; he 'conditions' the audience. If everything has gone according to plan and the dinner has been good and the drinks accessible in whatever quantity each person may desire, the audience is in receptive mood and the light 'aside' is received with thunderous laughter as though it were the jest of the evening. The speaker detects at once that he is among friends and, to return to golfing terms, the 74 that he has come prepared to deliver turns into a 69. Give him a fidgeting audience with uncharged glasses and three more speeches to come and the 74 becomes an 80.

I cannot see how you can fit in more than four speeches to a dinner. Indeed at two of the very finest dinners I ever attended there were only three. You can hardly ask any worthwhile speaker to come to your dinner and limit him to six or seven minutes—and the audience in any case would probably wish to hear more from him. If four speakers run for 12 or 15 minutes, you have already run for a full hour after the dinner and that is enough oratory—or 'ear-banging' as the Americans say—for anyone.

I think there is one golden rule for a dinner, a sermon, or an individual after-dinner speaker. It is: 'Stop when they could have done with a little more.' The moment the thought passes through people's heads that it has 'all been excellent but that is about enough', the peak of enjoyment has been passed.

In the world of golf the best after-dinner speakers happen to be among those who have been ennobled for distinction in other spheres—Lords Birkett, Brabazon of Tara, and Morton of Henryton. As a talker rather than orator I think all would rate Dai Rees high, especially for the way in which his patent sincerity transmits itself to the audience.

With memories of many happy evenings crowding the mind I end with another awful warning to chairmen. Let us hear only from those on the toast list, who have come prepared. 'We cannot let this splendid evening conclude without a few words from Charlie . . .' Cries of 'Good old Charlie!' But not from me.

17 March 1960

Long Service Records

I think it was the eminent Professor A. L. Rowse who said that the whole essence of English history was *continuity*. We have received our heritage over hundreds of years, and countless generations have done their best to hand it over to their successors intact before they themselves pass on. Only the wildest left-winger can take any satisfaction in seeing a place that has been the home of the same family for 500 years broken up by death taxes and turned into offices for the local council.

This continuity, for reasons which it would be inappropriate to go into here, is rapidly being lost in the English scene. Motoring cross-country from Birmingham to Mildenhall the other day I passed through the Bedfordshire village in which I was born. I remember, I remember . . . but that is about all. The 'big house' has long been a lunatic asylum and the once beautiful grounds are filled with hideous red brick barracks. The little stream beside which I walked since the age of five now trickles over tin cans between two housing estates and a forest of 'telly' aerials. Even the once famous nurseries of Messrs Laxton are covered with a vast anonymous red brick sprawl.

Continuity is as precious in golf as in wider aspects of life.

I should like to see every club that has had time to develop a character and atmosphere of its own have the same rule as that which applies to the Old Course at St Andrews, namely that no change, however small, may be made without six months' notice being given to an annual general meeting.

I remember vividly the thrill with which I returned for the first time after the war to two 'institutions' already mentioned. The Old Course, and indeed the hallowed precincts of the Royal and Ancient Club, were untouched. Soon afterwards, in this same month of March, I went to Mildenhall to play for the Society against Cambridge. We turned down the little lane to the club with a lively surmise overcast with doubt—but there it all was. The white posts with the chains behind the last green, the little farmhouse clubhouse, several of the same caddies we had known in Cambridge days, the same close-knit fairways and fiery greens.

And when we pressed the bell beside the little glass hatch in the clubhouse—the Royal Worlington must be one of the very few clubs that does not descend to having a bar, though they do now put out the drinks on Sundays on a help-yourself basis—the hatch shot up to reveal, unchanged by the years, the smiling countenance of Williams, the steward. All my playing life I had known no other. When I remarked on this to N. C. Selway, later to become chairman of the championship committee, he revealed that he and Williams had arrived for the first time at Mildenhall on the same day and had alternately been pressing the same bell and opening the same hatch for twenty-six years!

Nothing contributes more to the feeling of 'all's well with the world' than to arrive at a club and see the same familiar and welcoming faces. I first played for Cambridge against London clubs in 1928. John Hutchinson and Ralph Pawley were at Mid-Surrey then and it has never occurred to me in many visits since that they wouldn't be there again. Sheridan, of course, was caddie master at Sunningdale and Wainwright welcomed us in the locker room, just as he does today. I do not know his exact 'score', but I know that Sheridan, now an honorary member of the club, celebrates his half century this year.

Jack Barlow, when I first went to Formby thirty years ago, had already been there twenty years! In October last year they marked his fiftieth anniversary with a cheque and a television set. His courteous and helpful welcome must by now have endeared Formby to some thousands of visiting golfers.

Many professionals, of course, have contributed immense lengths of service to the same club. The great John Henry Taylor was, I believe, at Mid-Surrey for forty-six years. James Braid was for some forty-five years at Walton Heath and those who knew it in his day cannot fail to perceive his spirit pervading the club today. Nearer home to me, I learned the other day that my old friend, J. W. Moore, who used to teach me as a small boy, has been at the Bedfordshire club for thirty-nine years.

Before he came to Bedford he was assistant at Royal Eastbourne, where I remember him giving lessons on the ladies' course, I being then a preparatory schoolboy nearby and little thinking that soon he would be coming to my own home club. Royal Eastbourne itself had a trio with an extraordinary record of service amounting, some nine years ago, to one hundred and eighteen years. Alfred Huggett, the ranger, who has recently died, had at that time forty-two years to his credit; Fred Holly, the caddie master, had then completed fifty and went on for several more before retiring; Cyril Thompson, the professional still going strong, must by now have accounted for about thirty-five.

Fortunate indeed is the club—and the game—which inspires such loyalty and service.

28 April 1960

Get 'em Moving

There is not the slightest doubt in my own mind that golf as played in the United States is the slowest in the world. Should this reach the eyes of any of my American friends, let me say it at once that I consider this no affair of ours in this country and that a man is entitled to play with his own friends in his own country at any pace, in any fashion, dressed in any attire, under any rules and for whatever stakes that he may fancy.

We on the other hand are entitled to resist any importations from any quarter which we feel may cause a change in the character of golf which those who know it best feel may change it for the worse.

It is in a purely academic sense that I write not on whether golf ought to be so slow in America but on *why* it is so slow. There are two principal reasons and many subsidiary ones. The first is the climate. In the north the summer is hotter than ours and the winter so cold that the clubs close down. In the south it is agreeable in the winter but immensely hot, by our standards, in the summer. Broadly speaking, therefore, golf is played in the whole of America in what we should call hot weather. I should put the consequent difference at a minimum of half an hour per round.

Secondly, the Americans have always regarded golf as a scoring game, while we have always regarded it basically as a match-play game. I remember reading somewhere how this difference in attitude dates back to the very earliest days of American golf, when one of the first presidents of the United States Golf Association urged golfers to stick to their guns, irrespective of what might be done in Britain, and play their golf, as they wished to do, as a score-play affair—not 'Who beat who?' but 'How many did each of you shoot?'

This, like so many other aspects of American golf strange to us, is entirely logical. A man goes out for a weekend round of golf. He wants to play eighteen holes and see how well he can do, not whether he can beat a friend. All can then assess and compare their performances in the clubhouse afterwards, very much as in rifle shooting. You do not shoot a match against a fellow member of the rifle club. You see how many you can score.

Not so logical is the practice that has grown up in America of considering four players to be necessary to make up a game. (If there happen to be five, they will play a five-ball, whereas we should instinctively split up into three and two). In effect, therefore, the average Sunday morning game in America is a *fourball medal*, all holed out, with (naturally) indifferent players, just like the average club member here. How long would it take four of you in your club to get round, with everyone holing out at every hole? You would be doing extremely well if you got round in four and a quarter hours.

In certain respects I am frankly, though I hope without offence, critical of our American friends. They are just beginning to get past the idea that the man who has the biggest car is the biggest man. It has not yet occurred to them that the man with the biggest golf bag is not necessarily the biggest golfer. So every common-place, corpulent weekend golfer is liable to have a bag so vast, and filled with so many, to him, useless clubs, that I personally cannot lift it with one arm. It occurs to no one to carry a drainpipe bag containing as many clubs as he personally is capable of using. Indeed, when Chick Evans, one of the few men to win both the Open and Amateur championships of the United States, turned up with one for the Amateur a few years ago, a young caddie refused to carry it. The loss of face among his friends would have been insupportable!

This necessitates either a caddie, a trolley or an electric cart. Often the caddies will not go out without carrying two bags, on account of the money, and I have seen vast negro caddies shouldering four. Since no one ever thinks to assess what club he will want for his second shot and take it along with him, everyone waits for the caddie to come across with all the bags. I should put the time wasted at upwards of half an hour per round.

I think it is fair to say, too, that in the average club game no one is ever ready to play his shot when his turn comes. Every shot seems to take him by surprise—rather like a bad game of poker when no one knows whose deal it is or how many cards the others drew. The time lost on the eighteen tees, when everyone waits to pass remarks on everyone else's drive instead of the next man teeing up and getting on with it, is incalculable. On the greens the picking up, cleaning and replacing of the four balls in turn, again without the slightest sense of urgency, may well account for another half hour.

Then, of course, we have that ever-present menace, the Halfway House. Since the normal businessman golfer cannot stand five hours of play without a break for refreshment—and who shall blame him?—everyone has to stop in the middle of the round. Add for this at least a quarter of an hour, sometimes more. In many cases, since most American courses are intelligently laid out so that the 9th comes back to the clubhouse, they will retire to the club, have lunch and play the second nine in the afternoon.

There is much criticism of slow play in America, but I fancy that I alone have discovered the solution of this problem. It lies in the words, unknown in British clubs, the 'Men's Grill'. This splendid and insidious institution is open all day long. At any hour you can go in in your golfing attire and have anything from a sandwich to a pound and a half of steak, plus the accompanying refreshment. You can start at ten and have a steak at half-past three, or start at eleven and have the steak at half-past four.

The solution is, therefore: close the Men's Grill sharp at two as we do. That would get 'em moving!

International Illwill

It has long been my opinion, which I cannot claim to be a very original one, for it is shared by many thousands, that many forms of sporting contests do a great deal more harm to international relations than good, and either should never have been begun or should forthwith be abandoned. Foremost among these are the Olympic Games. These were revived by a Frenchman, Baron Pierre de Coubertin, who in 1894 addressed a circular to all the governing bodies of sport, in which he pointed out the educational value of sport to modern peoples, if practised in accordance with the ancient Greek ideals. The reinauguration took place two years later at Athens on the site where the ancient festivals had concluded 1500 years before.

In whatever spirit the Olympic Games are carried out today, it is quite evident that many nations have not the slightest conception of the 'ancient Greek ideals' or, if they have, have not the slightest intention of conforming to them. I believe, though open to correction, that the performers are meant to be amateurs. I wonder whether the Russians know, or care, what the word means? Indeed, I wonder whether there is a word for it in Russian at all.

I am old enough to remember the 'bodyline' controversy associated with the names of Harold Larwood and his resolute captain, the late Douglas Jardine—a man of high principle if ever there was one—and the bitterness of feeling between the Australian nation and ourselves at home. Only this year we have had the preliminary unpleasantness prior to the arrival of some young South African cricketers whom we ourselves had invited to our shores to come and play cricket with us. What the policies of their government, for whom most of them probably never voted and would like to get rid of, have to do with playing, of all games, cricket, I simply cannot see.

I read of, but have never attended, international football matches in South America where the goalkeeper is subjected to a hail of missiles of various kinds and the referee has to be escorted off the field, and when defeated British teams return home they seem to be greeted almost as traitors. This, of course, brings me to the absolutely cardinal point, namely, that only a few thousand people actually witness these contests and whether they engender goodwill among the many millions who follow them from afar depends wholly on how they are reflected by Press and radio.

Anyone who has worked in the Press in Britain knows that there are one or two newspapers who are simply not interested in reporting goodwill. Their correspondents must find evidence, however trumpery, of bad will—or get the sack and be replaced by someone more capable of detecting a bad smell in a garden of roses. Some correspondents who do this love it, and I do not love them. Others with a wife and family have my sincere sympathy, and I am not being smug when I say so.

On the other hand there are times to my mind when writers for the more 'respectable' papers take an altogether too lofty view of events which should be treated with levity—such as when a Test in the West Indies last year was broken up by a barrage of beer bottles on account of a Chinese umpire judging one of their players to have been run out. Pompous offers were made on high diplomatic levels to call the series off, but the English gallantly and chivalrously decided to play on. What rubbish it all was! I suppose it depends on how you look at these things, but to me it was one of the most splendidly comical incidents in the history of cricket.

Like anyone else who has been to the West Indies, I look upon the West Indians as one of the most attractive people in the world. Theirs is a simple, friendly, emotional world and they do not make rockets with which to destroy each other. Unlike mad dogs and Englishmen, they lie under a tree in the mid-day sun—or climb up it, thick as starlings, to watch cricket. I understand from a colleague who was present that those who threw the beer bottles were already boozed as linnets on the contents and I would give anything to have witnessed the splendid scene. To report it as a serious threat to the bonds of Empire (as the 'bodyline' business truly was) seems to me the height of absurdity.

Can we claim that golf is immune from criticism? On the whole I like to think yes. There was unpleasantness over the Ryder Cup match three years ago, but that again was largely due to one journalist overhearing and reporting one injudicious remark uttered by one man in the heat of the moment and then retailing it to millions. I do think, however, that amateur golf probably does more good in the international sphere than professional. My friends in the profession will not, I hope, misunderstand me. A professional is a public performer who lives on the quality of his performance, and on being paid to produce it. He cannot afford, though many are, to be charitable. He is there to earn his living.

Nevertheless, I am sure that the Canada Cup does good, even though old-fashioned purists could wish that it were not played by fourball stroke-play taking more than five hours for 18 holes. It brings people from no fewer than 30 nations together in circumstances where 'face' is not lost by the 29 nations whose representatives do not win, and the smaller the country the players come from the more keenly must they be aware, and convey to people at home, that golf does indeed make all men equal, in that the feeling of a man who misses a four-foot putt in Japan is identical (though the language may not be!) with that of another man who does it at the same moment in New Zealand or Ecuador.

8 June 1961

Falling Seeds

What is the object of holding a championship at all? Is it simply to establish a 'best match-player of the year'? Or to provide an annual gathering of the best players and those whose lot it is to administer the game, and to offer an opportunity to those less gifted to see the best players in action? There is, after all, no *need* to hold a championship. The game would go on in the same old way if we didn't.

Yet I think that almost everyone, including those who are never likely to be better than 24 handicap, would feel that something was missing if we did not hold an Open, an Amateur and a Ladies' championship. And if we are going to hold them, it seems indisputable that we should make them as good a 'show' as possible.

A bad draw can turn a potentially fine championship, full of the best possible entries, into an insipid affair, with an anti-climax for a final. How often one used to hear, or say, 'Of course, the final was really played last Thursday'.

The worst single draw I remember was in the Amateur championship of 1938 at Troon, when we had the American Walker Cup team over here. Two members of the team were drawn together, almost the first to go out, on the Monday morning. They were Charles Yates, who went on to win, and Johnny Fischer, who had won the US Amateur two years before, when he beat Jack McLean at the 37th in the final. By the luck of the draw one of these fine players had to be eliminated by about half past eleven on the very first morning. At about this hour Yates won with a wretched stymie on the 19th. That, of course, is strictly irrelevant, but it seemed to make it worse.

Year by year there was talk of seeding the draw, and Wimbledon, and the work-up to an almost always entertaining final, were often quoted in support. Year by year the championship committee could not quite bring themselves to institute so revolutionary a change in a pattern that had hardly altered in fifty years. At last the sensational news came that the draw was to be seeded. It caused no sensation at all, and indeed I cannot remember how many years ago it was that it happened.

Nowadays among the major amateur events only the Ladies' championship is not seeded and this year the draw turned out to be singularly unfortunate. In the first round, for instance, Mrs Innes Wright played Miss Bridget Jackson, and in the second round, after byes in the first, Mrs I. Robertson faced Signora Goldschmid Bevione. Added to these the unseeded draw meant that the Vicomtesse de Saint Sauveur and Mlle Brigitte Varangot met in the third round.

I should hesitate to offer advice to so formidable a body as the Ladies' Golf Union, but in view of the above it does seem fair comment to suggest that the championship would have been a better one if these inevitable clashes had come later in the week and that they should take a deep breath and try seeding the draw for an experimental period of, say, five years.

The Open championship, though by stroke-play, is also in a sense seeded. Only 40 people are allowed to play on the last day. (It used to be all those within ten strokes of the leader, till Henry Cotton, with a total of 132 at Sandwich in 1934, very nearly prevented anyone playing on the last day at all!)

The draw is then, if not seeded, at any rate manipulated, by pairing the leaders together and sending them out last. This seems to have everything in its favour. In the old days it was always held to be a great advantage to be drawn early, thus enabling you to get your blow in early and set up a target for the others to shoot at. Nowadays all the leaders have the same chance and the same conditions, which seems to be as fair as one can make it.

Apart from that, however, we do get a real build-up for the finish and the very slowness of golf makes it all the more exciting when so-and-so had 'four to win the Open'. Having a hand in television I am naturally biased, but I must say that this built-up finish does 'make our day'. I am sure that many readers who have seen the finish of the Open on television will agree that it can be one of the most exciting episodes in sport.

For this reason I should like to see one more change. Last year through the sudden storm at St Andrews the last round had to be postponed till the Saturday, thus having one round on each of four days as the Americans do. This not only added an extra 'gate' on a day when so many people were free to come, but it also meant that on television we could guarantee to see the winner winning, which, of course, is the very essence of sport on television.

20 July 1961

Why Not a National Course?

It may be taken, I fancy, that the money would never be forthcoming to build a new national course and that no club at present would consent to place its course and clubhouse at the nation's disposal. Nevertheless the idea gives rise to interesting speculation.

The first thing, since there would be an instant patriotic outcry from Scotland if the national course were in England, would be to have two of them. The Scottish national course would not be a matter of a moment's controversy, since in a way it already exists—at St Andrews. Knowing that I do not have to shoulder the responsibility for such a decision, I cheerfully go on record that if I had my way I should play the Open championship permanently at St

Andrews, just as the Cup Final is played at Wembley and the tennis championship at Wimbledon.

In England, since the national course would presumably have to pay its own way, it would have to be in Lancashire. Only in Scotland and Lancashire should we find sufficient crowds. If this is admitted, I do not see that we could do better than Birkdale.

One obvious requisite is plenty of accommodation at varying prices, for the competitors and camp followers—the golf manufacturers, Press and so forth—to say nothing of spectators who wish to combine the championship and their holiday. Southport in this respect is ideal. It has also at least one big hotel which can form the unofficial headquarters of those whose business it is either to run the championship or to meet and exchange views when all are gathered together.

For the above reason—quite apart from the fact that I should never choose an inland course—I should rule out London. Otherwise Wentworth, with its two courses for the qualifying rounds, would come at once to mind. With Hillside near at hand, Birkdale passes the test in this respect.

It also has a practice ground and a 'natural' car park for thousands of cars, to say nothing of a station on the Liverpool-Southport electric railway just beside the course. I think it is Hillside. At any rate I know from past experience that it is *not* Birkdale! This ease of access makes a great deal of difference. Perhaps the most difficult course in this respect is Hollinwell, which I revisited for the Dunlop tournament the other day. Here about a mile of narrow one-way road winds its way down to the clubhouse and, though the traffic was admirably controlled by the police by radio, it would not do for a championship—not, I am sure, that the members would wish to have the Open descend upon them in any case.

'Permanent amenities' would make an enormous difference to a national course. I can think of two which already exist. One is the laid television cable stretching out to the 9th at St Andrews, the farthest part of the course, which makes television far less costly and complicated than in the early days. The other is, strangely, at the Hon. Company's Club at Muirfield, where I remember being shown round by the secretary, Colonel B. Evans-Lombe, during the course of Gary Player's championship. Here they had laid on permanent electric points and hard-standings for the caterers, together with what are politely known as toilet facilities. The Colonel marched me boldly into the 'ladies' and, it being reasonably early in the day, we got away unscathed. I can report that everything seemed excellent.

Whatever catering is done at golf tournaments, you may be sure that some people will complain about it. For myself I do not, partly because, largely through the efforts of Mr Jock Christie, V.C., and Mr Gus Payne, it has so vastly improved in recent years, and partly because it must be so incredibly 'chancy'. Rain and perishing cold may keep the crowds away. A balmy July day may bring them out in shirt-sleeved thousands. In the Open there may be a tie and the whole organisation has suddenly to stay an extra day and pack up on Saturday night instead of Friday.

At any rate I am sure that no one would be more stoutly in favour of a national course than the caterers, if it meant that they could have permanent buildings for the cooking and washing-up and had only to plug in for all the light and heat they wanted.

A permanent Press room would also be a much valued amenity, with telephone points, tables, proper lighting and even perhaps a floor. The conditions in which the Press are asked to work are often disgraceful—but that is no one's fault but our own.

The more I think of it, the more I should choose Birkdale. It is a course of quality, right in the centre of a populous and golf-conscious area, and, not lightly to be forgotten, it is reasonably difficult to get into Birkdale without paying!

12 July 1962

Called to the Bar

My knowledge of golf club bars is somewhat limited, as I am naturally out on the course most of the time.

For the golf correspondent numerous human hazards lie in wait in the bar. There is always our old friend who says, 'Ha, I see you do your watching from the bar. Ha, ha!' Very witty, sir, and so original! Also, every kind of bore lurks in the bar, anxious to engage you in a one-sided conversation and tell you the story of his life or his round. Of these the worst—to me, though some people find it genuinely interesting—are those who come up and pose problems relating to the Rules of Golf. I feel rather ungracious in saying this, because very often they are flattering enough to begin by saying, 'Here—you'll know the answer to this one,' and I therefore have to maintain some sort of show of interest, difficult though it may be.

I do not know the Rules of Golf, I never have known them, and I am too old to begin learning them now. I think it is ridiculous that we cannot hit our little balls round with our little sticks without 93 pages of Rules and an ever-increasing volume of case law in the form of Decisions, many of them, so I am assured, contradictory to each other. I am afraid I am something of a spoilsport in this connection. I put a damper on the discussion by saying, 'Why not look in the book of Rules and see?' They have never thought of this—and anyway, as I say, it spoils the fun.

Nevertheless I confess to enjoying the period before lunch at the golf club bar on a Sunday morning as one of the most enjoyable times of the week and I believe that this goes for a great number of people to whom golf is their recreation after a hard week's work. I am always sympathetic with the clock-slaves who have to creep away just when the talk is getting interesting, for no better reason than that their wife's clock says five to one, or whatever it may be. The answer to this one is surely to alter the wife's clock.

I like to think of myself as something of a connoisseur of bars. What to drink presents me with no problem, for I have long ago settled for pink gin and soda before lunch—or champagne if I can afford it—and whisky and water after six o'clock (five thirty in winter), but I think that the surroundings in which you drink make a great deal of difference and that many golf clubs have been very unimaginative in the siting and decor of what after all is the 'happiest' room in the club.

Though it is not every club that is lucky enough to have the opportunity, there is nothing in my opinion to touch a bar with a view. The finest bar I have seen in any club in the world is at the Thunderbird Club in the desert in California, where the Ryder Cup match was played some years ago. The course is flat as a pancake, but there's a fine view of the mountains a few miles away, and as the sun sets behind them a magical peace comes over the scene, as in a tropical twilight, and even our American friends, if they will forgive my saying so, tend to fall silent.

The bar at Thunderbird runs the length of a big room, parallel with the window looking out towards the moutains, but here is what makes it different. You sit down to the bar not on high stools but low leather chairs and settees. Behind these the floor is raised so that those who sit at tables or stand up can see over the heads of those who are sitting down. Furthermore the floor behind the bar itself is sunk a foot or 18 inches, so that the barmen, as they stand up, are about on the level, face to face, with those who are sitting down and do not obstruct the view.

I have always wished that, while they were spending money on new bars at Turnberry and Gleneagles, where the views in their different ways are both 'out of this world', they would adopt this principle. Nor can I see why, if we have got to have these frightful skyscrapers which have now transformed our beloved London scene and in my opinion ruined it, we should not at least have the consolation of being able to sit in a bar at the top of them, just as one does in the 'Top of the Mark' in the Mark Hopkins Hotel in San Francisco. We have not yet come to skyscraper clubhouses. All the same, many clubhouses possess splendid views and it seems a pity that so few should make real use of them.

11 October 1962

Picking a Side

The modern golfer is frequently taunted with having no appreciation of the old traditions of the game. 'Real golf,' says the purist, 'is hole-play; stroke-play is a modern excrescence, a morbid growth induced by a diseased constitution.' 'So wrote the editor of *Golf Illustrated* on 12 March 1909—six days before I was born. I wonder whether it is the editorial opinion now?

Certainly it would not be the opinion of most of the leading professionals in this country or of any in the United States. It would, however, be the opinion of 80 per cent of the club golfers, on whom the very fact of having a card and pencil in their pocket has an effect akin to that of the snake on the rabbit.

However, we are talking of higher things, namely picking a Walker

Cup team, and here the selectors are, and will always be, in something of a dilemma. They have a certain amount of match-play form to go on—but their trouble is that a player on whom they have their eye may put up a good record on paper without ever encountering the sort of opposition against which they would have liked to see him in action.

This is particularly true of the internationals, in which a man may win all his three singles and still, as has been proved, not be worth a place in the Walker Cup team.

There is not the slightest doubt in my own mind that match-play requires higher mental qualities than medal. If you are keen enough on the game, it is not too difficult to develop an ability to isolate your mind in a kind of cocoon of concentration, taking each shot as it comes and thinking of nothing else. The fact that a fellow competitor several hundred yards away has just by some fantastic fluke secured a three when he looked like taking five is mercifully unknown.

It is impossible, whatever anyone may say, to ignore a living opponent who flukes a three when he ought to have taken five and it takes a special form of golfing courage to do so. I could tell of many a golfer of great distinction who, when this happened, would at once in his mind begin preparing his story for the Press when he got in. Once your mind works that way, you are vulnerable as a match-player.

There are in the professional ranks today two living proofs of the fact that the best match-player is not necessarily among the greatest of medal-players. Eric Brown won four successive Ryder Cup singles in a period of eight years and now, three years after that, has just won the Match-play championship for the second time. David Thomas—I wish they would not call him 'Dave': it is almost as bad as 'Arnie' Palmer!—tied for the Esso Round Robin tournament last year and won it outright this year. He and Brown should, of course, have been automatic selections for last year's Ryder Cup match, but by the grotesque system of selection then prevailing (but since altered) the team could be chosen only on the result of medal-play and they did not qualify.

Nevertheless, if you are going to have a general trial match, it seems to me that the best thing you can do is to pick a certain number of players on known form, match or medal, and bring them together to play matches against each other. This the Walker Cup selectors have done and a pretty rigorous affair it is going to be.

The fifteen players of their choice are to assemble at Turnberry during Easter and every one of them, in singles or threeballs over four days, will play every one of the fourteen others. Thus by the evening of Easter Monday the selectors will find themselves in possession of a complete points table and on the Tuesday they will announce their team.

I foresee two difficulties, which doubtless will not have escaped their own notice. What happens if in the meantime someone else does something which would appear to justify his inclusion in the first fifteen—though perhaps in the off-season this is unlikely?

Secondly, it seems that with a points table working itself out by Monday night the selectors need hardly be present at all, since, after all this business, anyone who finishes in the first ten may justifiably claim to have earned his place. At least, I should be extremely cross if, after playing eight rounds in four days against fourteen opponents, I finished tenth—and didn't get in!

11 April 1963

Country Club Impressions

Recent travels and indeed travel since the war, has convinced me that in almost every country in the world golf is played on a 'grander' and more expensive scale than in Britain and that there has arisen an almost standard form of country club which makes our own clubs seem astonishingly unpretentious by comparison. One cannot generalize in such matters and every reader will be able to point to exceptions. Nevertheless I believe that, broadly speaking, I am right.

One thing is certain, that Britain, and particularly Scotland, is the last stronghold of the simple little clubhouse; the simple little locker room (often slightly odoriferous and filled with decaying clothing and shoes belonging to members long since deceased); the pro, if any, tucked away in a small tin shed; the honorary secretary; and no lunch unless you order it.

The golf and country club in other parts of the world, though it may vary in degrees of lavishness, is very much of a pattern and derives, I suspect, largely from the United States. At its most expensive, in that country and in Japan, the annual subscriptions may be anything up to £250 a year and you may have to put up a £1000 bond (saleable on death or resignation) in order to get in.

In the locker room there are a number of attendants to look after the showers and see that there is plenty of warm oil, razors, after-shave lotions and what have you, and there may well be a resident masseur and/or barber. There will be a rather lovely drawing room (little used, in my experience, except for 'occasions'), plenty of attendants to bring drinks on the terrace, more than one bar, a mixed dining room and a swimming pool and tennis courts.

The country club, of course, represents a very big business—it may well have a staff of 70 or 80—and is run by a highly paid 'manager' rather than one, as they always claim, underpaid secretary. No money changes hands and everything is paid for by chit, including even the caddies' tips. This again is insidious since, as the evening wears on, it becomes increasingly painless to order another round of drinks, and maybe some supper, if you pay for it merely by signing your name. I have known some American clubs where, if you do not spend a set minimum in the club, they bill you for it anyway!

The club probably has two courses and perhaps a 'relief nine' and certainly has a practice ground where in most cases you can hire a bucket or basket of practice balls from the pro and leave them to be retrieved later.

Golf, as it has spread over the world, has taken on the American pattern rather than the British. Fourballs, almost inevitably stroke-play rather than match-play, though often a combination of both; inevitably fourteen clubs (oh, unhappy day when, in all innocence, they made that rule!), a huge bag, plus a trolley, caddie or electric cart; and that efficacious, though to the traditionalist still appalling, headgear, the coloured jockey cap.

In most countries, though again of course there are exceptions, I tend to associate the typical country club with golf in the sun—rather permanently in the sun or, as in the northern parts of the United States and in Canada, closing down in the winter and opening only during the warmer months. The subscription, heavy by comparison with British standards, tends to cover the whole family and with the weather reasonably guaranteed the whole family tends to use the club and get a great deal more out of it than would be feasible in this country.

Furthermore, though the cost is heavy, there are still many countries where much of it is allowed as a legitimate business expense and this again makes the signing of chits a less painful proceeding. Perhaps by the time this appears in print that once excellent golfer, Mr Reginald Maudling, will have done something for us in that direction—but instinct tells me that he won't.

For myself, I was brought up on 'simple' golf and simple amenities. Early experience dies hard and I am still content with them. I would rather have golf on the heath or the common and a farmhouse clubhouse like the Mildenhall or Piltdown than fifty-four holes and a mansion. Nevertheless, I have to admit that there remains many a clubhouse in Britain into whose changing rooms and wash rooms I should be far from happy to take my friends from country clubs overseas.

6 June 1963

Storming the Citadels

It is often assumed that it is the older people who are resistant to changes in the accepted order of things, but in my own case I find the opposite to have been true. For years, for instance, I was a solid supporter of the stymie, on the ground that it was 'part of the game of golf'. Later I realised that it was not part of the game of golf, in that probably 98 per cent of golfers (who after all *are* the game of golf) never played stymies at all and the only time they entered the game was in knock-out match-play competitions and the private games of the other 2 per cent.

Again when a worldwide code of rules was agreed between the R and A and the USGA in, I think, 1951, I thought it a magnificent idea and a great triumph for all concerned. Now I perceive that there are so many differences in the game as played in the two countries that it would be just as well if we each had our own set of rules—basically the same, of course, but by no means identical.

Similarly I was brought up to believe that golf clubs were very much a male preserve and, as my job of writing about golf—about eighty-seven years ago, as it now seems—began to take me around

the senior championship clubs, this impression was greatly strengthened. None of them admitted women to their principal rooms. At
some, like Formby, the women had, and still have, a clubhouse of
their own. At others there was a small mixed room in some distant,
inconvenient part of the building. At headquarters, in other words
the Royal and Ancient, women were not admitted at all—nor are
they now.

Strangely enough I had a letter only this week from a friend at the
Garden City Club in America, mentioning how they had managed to
maintain the ancient flavour of the game. Ladies, he said, were
permitted to play on two days a week before the hour of 11.30 a.m.
and not one of them had ever been allowed to set foot in the
clubhouse in any circumstances whatever! The same applies at that
greatest of American clubs, Pine Valley.

All the same, with the exception of the Royal and Ancient, which
is an institution apart, I must confess that I have completely changed
my views about 'mixed' clubhouses. *Tempora mutantur et nos
mutamur in illis*, which has been roughly translated, 'Times ain't
what they was and, come to that, nor are we neither'. Perhaps it was
the war that did it: the shortages of food and staff and the pleasant
habit of lunching at the club on Sundays to give the little woman a
day off from the cooker and the sink.

It took a good many years for the main citadels to fall. As good an
example as any, perhaps, was the Royal Liverpool Club at Hoylake,
which I was privileged first to know when we played a rather watery
University match there in 1929. At that time it is fair to say that any
suggestion of having *a* main, never mind *the* main, mixed room in
the clubhouse would not ever have got a seconder.

After the war there was a little room if I remember rightly—or am
I thinking of Royal Lytham?—from the end of a dark passage, where
the women congregated, tapping their tiny feet and awaiting the
coming of the lord and master. Sometimes they would send petulant
messages and, as the steward approached, the lords and masters
would turn quickly over their shoulders thinking, 'Lord, is it I?'
Taken by and large this sort of thing made both sides unhappy and it
would have been almost better to bar women altogether.

Now that bar takings (and fruit machine takings, to which I will
happily contribute until all available cash has been swallowed—
especially by that variety on which you can take a chance or double,

or even treble, or nothing and on which Joe Carr at Wentworth the other day got 500 and promptly doubled and got nothing!)—now that bar takings, as I say, contribute such a hefty slice of a club's income, no one in his senses would, I think, build a clubhouse today without making the main room 'mixed' with perhaps a small 'men only' bar adjacent to the men's locker room entrance so that they could 'have one' before changing their clothes.

17 February 1966

A Place for Women

It seems a far cry, though I doubt whether it is anything like a hundred years, since it was considered that 80 yards should be the maximum drive for a woman, since otherwise she would be subjected to the unseemly gesture of raising the club above her shoulder. So women started with little courses of their own, tapping the ball demurely round, encouraged by admiring gentlemen friends with side-whiskers. A far cry, indeed, between that and Mrs 'Babe' Zaharias!

The next step, I suppose it must have been around the turn of the century, was to give them proper courses of their own; shorter, it is true, than the men's but in every sense 'real golf'. Formby comes to mind, and another of the earliest clubs in England, Royal Eastbourne; and of course there is the rather prosaic-looking Ladies' course (though I may be doing it an injustice) on the other side of the railway from Hoylake. I have not played it but I have walked over it, with 'eyes down', like a bingo player. This was due to a senior member of the Old Hall Club in Liverpool betting myself and a friend of mine a fiver that it was too late in the season to find a plover's egg.

The only place where we knew to look was the Ladies' course at Hoylake, where my friend was a member and where I was not unknown myself. I am afraid we did not pay a green fee, or perhaps a 'search fee', but we must have covered pretty well every inch of the rough when at last my eye fell upon a solitary egg. We gazed down at it with childish satisfaction. 'It's not a plover's egg,' I remember saying to my friend. 'It's a fiver!'

The earlier 'senior' clubs—and I suspect that the less distinguished were very much the same—did not think of admitting women any more than they thought of admitting professionals. Nor was this resented at the time by either party. That was how life was. When sometimes I hear people suggesting that it was 'snobbish' that professionals should not be admitted to the clubhouse, I ask them whether the caddies are admitted to theirs today. In twenty years' time they may be. Nobody considers it snobbish that they are excluded now—least of all the caddies themselves.

The senior clubs which I have in mind are such as Muirfield, Hoylake, Lytham, Formby and Sandwich—the Royal and Ancient is somehow in a different category. All these clubs exercised the inalienable right (fast being eroded) of a number of persons joining together to form a club, whether for golf or anything else, and running it as they wish to. All clubs, by definition, are 'exclusive', otherwise they would not be clubs. So far as I am concerned they have an absolute right to exclude women, professionals, caddies, negroes, house furnishers—or H. Longhurst. If, in the case of golf, they are public courses, they have, in my opinion, no such right.

At some clubs the women (encouraged and financially assisted, I will bet, by the men!) possessed not only courses but clubhouses of their own. At Formby, for instance, their clubhouse, in which I have sometimes been kindly invited to take refreshment, is as delightful as their course.

At another of England's oldest golfing institutions—that really is the right word for it—namely the Brighton and Hove Golf Club, of which I have the honour to be a member, the women still have a clubhouse of their own, some fifty yards across the bare Downs from what used to be exclusively the men's but is now used equally by both sexes. Until a week or two ago, however, the women, if they wished to powder their nose, still had to get the key from the steward and battle their way across the Downs in wind and rain to their own little retreat. Now, what with running water having been installed in the clubhouse in the 76th year of its existence, a modest 'Ladies' has been installed in the main clubhouse. With all this, and a diesel apparatus to make electricity instead of the old Calor gas, many a senior member threatens to resign on the ground that the club is not what it was when he joined it.

Very few clubs still relegate the ladies to the equivalent of the servants' quarters and I am sure it is, and was, a mistake to do so. I think you should either keep them out or make them welcome. Perhaps as good an example as any of the unsatisfactoriness of the 'half and half' method—and I am sure that the members will forgive my suggesting this—was the Royal Liverpool Club at Hoylake. Here, after all, was the tournament in 1885 which later became the Amateur championship. Together with Westward Ho! in the remote south it was *the* club in England and no woman, I am sure, would have claimed the slightest right to set foot in it.

I cannot put a date to the year when women were allowed into a little remote room overlooking the caddiemaster's premises but I do not believe that this had happened when I played in the University match in 1930. At any rate the 'half and half' situation did prevail after the war and, as at other clubs, led to the uneasy situation of the male enjoying the company of his witty friends at one end of the clubhouse and the female tapping her tiny foot in isolation at the other, eventually plucking up courage to send the steward along with her dread summons.

A few years ago Hoylake took what must have been a very deep breath indeed and created a mixed lounge and bar on the ground floor as a truly integral part of the clubhouse. The original big room, with the pictures of the red-coated past captains round the wall, remained sacred upstairs. When I last went there, for the Amateur championship of 1962, the mixed room was packed and animated all the time. And the biggest number of people I saw in what used to be the holy of holies was four.

Times have indeed changed. The women are with us now and most of us, I suspect, in our hearts view their presence with pleasure.

15 December 1966

The Secretary's Lot

I wonder how many golfers have *not*, at some time or another, fancied themselves in the role of golf club secretary. Precious few, I am sure. It is one of those jobs that everyone imagines he can do. Nothing to it. Nice quiet office in which to write a few odd letters and notices until it is time to proceed in leisurely fashion to the bar for one or two free drinks before settling down to a nice free lunch and perhaps a glass of port—what more can a man want?

There may still be clubs where such a life is possible but they must be increasingly few. I should envisage them as being mainly on the southern coast, adjacent to not too big towns inhabited largely by retired people, with perhaps an influx of visitors in August, these being regarded as a most frightful nuisance mitigated only by the fact that they bring enough money with them to enable the club to avoid increasing its subscription. I sometimes feel that it is about time I stopped writing about golf, so if a vacancy occurs in such a club I hope someone will bear me in mind!

Of course, it is impossible to generalize. I could see leading an immensely happy and worthwhile life as a golf club secretary. On the other hand to be stuck with an 'awkward' committee and/or captain must be a fate worse than death. The man to beware of is the man who *wants* to be on the committee. He is always liable to be a menace when he gets there. What the secretary wants is a man who joins the committee with the utmost reluctance and is therefore likely to be only too pleased to let him, the secretary, get on with his job. No sooner, however, does he start getting on with his job unhampered than somebody starts muttering the word 'dictator'. In some cases which I have known, but which it would be tactless to mention, this would not have been far from the truth, at that.

The best thing ever written on this subject is, without any doubt whatever, the *Letters to a Golf Club Secretary* written by George Nash when he was in fact secretary of the Royal Portrush Club. How near that splendid cast of characters—General Sir Armstrong Forcursue, KBE, CSI, Admiral Charles Sneyring-Stymie, CB, Commander Harrington Nettle, CMG, DSO, and the rest—were to the truth, and to what extent they were drawn from life at Portrush when the book was first published in 1935, we shall never know, but one suspects somehow that they cannot have been drawn wholly from imagination. On the other hand, with the general levelling-down process that has gone on since the war, I doubt whether many such characters exist to harry the life of the club secretary today.

There can be little doubt surely, of one thing, namely that the secretary's job has become increasingly onerous in, say, the past 20 years. Smaller clubs can still be run on an 'honorary' basis by some well-wisher but a bigger club is now more of a business than a club. The money involved is much bigger; the bar has to be watched a great deal more carefully; the fruit machines, the very lifeblood of the club as likely as not, have to be supervised; stamps and now Selective Employment Tax for the staff have to be taken care of and a whole host of other things.

Not least of the secretary's headaches must, I imagine, be that second lifeblood of the bigger clubs, the 'visiting societies'. One after another they come and there must seem never to be a day free from them. All have to be welcomed and taken care of and when the last one leaves on a Friday, well, tomorrow's the weekend once more, the club's busy time. Should the secretary take a couple of weekends off in the course of a year, almost immediately it is a case of 'Quite a good chap but he's hardly ever here'.

To be secretary of a really big 'business' like Wentworth, where you have not only a vast membership but a whole host of tournaments to organize, must be absolute hell or a stimulating challenge, according to temperament. The last man you would have thought to be good at it was that splendid character, the late Peter Roscow, whose death was such a loss to the golfing world as a whole. We were great friends and he once confessed that his secret ambition had been to be an actor—yet I thought he was a wonderful secretary and presented a perfect 'image' of the club to the outside world.

Are secretaries underpaid? I was once alleged to have said that they were overpaid. I don't believe I did, but I am afraid my rating among the fraternity dropped alarmingly, so let me now say that on the whole they probably are underpaid—but nothing like to the degree that I am!

12 October 1967

Ridiculous Rules and Decisions

I am always, I am afraid, liable to bore on the subject of the Rules of Golf but really it does seem to be ridiculous to have 93, and after the last lot of changes, possibly 100 pages of Rules of hitting a little ball about with a stick. The whole thing has become so ghastly solemn—

and who can wonder, when a man may have a single putt for £20,000? With this sort of thing going on you have to have a whole code, like the law itself, to cover almost every known contingency, and then an ever growing volume of case law, so to speak, in the form of Decisions on the Rules.

It is natural that the ruling bodies of golf, the Royal and Ancient and the USGA, should wish to keep a hold on the game and steer it along what they consider to be sound lines, rather than let control slip to a body like the World Council of Golf or to have the millionaire professionals of the various Professional Golfers' Associations establish a set of Rules of their own. We all like to retain positions of prestige and the power to do what we think is for the general good and I yield to absolutely no one in my appreciation of the hard work put in on the Rules by volunteers on both sides of the Atlantic, and indeed all over the golfing world.

Nevertheless the time may come when it will be better to have an ordinary, simple intelligible code for ordinary golfers and let the professionals go their own way. Their numbers are trivial by comparison with the rest of us and, after all, golf is their business and their livelihood. It is very important indeed to a man to know whether he is permitted to 'obtain relief', as the saying is, and get a free drop. It is also important to his fellow competitors, when it may make a difference of several thousand pounds. So the custom is for professionals not to interpret the Rule there and then but to sit down on their vast golf bags and 'send for a ruling'. Out comes an official in a mini-Moke or some such, having been summoned by radio, and gives a decision.

For the rest of us we could easily play to an ordinary code, containable on the back of a score-card and therefore consultable at any time. I should look forward to the day when it became 'the thing' to have one in your golf bag and even, strange thought, to have read it and perhaps in the end know the Rules of Golf without having to consult it, just as our forebears presumably knew the original twelve Rules which were then held sufficient.

I am against constant changes in the Rules and am glad to emphasize that the authorities do indeed feel the same way and have agreed to make changes only every four years. Even so, most people do not follow the changes and it will be interesting to know after 1 January 1968 how many people know whether they are entering a four-year period when you can now hit the flag-stick with impunity, or just leaving one! Or what is the new Rule about the provisional and unplayable ball.

I should like for a start to go through all the Rules and examine some of the really savage penalties exacted for trivial offences, committed palpably by mistake and gaining no possible advantage to the perpetrator. I have just been sitting in the R and A and idly glancing through some of the Decisions, and really the Rules do seem the more remarkable the longer you look at them. The original sacred Rule of golf was that the ball should be played where it lies and you must not touch it during the course of play. My researches, on a very modest scale, reveal that if you move your ball when moving a movable obstruction, you replace it without penalty. If it falls off the tee-peg, or indeed if you knock if off, you replace it without penalty: but if the wind blows it a fraction of an inch after you have addressed it, instead of putting it back where it was, perhaps half an inch away, you lose a stroke; and the same if you turn it over by mistake when addressing it.

A lady who touched a piece of sand in a bunker in making her back-swing was held to be fined *two* strokes (or loss of hole) because the club 'shall not touch the sand before making a stroke'. Yet a fellow who dropped his club in the sand before playing suffered no penalty. Nor did another culprit who missed the first shot, then threw his club down into the sand in disgust. Another man in a bunker found a dead branch projecting into it but nowhere near his ball and not in any way interfering with his stroke. His caddie, seizing it by the part that was not in the bunker, removed it, together with, of course the bit that was projecting into the bunker. For this the player was adjudged to have lost the hole (or *two strokes* in stroke-play). The same is the penalty for 'testing the surface of the green' by rubbing the putter head across the turf. Such penalties are to my mind rubbish and could be completely abolished. Such situations could all be covered by the final words of a set of Rules I once devised to go on a score-card, namely *'ensuring, as always, that no advantage to himself shall accrue'*.

P.S. I have just come across a Decision which, I am sure you will be glad to know, defines a bird's nest as an immovable obstruction. So these Rules of Golf committees do not have hearts of stone after all!

CHAPTER NINE

Traveller's Tales

Unpronounceable Names and Berets

I am indeed set pleasant tasks in writing on golf. What, for instance, could be more congenial a subject than golf on the Continent, the background of some of the happiest memories that the game has given me and still waiting there for those yet to discover it?

My own appetite was whetted when, having passed into Cambridge—a somewhat easier task, I suspect, in those days—I abandoned the last term at school and went off instead to 'learn French' at Lausanne. Here I found a splendid golf course up in the hills above the town, with the inevitable result that, while my golf improved a good deal, my French remained stationary. There were a number of gay spirits in the club in those days, and some pretty good players at that, and sometimes we would set sail in the steamer and cross the lake to play a match at Evian.

In the following year Eric Martin Smith and I went out for the Swiss championship at Geneva and by some miracle I reached the final, where I was beaten by D. Welsh. By a coincidence, I had a letter from Commander Hallowes, who was then secretary at Geneva, reminding me of the championship 'which I should probably have won if I had taken it more seriously'. As a matter of fact I tried desparately hard, and it nearly broke my heart when I lost!

Anyway, the appetite was still further whetted, indeed I may be said to have been since that time an addict, and before the war some of us used to make trip after trip to the continental championships. We tried like the devil while we were on the course and increased our stock of knowledge in devious ways when we were not. It was an experience which I cannot recommend too strongly to any young players who can find the time and the wherewithal.

How good, on the whole, are courses on the Continent? From what I remember, the New course at Le Touquet, now I believe defunct as a result of the war, was just about as fine a seaside course as you would find. It was here just before the war that Tom Odams, professional at Grim's Dyke, led the field in the French Open by six shots. He did a 75 in the final round, only to be nosed out by the Argentinian, Martin Posé. I always look on this as one of the most extraordinary rounds ever played.

On the whole, seaside courses are rare on the Continent, though there are one or two in Holland, and, of course, Zoute, not far from Ostend, is very highly to be recommended. Inland, however, there is an almost standard continental course and you will find it in France, Holland, Belgium and Germany. It is about the length of Woking, possibly a little shorter and its fairways are very narrow, enclosed by woods, off which balls may be heard bouncing in the silence of the forest several holes away. The course is intelligently laid out and in excellent condition, the clubhouse is most congenial, meals can be had at any time, the cooking is exceedingly good, making you wonder why the dickens people cannot do the same at home, and champagne is cheap.

The idea got around at one time that championships on the other side of the Channel were money for old rope—probably because I once won one. This was not true, as many a 'big shot' found when he got there. On a shortish and very narrow course you may well do a 68 in the first practice round, but gradually the place is liable to close in on you till in the end you feel as though you are playing in blinkers. Then the jitters set in and you begin calculating how many hundreds of miles you have come for all this. Before you know where you are, you have been beaten by a man with an unpronounceable name and a beret.

Being of the cowardly disposition that prefers medal play to a flesh and blood opponent, I used greatly to enjoy the open championships and played at various times in the French, Italian and Dutch. On two occasions I partnered Marcel Dallemagne who in those days used to hit the ball the most fearful crack. The first time was at Mandelieu, near Cannes, where the flattened fir trees are so thick with pine needles that your ball often stays up them. Here Dallemagne started 7, 2, 8, 6, 2. The other occasion was at an even narrower course, The Hague, where Dallemagne hit a number of strokes still spoken of with awe, completely cutting off the dogleg at one or two holes.

A great deal of fun, to say nothing of some very fine courses, used to be had in Germany. Winning the championship involved having one's hand pump-handled up and down by Karl Henkel, Ribbentrop's uncle-in-law, while he poured out a torrent of unintelligible German. Poor Henkel was killed by a bomb. A good fellow in his way, he owned a champagne business with gigantic cellars at Wiesbaden, which we duly inspected one year. I mentioned this in a book and years later, when I stood for Parliament, I arrived one morning to find the place festooned with posters saying 'Longhurst feasted with the Nazis!'

I defended the championship at Bad Ems, where life was made more than agreeable by the fact that General Critchley had brought over his remarkable caravan and in this luxurious appliance we used to go over in the evenings to Coblenz to dine on Rhine salmon. At Bad Ems against that fine young German player, von Beckerath— did he survive the war I wonder?—I was three down with eight to play and finished 3, 3, 5, 3, 3, 2, 3, squared the match and lost on the twenty-first. The London evening paper for which I was then working said 'Longhurst was three up with eight to play but cracked'! It rankles still.

The main charm of continental golf, to me, has always been that it is the ideal excuse for travel. I am not sure that I should deem it worthwhile to join a party to go and simply sit around the Lake of Geneva. To go and play in the Swiss amateur is quite another story. Even Paris itself would not have quite the same charm if one were not getting fresh air and exercise on the golf course during the daytime, and with a purpose sufficiently serious to make you determined to do your best. Only the other day at the University match some of the boys were mentioning that they had been to play in the Swedish championship, and immediately my train of thought was one of regret. I had been going to play at Malmo, where Swedish friends, met playing in Germany, had given ecstatic descriptions of the long golden sands with long golden ladies lying on them—and then the war came!

Of course one does not need a championship as an excuse. The ordinary golfing holiday will do, or you may be a member of some touring team. Last year some of us had a most delightful week in Belgium, representing the Royal and Ancient. Before the war I was fortunate enough to be regularly a member of a team which Joe Fairlie used to take over to play a French side at Deauville. It was at one of those earlier matches that Dale Bourn arrived on the first tee for the singles attired in a dinner jacket and on his way home!

Geneva, St Germain, Chantilly, Morfontaine, Le Touquet, Nice, Mont Agel, Wannsee, Frankfurt, San Remo, Ghent, Spa, Waterloo, Noordwyck, The Hague—the list could go on and on. What an accumulation of happy memories! Hospitable folk, new friends, new scenes. How different a world it would have been if Stalin and Hitler had played golf!

3 March 1955

Filling in the Chapters

All my life I have gone on the principle of trying anything once. I have always thought of it to myself as 'filling in chapters'. I thought it was my own expression till—since great minds, especially with the same name, think alike—I was talking with Henry Cotton the other day and he remarked of something: 'Oh well, it makes another chapter.' At any rate what I am driving at is that, whenever you get a chance of going somewhere where you have not been before, or doing something, however trivial, that you have not done before, you should automatically take it, even if it seems a bit of a bore at the time.

If you get a chance to go skiing, go. If you like it, it will give you the greatest thrill that is open to an ordinary amateur performer in sport. (One of the greatest regrets of my life is that I started too late; the war intervened; and now I am too old and too fat!) If you don't like it, you will have filled in a blank and for the rest of your life, when you read about it or hear people talking about it, you will be able to imagine the scene and know what they are talking about.

This simple example can be multiplied a thousand times. New people, new places, new experiences—they are all to be had for the asking. The more you have seen, the better company you become to other people and therefore the more you see. It is a cumulative process.

In some ways this wide variety of experience is more difficult for young people to attain than it was between the wars; in others it has become easy beyond the dreams of previous generations. High taxation and impoverished parents mean that if you are to travel the world you must do it some other way than simply 'on father'. On the other hand, if you can wangle the trip somehow, you can spend more than a fortnight in Sydney and still be back within a month. There are all sorts of ways of wangling these things so that you travel 'on the house', which nowadays is the only way to do it, but here I am talking only of golf, which of course does not come under the heading of wangling!

Golf is just about the best excuse for travel yet discovered. It gives you a purpose in the background, brings you in touch with the most influential and amusing of the natives, and gives you plenty of time for activities other than the golf. I first discovered this when in our first year at Cambridge, the late Eric Martin Smith and I went off to play in the Swiss championship—a fact which I mention largely as an excuse to remind readers that I reached the final. This splendid outing whetted the appetite and I find on reflection that I have now played golf in 22 countries and on something approaching 400 courses. If you won every treble chance from now to the end of the season you could not buy a single one of these memories. Some people, of course, do not think this way, while others come round to it but realise too late.

It is not only abroad that you 'fill in another chapter'. Most of them are filled in at home—but, reverting to golf, how blind so many people seem to be. Even with that scheme which used to operate before the war—I don't know whether it does now—the vast majority of golfers have not played on half the other courses in their own country.

The outstanding single instance of blindness to opportunity within my own experience was when the majority of the 1953 British Walker Cup team, having played in the match, failed to go on to the US Amateur championship at Oklahoma City. When I chivvied one of them about it, and a young bachelor at that, he said he 'thought it would be a bit hot there'! They were all entered for the championship; they were to be put up at private homes; an unknown benefactor was sending his private aeroplane 1500 miles to fetch them from New York; and none of them had ever been to Oklahoma before. If that isn't dishing it up on a plate, what is?

Of the golf at Oklahoma City I remember little or nothing except that John Morgan did well and that Gene Littler won, but what I remember of Oklahoma City and the people I met would fill this entire edition of *Golf Illustrated*. The city itself is six years younger than my mother. They founded it in one night on the famous 'Run' from the Kansas border—an episode in which the grandfathers of many of our hosts had taken part. When they had been there forty-odd years, they found they had put it plumb on top of one of the biggest oilfields in the world. Now even the main street has great pumps going up and down within the derricks and people have them in their back yards—'seven times up and down for the oil company and the eighth for me'. One member of the club, of direct Indian descent, admitted when challenged that he did not know exactly how many wells he had got.

Well within a middle-aged man's memory the sheriff wore a broad black hat and carried a gun on either hip. Now, while we argue about building motor roads, they have the Turner Turnpike, 88 miles to Tulsa for a dollar-fifty, and the bus is scheduled to do it in 72 minutes. I never met a richer assortment of characters and I could not have been more thrilled than when two different parties of them looked me up in London.

8 March 1956

Desert Golf

To play in sand or desert is always an entertaining and—like the game of golf anywhere in the world—a humbling experience. I saw it for the first time in the oilfields of Persia, which for ten months of the year are a howling wilderness with shade temperatures up to 127 degrees. Here the members of the then Anglo-Iranian Oil Company had made themselves a first-class clubhouse and, considering the conditions, a first-class course. They were helped, I remember, by unlimited quantities of asphalt, which is a residue of the oil—the 'pitch' mentioned in connection with Noah's Ark—and which they used as a basis for the greens. Later on I experienced desert golf at Khartoum, where not a single blade of grass or anything else grows at any time, and El Fasher, in the heart of the Sudan, where they had nine holes, no tees, and only one flag, with which a boy in a nightshirt dashed ahead from hole to hole.

Tripoli and Benghazi, where I had the pleasure of playing a week or two ago, are of a much higher order than this, and golf, with a strong nucleus of local Scotsmen, is a matter to be taken with proper seriousness. Tripoli, with 18 holes and a firmer substance underfoot, is perhaps the superior of the two. Benghazi suffers from more sand and I can well understand that summer golf there is rather like something out of *Beau Geste*. Nevertheless, both to a remarkable degree make the most of what they have got.

The only shots that are really spoilt are those to the green from 80 yards and upwards. Some of the drives, from solid raised-up tees, are magnificent, with the blue Mediterranean as a backcloth and just enough greenery mixed with the sand at this time of year to remind you of the best undulating seaside courses at home. The greens again are perfectly all right, once you get used to them. At Benghazi they are positively flattering, as nothing that anyone can devise can prevent the holes sinking into a miniature basin. If you get the strength right, you can be as much as four inches off the line and have the supreme satisfaction of watching the ball 'die' sideways into the hole, thus defeating the man who on the old principle of 'never up, never in' has made a bold, firm putt and sees it skid round the rim of the hole and go on.

It is the 'middle' shots that are the problem because no one yet has devised a satisfactory 'apron' on which to pitch the second shot—though an engineer with whom I played at Benghazi declared, in terms which were technically over my head, that it would be perfectly possible. At holes where you have hard ground in front of the green, a splendid 'bumbling' shot is always on and sometimes brings a supremely satisfying reward. At other times, when the apron consists of loose sand, nothing is on. You either pitch short with a splash in the sand, or pitch on the green and go careering over the back, to the left with a tantalisingly difficult little pitch back.

The desert, where naturally you play 'winter rules', even with the temperature in the 120's, is supremely the home of the 'had only' shot. This expression, now I think widely known, was born of the writings of the late George Greenwood who so often recorded that 'He had only to play the simplest of . . . but, alas, up came his head and the ball, feebly struck . . ., etc.' Faced with a shot with a 'carry' of anything from three yards upwards to the green, you tee your ball up high in the sand, take a lofted club (till you learn better), catch the sole of the club in the sand, and hit it a yard. Time and time again—maddening! Later, of course, you learn to look on any club with a rounded sole as the invention of the devil.

On these desert courses, if you use your head, you can beat a man immeasurably superior to yourself in normal conditions. It depends on whether you can 'make up' the shots as you go along. If you think that golf consists of one basic shot, the only question being to make up your mind which club to play it with, you have had it. Henry Cotton, the supreme 'maker-upper' of golf shots, would be a superlatively good desert player. Ben Hogan, with great respect, I think, would not. Indeed, I would back the Controller of State Properties, Libya, whose handicap is 8 at Llandrindod Wells and scratch at Tripoli, to beat Hogan first time round by not less than 5 and 4.

14 June 1956

Ex-Cadet Longhurst, 1737288

'Mr Howard, your cap badge is too high . . .' 'Mr Fisher, your lanyard is crooked. . . .' 'Mr Longhurst, your bootlace is twisted.'

Could it really be true? Could it really be that ex-Cadet Longhurst, 1737288, was back at Shrivenham after fifteen years, this time as an honoured guest instead of a unit of officer-material?

Such, indeed, was the case and, if I have enjoyed another afternoon's golf as much this year, I do not remember it. The vast barracks at Shrivenham, in the heart of the Vale of the White Horse, were built in Mr Hore-Belisha's day before the war as a model for the future. I suppose that of their kind they are the finest in England. During the earlier stages of the war they became a Royal Artillery OCTU. Later they were handed over to the Americans. After the war they became, as they now are, the Royal College of Military Science. Some of the students are newly commissioned young officers; others have come back later in life as captains and majors.

With this grown-up element it was natural that at some time someone should think of starting a golf course, especially as there is none within the immediate vicinity. They began with half a dozen holes, which were designed by C. K. Cotton. Now, by redesigning one and creating two others, they have got the full nine and it was to the opening ceremony that, having heard that I was an 'Old Boy', as it were, they kindly invited me. I was not only to be honorary captain of the students' team against the staff, but I was to drive a ceremonial opening ball.

As I drove over the top of the ridge and saw again the wonderful panorama below, not greatly changed, I dare say, since the Romans marched down into what they called Corinium and we call Cirencester, my heart was full. Here, come to life again, was the pattern of Sheet 104 of the Ordnance Survey, a document which I carried with me for five long months and came to know by heart. It was that wonderful week at the end of May and, as I drove along, I found myself reciting the magical names of the hamlets in the Vale and seeing each of them in my mind's eye again . . . Compton Beauchamp; Kingston Lisle; Coln St Aldwyns; Ampney Crucis, Ampney St Mary, Ampney St Peter; Stanton Fitzwarren; Blunsdon St Andrew; Stratton St Margaret. What a pageant of English life!

The golf course turned out to be quite exceptionally good by comparison with what I had imagined possible. It finishes, it is true, with four holes, two of which are short and the other two reachable by a goodish player enjoying both good form and good luck. These holes thread their way narrowly between the cedars and other giant trees that surround Beckett Lodge, which used to be the 'big house' and is now the officers' mess—a sanctum to which as a mere cadet I never, of course, graduated. The other five holes offer shots with pretty well every club in the bag, including the brassie. They lie in the park and the fairway of one of them, close beside the stream, is the best I have seen anywhere this year. I cannot believe it possible to fulfil more completely than Ken Cotton has done their desire for an adult, enjoyable, not-too-long course right at their front door.

The opening ceremony was no small ordeal and I now have even greater sympathy with captains of the Royal and Ancient, who have to make their solitary stroke before a larger and more critical audience, and furthermore at eight in the morning! Thoughts of complete fluffs, tops, and even air shots flashed through my mind. The only thing to do, I thought, was to hold the club short, take a very slow swing, and try to finish on both feet. Next moment the club had flashed up and down before I could stop it and the thing was over. And the result? How did you guess? High slice.

This being over, we set off in a foursome to play in the match and I had time to take stock of my surroundings. I could still hardly believe it to be true. The place ought to be filled with the white cap bands of cadets. Behind one of those very windows we used to scrape the floor with razor blades, prior to 'bumping' and polishing it for the barrack-room inspection on Saturday mornings—at least the others did: I am happy to think that I declined, on working out that we had 10,721 square inches each. Somewhere behind the big building on our left ran the muddy stream over which the fiendish PT instructors had constructed the obstacle course, and as I wandered along the first fairway I could see again the splendid spectacle of an ex-schoolmaster-cadet hanging wrong way up like the giant sloth on a rope suspended between two trees. Coins are falling from his pocket, his knuckles are whitening, his head is hanging back. Any minute now . . . splosh!

Away on the right the White Horse itself stands out on the hilltop, crudely carved, as it has been these many centuries. The inhabitants of the village of Uffingdon have an annual 'scouring' to keep it white. In my day it was 'blacked out' with turf. Uffingdon, incidentally, was the home of Tom Brown of 'Schooldays' fame.

I am afraid my partner and I were defeated but perhaps I had some excuse for mind-wandering. Could it really be true that there was a time when, only a few hundred yards from the first green, I was to be seen charging at a great cluster of barbed wire, jumping headlong into it with a rifle held out horizontal in front, turning head over heels, and emerging miraculously unscratched the other side? No, no. Some other person, some other world!

Still, my team of students did me proud and we won by the odd match. Lt-Col. R. N. Syme, who I fancy inspired the golf course in the first place, had presented a most beautiful old silver-embossed tankard as a trophy for this annual match and in the mellow evening sunshine I found myself stepping up to receive it from the wife of the Commandant, General Richardson.

Casting my mind back over the years, I thought 'If only my friends could see me now'!

12 December 1956

Golf by Train

The very best that can be said of petrol rationing in so far as it affects golf clubs is that it could not have come at a better time. Heaven knows how long it will last—my own guess is that it will be with us in some form or other for the best part of a year—but, if this should prove to be an unduly pessimistic forecast, then the months of December, January, February and March are the very ones in which we would have chosen to go short.

Nevertheless it is going to prove a real hardship to a great many clubs, and the more congenial they are, in offering a chance to 'get away from it all', the harder hit they are bound to be. At the moment of writing it seems that even 'sharing a taxi from the station' is going to be a chancy business. In Brighton, for instance, there is a great fleet of yellow-topped taxis. Each vehicle supports two drivers and is kept in continuous use. Normally each uses six gallons a day. Now the ration is 1½ gallons, or about 30 miles a day, and this will not even support one man.

In the end I suppose we shall all have to follow the example of Jack Burns, who won the Open championship in 1888. Shortly afterwards he returned to his job as a platelayer on the railway and is credited with the observation that he was 'never off the line now'. There must be innumerable clubs which are 'on the line', yet I can only think of half a dozen or so. Prestwick is an obvious example and perhaps the best, since you can slice your opening tee shot straight on to the platform at which you have just alighted. Then, of course, there is Formby, where the stranger, having heard that the clubhouse is right against the station, not unnaturally gets out at Formby only to find himself in the middle of the town, the club in fact being adjacent to Freshfield, the next station down the line.

Perhaps the best 'golf by train' I ever enjoyed was when the Army saw fit to post me as a cadet to a camp on the coast of Merionethshire, which had a little halt actually inside the camp. We used to put our bicycles in the guard's van and alight at the first tee at Aberdovey, pedalling dangerously home late at night over the golf course at Towyn. Nearer home, some of the London courses are fortunate in the current misfortunes, notably Sandy Lodge, Beaconsfield, Denham, Sunningdale, and, if you don't mind the discouraging walk back through the cemetery, West Hill.

In the old days, before it became a wartime casualty, Bramshot was a great 'train course' and several of us used to go there by train in preference to car. The golf club halt was at the foot of a high bridge on which a small boy was stationed in the evenings, looking down the main Southampton line to Fleet. He had a bell which rang in the clubhouse to signify that he had seen, or in the dark heard, the train leaving Fleet station, and it was a stimulating sight to watch the 'regulars' judging the final drink to a split second, gathering up their things, dashing frantically into the night, down the long flight of steps and into the last carriage as it began to move out.

The Universities will, I fear, be badly hit, both domestically and in their weekend matches. I suppose it will be a case of the old 7.47 a.m. from Cambridge station all over again and that frightful thing home in the evening from Liverpool Street panting along through the fog via Bishop's Stortford and Audley End. Oxford still have Southfield near at hand and Cambridge the Gog Magog, but maybe a bus will be laid on to Mildenhall two or three times a week. I remember writing once about the early days when it meant taking a train to Mildenhall and walking back to Worlington along the line. Then came the days when the guard would let some steps down for the golfers at Workington Halt. I thought they were over but a Cambridge correspondent wrote: 'We do not await events in Persia to reach Worlington by train. I often travel by it. It still leaves Cambridge at 10.28. You get in the Worlington coach and the guard still lets the iron steps down to enable you to descend in safety.' Still, the communal bus is still probably the answer in most cases. They ran one from Sheffield to Lindrick during the war and were talking of it with nostalgic affection when I was there the other day.

As to the championships, those responsible are in an awkward position indeed and all depends, so far as I can see, on how long notice is required to change the venue. A club can probably accept a championship at a couple of months' notice, but for hundreds of

competitors, Press and assorted camp followers to 'unbook' their
rooms and find accommodation in another place, which will probably be booked up by holiday visitors in any case, is no mean
business, especially when some of them are coming from abroad.
The Open and Amateur are at Muirfield and Sandwich and the
English championship is at Hoylake, and a more unfortunate trio
from the point of view of access by train it would be difficult to
imagine.† Do you change these venues now, only to find yourself
accused of panicking when petrol rationing comes off in a few
months' time? Or do you let them run, only to find that no one can get
there and the whole thing is a flop on account of your wanton lack of
forethought?

In the meantime, hats off to the Ladies' Golf Union. They fixed
their championship for Gleneagles. Clearly collusion with Nasser!

27 June 1957

Brilliant Flashes of Silence

I wonder what Tom Kidd, who, in 1873, won the first Open championship to be played at St Andrews against 25 other competitors, or
Bob Martin, who, in 1876, won the second against 33 (his entry in
the *Golfers' Handbook* is followed by the delicious reference 'David
Strath tied but refused to play off'!) would have thought if someone
had assured them that within the lifetime of infants yet to be born the
competition for the very trophy that they were holding so proudly in
their hands would be contested by players from almost every country
in the world, and furthermore would be watched by unseen millions
sitting in their own homes hundreds of miles away.

The televising of golf has attracted a far bigger audience than was
at first anticipated. Even housewives who do not know one end of a
club from another have been found to watch it—a favourite comment
being, I gather, 'It seemed to be such a lovely place'—but it is still a
chancy business by comparison with other games. In cricket, tennis

---

† The Open and Amateur championships were switched to St Andrews and
Formby respectively in 1957—Ed.

or football you know what you are going to get, and where and when you are going to get it. In golf you are at the mercy of circumstances. At St Andrews for the Open all concerned are keeping their fingers crossed in the hope that we shall be able to fulfil the supreme purpose of television, namely, to show the winner winning.

This year we have been frustrated in the purpose, since the two tournaments so far televised on a Saturday and the precious hour of 6–7 p.m. has been taken, and retained through the summer, by a 'skiffle' programme for teenagers. Scotland 'opted out' of this pro- gramme for the Swallow-Penfold tournament and Scottish viewers were able to see Weetman winning. In England we had to shut down just as the leaders, going out last, were due to drive from the first tee. What is worse, we made arrangements for them to drive at 4.58 instead of 5.0, as we should then have probably the biggest audience ever to see golf—all tuned in for the Duke of Edinburgh! And then at the critical moment one of the players was missing and we faded out on some hopeless shots of players partly obscured by trees.

So many people ask me what goes on in these transmissions, and are so surprised at the answer, that I am glad to say something about it here, if only to pass on the credit to the man who deserves nearly all of it and never gets any, namely, the producer. In most cases this is Antony Craxton, a keen performer himself, who pioneered golf television. In Scotland, it is Jim Buchan.

The producer is the spider in the centre of a truly fantastic web, and the point to be borne in mind, should you find yourself in critical mood, is that he *cannot see a thing*. He sits in a sort of mobile 'Ops Room' surrounded by a mass of dials, screens, plugs, telephones, microphones, clocks and assorted paraphenalia beside which the cockpit of a Stratocruiser seems almost child's play. In front of him he has four screens in a row, and below them two others. The four screens show the pictures that four of his cameras are showing. One, or even two, of them may not be in use at the moment but they are still 'going'. To make it difficult, at Wentworth he had five, two of which were at the 18th, a mile and a half away, but only one of which was received at a time, as decided by the people at the 18th.

The two lower screens each show the same picture, identical with one of the four above. The left-hand one is what he is transmitting. The right-hand one shows what the public is receiving. If anything goes wrong with the one on the right, but the one on the left is alright, he knows it is not the fault of any of his own equipment but of some apparatus somewhere down the line. From Wentworth the picture went out from a dish-shaped object on the tower to a mast at Chobham nearby and from there by air to Highgate. From here it went by land cable to Broadcasting House, thence to Lime Grove, thence to Crystal Palace, and from here by air back to his right-hand screen, the whole process taking of course the merest fraction of a second. Don't ask me how it works, but that is what happens.

Inside the 'Scanner', the producer's nerve centre, there prevails a sort of controlled babel, all of which is heard by the commentator through his earphones as he endeavours to make his brilliant and revealing comments on the play. This, though at first disconcerting, is to me fascinating. A good deal of it consists of directions to the various cameramen, exposed in all weathers on the top of their towers and doing, if I may say so, a quite remarkable job. These directions are not merely, of course, to the camera now showing but to the ones that are to show in a few seconds' time. They include not only what to get on to but also what lens to use. In addition to this you hear, as commentator, the talk with your fellow commentator on his distant tower, asking whether he has got anything special to show; constant technical jargon going on between technicians in the Scanner; telephone talk between the producer's secretary and Lime Grove, often telling her to tell you to say such-and-such when you hand over or to interpolate at a suitable moment that the West Indies have lost another wicket and are now 148 for 3, or giving changes of instructions that, as it is raining at Lord's, you had better go on until further notice. And finally, of course, you hear the producer's instructions to yourself, which above all things you mustn't answer or it will go out as part of the commentary.

Being totally in the dark, the producer is often at a loss as to 'where to go next' and up till this year we have all had to resort to veiled indications like 'I am hoping that when we have seen these three hole out we shall be able to go over to the 8th where so-and-so . . ., etc.' Now, thank goodness, we are given a second microphone by which to talk to him direct, 'not for publication', and this is a great improvement.

The essence of golf television, of course, is to be up to date with the scores, and this presents a problem indisputedly more difficult than in other games. It is solved mainly by a system of walkie talkies, operated by local Signals regiments—much enjoyed by them and ideal for practice. The scores come up to the towers by telephone and the whole thing stands or falls by their efficiency. At Wentworth, mercifully only five minutes before the finish, I incautiously lifted the binoculars which were anchoring the main score sheet and in a second it was floating in the wind 100 yards away beside the 9th green. At Hoylake last year the gale blew away our tarpaulin overnight and the rain soaked us and the score sheet to such an extent that when we turned the pages they merely peeled off in our hands.

From this it will be seen that, while the commentators often receive the lion's share of the attention and their names are quoted at the end of the day's transmission, they are, in fact, cogs in an incredibly complicated machine and their job is a very simple one by comparison with some of the others. And if they think they are beginning to get on top of their job, there are always kind members of the public to correct them. Having held forth recently that the commentator's main job was to ensure 'brilliant flashes of silence', I received next morning an anonymous postcard from a gentleman in Doncaster saying 'You open your big mouth too dam' much'.

22 January 1959

The Passing of 'Kettledrummle'

The trouble with allowing yourself to become too fond of an institution is the same as allowing yourself to become too fond of a dog. When nature takes its course and the dog departs this life, it leaves a gap too painful to contemplate. In the case of the more material things that we cherish, there remains the virtual certainty that someone, sooner or later, will contrive to muck them up.

I am a great fan of British Railways. I think the meals on trains are capital, considering the price, and the staff are long-suffering and civil. It seems remarkable to me not that trains are sometimes late but that they are so often on time. At the moment, however, British Railways and I, though they may not know it, are not on speaking terms.

The trouble is that, when they have a guilty conscience, they are so damnably surreptitious. I do not know to how many hundreds of people I have enthused about my own service from London to Haywards Heath. Americans simply won't believe it. 'Yes,' I say, 'I can go home at 8.0, 8.45, 9.0, 9.25, 9.45, 10.0, 10.45, 11.0 or midnight and on every one of these trains there is a Pullman, on which for rather less than 50 cents I enjoy an armchair, table, light, private butler and private chef.'

And what do British Railways do? Silently, furtively, and without a word to a soul they cut off the lot and now all these Pullmans, locked, unlighted, and without their ever-courteous staff, run barrenly to and fro, dead links in the chain. They 'didn't pay their way'? No one who has known the midnight to Brighton would stand for that one. There was an 'institution' for you!

Now it's the institution—for so it was—from Leuchars to St Andrews. 'Change for St Andra's!—the most magic words in a roving golfer's life. We shall still hear the words but the magic will be gone. Instead of stepping across into the ancient familiar carriages hauled by our old friend 'Kettledrummle', which used to go so fast in reverse round the bend opposite Hell bunker that one day, one thought, it must surely fall over backwards. What do we find? A horrible, impersonal oil-fired thing that hoots instead of whistling. Tschah!

And what happens to poor old 'Kettledrummle'? Relegated to dishonourable retirement, no doubt, in some anonymous goods yard.

Supporters of lost causes are never wholly fair and, though I shall never forgive British Railways for the Pullmans, I can see the point of this one. Perhaps I am prejudiced through my first Diesel experience being unfortunate. I had to go by day from St Andrews to Little Aston, which you might think to be impossible; the solution turned out to be taxi to Thornton Junction for the 6.50 a.m. Diesel to Glasgow and aeroplane to Birmingham.

The taxi man got me there 40 minutes early. I will not harrow the reader with a description of Thornton Junction at 6 a.m. Suffice to say that the train had been there overnight and after half an hour or so the driver arrived and started it up both ends—which you do by pressing a self starter under the running boards. It started at the first push and I made sure, being the first arrival, of getting the seat just behind the driver, where I looked forward to a clear and hitherto unique view of the journey.

Unhappily my geography turned out to be at fault. When the train moved out, I was at the wrong end.

Still, I have since done the journey from Edinburgh to Leuchars by Diesel and this time even I knew which way it was going. I secured the coveted seat and I must confess it was a memorable experience. And so, when I come to think of it, will it be on the way to St Andrews. The thing will be to jump out at Leuchars almost before the train had stopped and run across to fling one's hat on the front seat of the waiting Diesel.

From there we shall see the beloved scene unfolding as no one, even 'Kettledrummle's' driver, has seen it before and perhaps in the end we may live to be grateful.

18 February 1960

Getting There is Half the Fun

The fact that I am writing from Enton Hall in the leanest period of a starvation cure and only a quarter of an hour ago passed the West Surrey Golf Club on returning from a solitary, though legitimate, cup of tea in Godalming (flanked by two fat women eating buttered crumpets and surrounded by a positive sea of iced cakes, fancy pastries, sausage rolls and the rest) reminds me that there were indeed trials and tribulations in reaching and especially getting back from West Surrey in my schooldays.

This involved about four and a half miles each way on a bicycle with the clubs slung over one's shoulder. My own steed was a vast affair, more suitable for the village constable, known, I remember, as the 'Golden Sunbeam with the Little Oil Bath'—the latter enclosing the chain. The journey out was comparatively simple. We raced at hideous speed down the steep hill from Charterhouse and then 'lay up' for a few minutes in Godalming in case a passing lorry could be found to give us a pull, hanging on the back. The fact that the left arm (so important in golf, etc., see textbooks) was nearly pulled out of its socket did not seem to matter. Far more dangerous was the prospect of being detected by a golfing master passing in his car.

It is one of my most cherished memories that I once secured a coal truck which not only took me along the Portsmouth road to the turning off to the club but actually turned off itself and delivered its coals to the clubhouse. No such chances could be relied on however for the return journey, with the ever-present thought of lock-up and dire penalties for being late. It ended with half riding and half pushing an enormous bicycle and one's clubs for the best part of a mile up one of the steepest hills in Surrey. I wonder how far I should get without a heart attack today!

From Cambridge we had some really agonising battles to get to our Saturday matches with London clubs, some of them 90 miles away. Marshall's garage 6.30, and an open two-seater Morris Cowley (£25 second-hand and an excellent runner; petrol 1s 2d; beer 7d a pint). Often it was snowing and nobody knew whether the course was playable. No use ringing up at this hour of the morning. Better start off and chance it.

One by one we would turn up for breakfast at the Peahen at St Albans—where I remember one celebrated, if eccentric, Cambridge golfer, who was still wearing his scarf, turning to the assembled company and saying quietly 'Have any of you - - - - -'s got a spare collar and tie?' His own, it transpired, had been lost in an all-night outing near Newmarket. (No, no. Cambridge golf was not always like that!)

When we got to the club, I always remember our own astonishment at our host's astonishment that we should already have driven 90 miles. Some of them, one supposed, must be every bit of 40. One hoped one would not get as soft as that if one ever reached that age.

Sometimes the journey home was even worse. Crossing Royston Heath in a snowstorm one night, my old friend, W. H. Bermingham, as well might anyone, left the road and, turning in the wrong direction in the blizzard to retain it, found himself half-way across the heath to the Royston golf course.

Later, of course, one came to realise that driving anything over 15, or at the most 20, miles simply did not go with really serious golf, i.e. when one was trying to do one's very best, however humble that best might be. Henry Cotton, who in his finest days had one of those Mercedes, with ironmongery sticking out from the bonnet, would not drive himself more than a mere mile or two to a championship for fear of shaking up his arms and hands.

I often wonder, incidentally, whether the younger generation of professionals realise what an immense, untiring perfectionist he was. Of course, he started with certain advantages, but his success was 'all his own work'. If I were a young and truly aspiring professional today, the first thing I should do would be to seek a few private talks with Cotton. Nothing, I believe, would give him greater pleasure.

In later years I do not recall many 'trials and tribulations' in getting to golf, though it amuses me to think of a journey in a friend's car to play in some match at Rye, where for the first time since we first met years before the war I was to play General Critchley in a single. We had travelled thousands of miles together but had never come into direct combat. The car broke down in an obscure lane near Peasmarsh and I never did get there.

I had to stand a great deal of banter about this and I think that 'Critch' did at one time think almost seriously that it had been done on purpose. We each declare that we should have won but now we shall never know.

Finally, though I now admit it for the first time, I nearly put up a performance in my recent voyage round the world which would have justified instant promotion to 'King Purchaser'—the Purchasers being members of a club for those who have 'bought it'. On my way to Australia for the Canada Cup, I stopped for a few days in Honolulu with Francis ('Pineapple') Brown. Casually inquiring for a seat to Australia, I was told that they were fully booked up for three months and there was a waiting list so long that it was not worth putting my name on it. The only suggestion was that I report at the airport each morning at 4.30 a.m. and offer outgoing passengers £100 for their seat.

I was rescued in the end by the long arm of BOAC, but it was a nasty period. I can still see my report on the Canada Cup: 'We regret that our correspondent failed to book a seat and is now in Honolulu.' A nice place to be stuck in, but even now my mind hardly likes to dwell on it.

13 April 1961

The Land of the Rising Golf Course

It has often been suggested in this country that club members having already paid an annual subscription should also 'pay as they play'. A shilling a round is the sum usually mentioned. This always sets going two opposing arguments. One side says that the numerical minority who are constantly at the club, supporting it in various ways, are doing their whack already and it is not up to them to bolster up the backwoodsmen who scarcely turn up at all.

The backwoodsmen reply, also with logic, that they continue to pay their subscriptions and get in no one's way cluttering up the course and you can hardly ask anything fairer than that. Those who batter the course about should pay, in direct ratio, for its upkeep. If they did so the basic subscription could be lowered for everyone.

I have seen people get quite hot under the collar arguing about this one. I suppose the deciding factor is that no one has yet devised an effective and at the same time economic method of collecting the shillings!

The Japanese, I gather, tax the playing golfer in this way to the tune of anything from four to eight shillings a round, according to the prestige of the club. This is, of course, a government tax, not a club one. Now members of the opposition party are demanding that all golfers be taxed £10 a year however much or little they play. This is apparently in addition to the 'green fee tax' when they do play.

I do not expect these worthy gentlemen have heard of the law of diminishing returns. As a director of the Japan Golf Association put it, the total revenue would be more likely to fall through so many people deciding that they could not afford to pay.

The real reason behind the move is not a social but an economic one, as would become apparent at once if you had the luck, as I did after the Canada Cup week in Tokyo, to travel out to that lovely kind of Gleneagles-by-the-Sea, Kawana.

This involves a train journey of two hours, which might be along the coastline of the south of France. The train makes its way alongside the water, skirting little bays full of fishing boats and plunging into short tunnels to repeat the process on the other side. Fir trees grow beside the shore, reminding you of pictures you seem to remember, which turn out, not unnaturally, to be Japanese prints.

The trains, incidentally, depart from each station, as a point of honour, not to the minute, but to the second, and are scrupulously clean. When you buy a net of oranges from a girl on the platform, you find that it includes a bag in which to put the skin.

All this leads up to the fact that, as you look out at the slopes above and below the train, you find that every conceivable space has been terraced out and covered with soil. Some of these little terraces are hardly the size of half a billiard-table, but they are tended with the most loving care. After all, if you are prepared to take the trouble, you can grow 30 or 40 lettuces on half a billiard-table.

It soon dawns on you that land is so desperately short in Japan that every little plot is precious. Not a square foot is wasted. Now a golf course takes up, I suppose, several million square feet. Kasume-gaseki, where they played the Canada Cup, has two absolutely full-sized courses—each incidentally with a summer and winter green for each hole, making 72 in all—and a small prize for anyone who can detect a weed on a fairway.

The Japanese have taken to golf like ducks to water, especially since their pair, Nakamura and Ono, won the Canada Cup. There will doubtless be constant pressure for more and more golf courses and I have no doubt that it is as much to preserve the land as to soak the 'rich golfers' that the politicians want to keep the poor man away from golf.

17 August 1961

I Gotta Horse!

I remember receiving a book of raffle tickets with a horse as the prize and making a mental note that it would be great fun to win a racehorse and that I must remember to send the money. Of course I never got round to doing so and now I have just applied my mind to what I should do with the creature if I won it, I am thankful indeed that I did not. It costs, so I am told, a minimum of £500 a year to keep a horse in training, plus entrance fees, horse boxes, jockeys and your own expenses to go to various racecourses to watch it lose—in other words the taxed residue of about £1500 a year.

On the other hand I know perfectly well that, if I did win the horse, I should never have the moral courage to do the right thing with it, i.e. sell it instantly without so much as setting eyes on it. The temptation to let it run once would be too great. Think of it. Choosing one's colours . . . light blue and white hoops I think, with a dark blue St Andrew's cross on back and front. Getting one's 'owner's uniform' . . . bowler hat, lined waterproof coat, narrow tweed trousers, suede half-boots and a vast pair of binoculars captured from a German submarine officer. Turning off in the hired Rolls to the park marked 'Owners and Jockeys'. Why, one might appear on the telly. I can just hear the smooth tones of Peter O'Sullevan: 'And there, talking to Boyd-Rochford, or there, giving final instructions to the jockey, is the well-known owner, Mr Henry Longhurst—the good looking one in the bowler hat.' Hang it, I am beginning to wish that I had gone in for the thing after all!

I should not have been the first owner in the family. In the 1880's my mother's uncle won the Royal Hunt Cup at Ascot with his horse, Despair. He also had another horse running called Sailor Prince. Being in severe financial straits at the time, he plunged with everything he had. Unfortunately he placed it on Sailor Prince. It is always said that the youth on Despair passed the post with his feet stuck out in front, pulling for all he was worth, and apologised afterwards with 'I couldn't 'old 'im, sir'. This was, I believe, the only occasion on which the Royal Hunt Cup has been in pawn.

There was a time, in a Bedfordshire village, when no one would venture a wager on a big race until it was learnt, via the local hairdresser, 'what Mrs Longhurst Senior was on', but I myself have not inherited the urge. In my earlier days I associated a good deal with a bookmaker friend, the late Mr Ted Durling. For six nights a week at Harringay and the White City I noticed that he invariably gave the cloakroom attendant a pound for looking after his hat. When I won ten shillings from him at golf at Addington one day, he pulled an enormous wad of notes from the right hand front pocket of his plus fours. (Bookmakers always seem to keep their money in front instead of behind.) There was no ten shilling note, so he stuffed the notes back and produced a similar wad from the left hand pocket.

When he had paid the humble debt, I said to him, 'As a matter of interest, Ted, how much have you got there?' 'Oh,' he said, 'about twelve hundred and fifty.' I decided from that moment onwards that I should not have the occasional pound each way on a horse I had never seen and knew nothing about, merely to pay for his hat for one third of one week.

We often dream of drawing a ticket in the Irish or Calcutta Sweep, but it leads to great complications and the agonising decision has to be made about selling it. In the years between the wars the hottest favourite for the Derby was Orwell, and a well-known Midlands golfer drew it in the Calcutta. The figure offered for the whole ticket was, I believe, £6000. At any rate, after much heart-searching he sold half of it for £3000 and let the other half 'ride'. Orwell finished plumb last and it was not until afterwards that the luckless holder of the ticket realised that what he had done was, in effect, to bet £3000 on Orwell. 'And I've never had a bob on a horse in my life,' he said sadly.

Sometimes, however, these tales have a happier ending. As I got out of the train one evening at Haywards Heath, I noticed a certain amount of commotion farther up the platform, the centre of which was a rotund figure brandishing a walking stick and crying genially to the assembled company 'Sundew! Sundew!' This proved to be an old friend and past captain of the Brighton and Hove Club, Mr Tubby Ionides. He unfolded a curious story. His sister, it appeared, had drawn a horse in the Irish Sweep for the National and was in America.

Acting on her behalf Mr Ionides had obtained an offer of £1800 for the ticket and had cabled her accordingly. Successive cables had elicited no reply and at last he had taken upon himself to sell the ticket. By this time, however, the bookmaker was offering only £800-odd. Affronted at this, Mr Ionides turned it down and, after a good lunch in the office—he is a wine merchant—he and a number of friends settled down to watch the National on the television. The sister's ticket, needless to say, was for Sundew and it won her £51,000.

27 July 1967

Trans-Atlantic Comparisons

There is a tendency in some quarters in the United States to look slightly askance at the fact that the Masters may steal some of the US Open's thunder. This it undoubtedly does, but not, so to speak, on purpose. The fact is that it is unique in more than one way and there simply is not another one like it. For a start it is the first major event of the season and this means that the winner has time to cash in in a way denied to one who wins a tournament in, say, June.

Again, the background to the tournament explains why it is different from any other. In the early 'thirties the comparatively few members of the Augusta National Club, all of them successful men and pretty well-to-do, decided that they would like to see the master golfers in action on their course and decided to stage an invitation tournament. This was such a success that it turned into an annual event, but at what time it first become known as the Masters, and who gave it this name, no one seems to be quite sure.

Thus it has no 'sponsor' except the Augusta National Club, who simply run it and make it pay for itself, as it does with increasing ease every year, to the extent that it is now an all-ticket affair and the tickets are all sold long before the day of play.

When I say that the club 'simply run it', I do not mean that they run it simply. An immense organisation lies behind it and before one tournament finishes they are already planning its successor for the following year.

The best way to run a club, or a tournament, is through a benevolent dictator, and this the Augusta National Club possesses in the person of Clifford Roberts, joint founder with Bobby Jones. He even tells the television people, who have paid colossal sums for the rights, what they can and cannot do, and that really is saying something. This means that the club stands no nonsense from anybody and therefore does not get any. Though there is an automatic qualifying list, this does not mean that anyone who puts a foot wrong one year would necessarily get the much prized invitation for the next, so an impressive air of decorum prevails.

What really makes the Masters memorable, though, in a way unequalled anywhere in the world, is that it is always played on the same course at the same time of the year. I have now been four times, but I could not for the life of me tell you, as I sit in the same chair on the balcony looking out through the wisteria and being served with the same drink by the same coloured waiter, which year it is. The only way of telling is to look at the big scoreboard and see whether it is Palmer's year or Nicklaus's or Brewer's. The same people turn up every year, bringing their chairs with them, and sit for the whole day in the same place by the same green.

I remember how impressed I was when I went down to the 16th to record a small piece for the television at about 10.30 on the morning of a play-off which was not due to start till 1 o'clock. This meant that there could be no play at the 16th before at least 4 or 4.30. Yet the faithful were already assembled there with their chairs and rugs, perfectly happy to wait six hours to see their heroes play one short hole.

This continuity cannot be achieved with national championships on either side of the ocean if, as is inevitable, they move from one course to another. The problem is greater in the United States because it is such a large country and so many areas put in a legitimate claim to be included on the list. This year's US Open emphasised this point, in that it was the fifth to be played at the Baltusrol Club and there has already built up an air of 'continuity', such as one finds also at the Country Club, Brookline—the scene of Francis Ouimet's historic play-off against Vardon and Ray in 1913. How different our own Open would be if, for instance it were always played at St Andrews! I am not saying that it should be: I merely say how different.

I think it is true of the Masters and of the two Open championships, and of no others, that they are bigger than the players and bigger than the winners. They do not pay 'appearance money' or expenses and are beholden to no one.

By way of contrast one could quote the Carling tournament, due to be played this year in Toronto at the end of August. Here the sponsors put up a gigantic sum of money and by a meticulous system of zonal qualifying produce what could almost be called a world championship—incidentally guaranteeing not only his fare and expenses but quite a sizeable sum in cash to even the worst player in the field. Recently, only two months before the tournament, the USPGA informed Carlings that they were to alter the conditions of qualifying and bar from the tournament a number who by the conditions laid down had already qualified. What damned business it was of the USPGA is not disclosed, but it shows how they reckon to control professional golfers like puppets. It is easy, of course, to give opinions from the sidelines, but I must say that if I had been Carlings I should have told them precisely what they could do with themselves, adding 'And one word out of you and I cancel the tournament for ever'. My word, I'd like to see them try that sort of thing on old Cliff Roberts at Augusta!

As to differences in the running of events in America and at home, it is natural that the general scene should be rather more lavish over there partly because the events are liable to be played at the more lush and expensive country clubs (which are by nature and climate part of the American scene and not part of ours), partly because the Americans are the most hygienic-minded people in the world, and partly because of the sheer weight of money involved.

Our own Open loses little in comparison these days by way of the effort put in by volunteers from the R and A and the host club and, if there are deficiencies, it is generally because the British have never quite got over 'There's a war on' and are liable to put up with what they get. Accommodation for the Press improves year by year, but if I worked for a 'daily' instead of a 'Sunday' I should raise merry hell when I found that the scores were not visible, let alone readable, from every seat in the tent.

As to the television, with which I have been mildly concerned for more years than I care to be reminded of, in America it is, touching wood, a piece of cake, since they have a commentator, or 'announcer' as they call it, at every hole they are covering, together with experts like Byron Nelson or Cary Middlecoff to pronounce on points of style, etc., and instant slow-motion playbacks and sundry other gimmicks, not all of which I personally like. However, the point is that if you are allotted, say, the 16th hole you know that nothing else is anything to do with you and you need do absolutely nothing till a voice says in your ear, to some other announcer, 'Throw it to 16'. For the rest of the time all you have to do is sit back and enjoy it on the telly!

27 February 1969

African Contentment

More than half of my present journey to Southern Africa and Kenya has now, alas, passed and I confess that, as I sit in the sunshine looking out on the surf rolling in to the vast beaches of Durban, I am sorely tempted to call it a day and not come home at all.

This is indeed a beautiful country and a wonderful climate either to grow up in or retire to and I confess that so long as the wherewithal can be found I do not intend to spend another winter in England. I only wish I had thought of it before!

I have watched two tournaments, one at the Cape and more recently the South African Open at the Country Club here, but it cannot be said that any of the British players, with the exception of Oosterhuis, have really distinguished themselves or lifted themselves above the run-of-the-mill South African professionals.

None of them seems able to keep the odd 76's and 77's off the card and these are the sort of scores you expect from a good club amateur. On the other hand I should not like to appear too censorious because nearly all good scores depend largely on 'turning three shots into two' and on strange greens and the kind of grass you have not seen before it is easy to hit the ball perfectly well and yet finish six feet away instead of three, and then just miss the putt.

Thus you can hole out time and again in four and a quarter, so to speak, but alas there are no fractions in golf and they all count five.

Golf here is still a very 'British' game and one really might be at home, apart from the sunshine, the occasional exotic vegetation and the service in the clubhouse. Not to mention the notice at the Royal Cape Club saying 'Please do not kill our snakes', these being, it seems a special variety which live largely underground and have been imported to kill off the moles. Every time one shows its head above the ground someone is liable to go after it with a niblick.

Many of the new courses in other parts of the world follow the American pattern, with huge greens each with four or five separate 'pin positions', so that you are nearly always either trying for one putt or trying to avoid taking three; also with single tees sometimes as much as fifty yards long, which it is claimed save money on maintenance. Perhaps because I was brought up with them, I prefer the smaller greens and separate tees, and this is the pattern here.

A second purpose of my visit was to spy out the land and offer some comments for BOAC, who are contemplating inclusive holidays for golfers from Britain, and I must say that the results so far are very encouraging. I have become much addicted to the 'package tour', now that there is no question of being herded about with people you have never met before. You can in fact constitute a package tour of one person.

The other day I went to Cyprus on such an arrangement and had fifteen days at the best hotel with all meals, transport to and from the airport, a day flight and a single room with bath, all for about ten pounds in addition to the advertised fare.

No golfer expects to play on a course as a visitor at what is the peak period for the members but in this country this only means about a couple of afternoons a week. Otherwise, what is so splendid is the genuine welcome given to visitors, especially from Britain, by every club that I have so far visited.

They are abolutely delighted to see you. This means that, even if the package deal includes free golf at one club for five days a week, you can still add variety by playing on several others. And on the off-days there are all manner of 'outings', such as driving through or flying over the game parks. Or you can play bowls, which is almost the national pastime here; or bathe; or fish; or just sit under a tree, at which I am becoming remarkedly adept.

One time at which you can certainly not play in this country is ladies' day, or at any rate ladies' afternoon. All the clubs have a weekly period exclusively for the ladies and they come out in swarms. On other days they can play at any time so long as they take their turn.

My own feeling of being 'at home', though thousands of miles away, was increased during the South African Open by meeting the professional and finding that his name was Jimmy Ockenden. It took me back to the very first time I set eyes on great golfers, when, as a small boy, I watched an exhibition match at Letchworth and one of the four was Jimmy Ockenden's father who was professional for many years at North Middlesex.

I am now off to the little independent state of Swaziland—almost exactly on the right of Johannesburg in case your geography is not too up to date—where I am told there is magnificent scenery, a pleasant golf course and even a casino. What is more, I am promised a day's trout fishing.

As for the snow at home, it almost breaks my heart to read about it!

CHAPTER TEN

Professional Qualities

26 July 1956

Losing Has to Hurt

I suppose that at any given time there are two or three potentially very great, as against merely potentially great, golfers in Britain, and say six times that number in the United States. This is perhaps a parochial attitude since there are clearly more in South Africa than in Britain, more in Australia and South America and, judging by the Canada Cup, more in Japan. However, let us not rub it in. The point is what turns the potentially very great into truly very great?

One thing assuredly is that they must be bitterly hurt by failure. They must hate, to the depths of their souls, being second to any man. They can be hurt—all this sounds very savage, I am afraid—either in the stomach or in the mind. It is said sometimes of players who seem destined for the highest honours and just fail to attain them that they are 'not hungry enough'. I should say that most of the regular performers on the American circuit start 'hungry'. They go from tournament to tournament in trailers, hoping to finish 'in the money' sufficiently often to pay their bills while they fight their way to the surface—or drown unrecognized and unsung.

Ben Hogan certainly started that way and it was not until he was well past thirty that his future—and his meals—were really assured. It is the American way to pay heavily for success. One good thing leads to another. The sky is the limit, but there is no convenient 'floor' to sustain a man on his way up.

The alternative to those who are fortunate enough to have a ready-made temporary 'floor' to sustain them on the way up, is mental hunger, or ambition. This, I hope he would agree, was what drove Henry Cotton on. He could afford to travel first class and did so, not on the assumption that the world owes him a first-class ticket—only an idiot in my opinion reckons that the world owes him anything at all—but on the ground that you probably play better in the afternoon after a meal that suits you, followed by putting your feet up in a private sitting room for half an hour, than by sitting around the clubhouse or the locker room answering damn fool questions about your morning round. Apart from American visitors, Cotton was the first in this country to adopt this kind of practice, though a good many others could in fact have afforded it, if only as an investment, and I remember how he used to come in for a good deal of jealous criticism. He was right, of course.

Nevertheless, 'the acid test is the figures'. First-class tickets may help towards first-class scores, but they do not make them. Only burning, blazing ambition does that. Practice makes perfect, they say, but in golf it makes only near-perfect. A man who practises eight hours a day, as Gary Player has quoted himself as doing, will almost certainly win tournaments. Whether he joins the immortals depends on some deeper quality. Frank Stranahan must have hit as many practice shots as any man of his age alive. Yet his total quota is two post-war British Amateur championships, and one major tournament since he turned pro.

No, the answer is that it has got to really hurt! If you are not hungry, you must be a perfectionist. Cotton always was. It must normally be a greater joy to win your first Open than any subsequent one, but I will bet my bottom dollar that that was not so in his case. In 1934, you may remember, he not only started at Sandwich with 67, 65, but set an entirely new standard for first-class golf. He went on with a 72, was ten shots ahead, and then, crash bang, 79. Certainly he had made a noble rally from the 12th onwards, but it finished with a miserable four-footer missed on the last green.

Cotton is too honest a golfer to have let the universal adulation, the congratulations that 'at last the American supremacy was broken'—when no notable Americans were playing—blind him to the fact that this had not been a 100 per cent job. It had been good enough, yes, but at the same time manifestly imperfect.

With what different feelings he must have left the rain-sodden 18th at Carnoustie in 1937! Here indeed was the full treatment. The full force of the American Ryder Cup team, who had beaten us two weeks previously, were lined up against him. On the final afternoon the rain was so heavy that you could not hear the typewriters clattering in the Press tent. In these truly hideous conditions Cotton got round in 71—to win by two strokes. That was *it*!

What else sparks off genius? So many things. One of them is an ability not to be 'put off', either by a bad lie at a crucial moment or by more obvious things like newsreel cameras—or, as P. G. Wodehouse has put it, by the 'roar of the butterflies in an adjacent meadow'. From reading his book I fancy that Von Nida would have won a post-war championship if part of his mind had not been engaged on looking for things or people which could later be held to have put him off. Easy to write—less easy to put into action.

Again, do you need imagination—to extract from you the inspired performance at the moment of crisis? Or no imagination at all, so that you did not realise it was a crisis till it was over? Jones, Hagen and Cotton surely had this golfing imagination. Does the current third-time champion, Peter Thomson, possess it? As a mere observer I should say not, and I write it in no derogatory sense. Does the modern maestro, Ben Hogan, have it? Probably—but, from what I know of him, it had better keep out of the way!

10 January 1957

Four New Professionals

In the recent past no fewer than four internationally-known American golfers have turned professional. In two cases it greatly surprised me. In two it did not. The four are Doug Sanders, Joe Conrad, Ken Venturi and Miss 'Wiffi' Smith. The latter, of course, is the British and French Amateur champion of the moment.

I did not come to know her particularly well when she was over here for the Curtis Cup and the championship, but what I saw of her I found, like everyone else, to be most appealing. This sturdy teenage girl seemed to have the right approach to golf and a more complete amateur it would be hard to find. I can't believe that she would turn professional by choice. It so happens, however, that her home life is somewhat divided and as she has to get down to earning a living, golf is an obvious choice.

Not many of the girls on the regular American tournament circuit make money out of it. A bare half dozen, I should say. Last year Mrs Marlene Hagge, who was one of the good-looking young Bauer sisters before she took over the husband who was already married to her sister, made 22,000 dollars last year and, even allowing for the fact that expenses pile up all along the trail, she must be well in pocket. Most of them, however, don't make ends meet. Miss Smith, I should say, will do so from the start. She is physically strong and is blessed with an ideal not-to-worry temperament which will stand her in good stead in a line of life which has already broken the spirits of quite a number of women.

Doug Sanders, a lithe young man in his early twenties, was almost a certainty for turning professional. He played in the Amateur at Troon last year but was put out in the first round, in conditions which will have been completely strange to him. He was obviously a first-class player and one would have liked to see more of him. Soon after returning home he won the Canadian Open from a field of top-class pros and has been playing, as an amateur, in a good many of the tournaments, so it is a line of life to which he will be no stranger.

To so gifted a golfer of this age, life as a professional offers fine prospects. Hogan and Snead are still at the top of the tree in their middle forties, so, all being well, a young fellow like Sanders can count on the best part of twenty years of competitive ability. Then, if he has played his cards right, he may continue, like the amiable Jimmy Demaret, as professional to two wealthy clubs, one for the winter and the other for the summer, and pull down an annual income, in cash and in kind, which would make a British Prime Minister gape with envy.

Joe Conrad, who won the British Amateur at Lytham the year before last, is rather older, though still under thirty, but I should not have thought his prospects in tournament golf quite so bright—but perhaps after a year or two of the competitive stuff he will settle as a club professional. An admirable fellow, well liked by all who met him over here, he would do extremely well in that line.

The real surprise, to me, is Ken Venturi. I should have thought that he and Harvie Ward were two of the only near certainties in the top amateur ranks to remain amateur. They have a wonderful job, and prospects, with Ed Lowery, who is mad keen on golf and a member of the executive committee of the USGA. He runs an extremely prosperous motor agency in San Francisco and for a year or two now the two young fellows have been working for him. Though he allows them time off to play in all the worthwhile tournaments, he also, he has often assured me, makes them work as well.

Venturi says that his decision has not been taken without much heart-searching and I can well believe it, but golf is in his blood and he sacrifices a sure position with outstanding prospects for the hazardous life of a tournament professional. That is the privilege of youth. To back his resolve he has the knowledge that he is undoubtedly one of the finest golfers in the world today. For some 63 of the 72 holes he had the Masters tournament in the palm of his hand. A nervous final nine, poor fellow, saw him eased out at the last minute by Jack Burke, but the form was there for all to see.

In wishing them good fortune in their new line, a final comment comes to my mind, namely what an excellent thing it is that it should be so simple a matter for both men and women to turn professional in the States. The cost of playing as an amateur in the top flight is far beyond what most young men can afford. If we played the British Amateur championship in, say, Philadelphia, we should still have less far to travel than Ward and Venturi. This makes it prohibitive for most people and, if the way is not easily open for turning pro, a race of subsidized amateurs, as in tennis, becomes inevitable.

24 January 1957

Further Still and Further

Say what you like, long driving is *the* fascination of golf. People will talk for hours on the theory of putting, on lateral hip shifts, forward presses, delayed wrist action and all the rest of it, but the thing which appeals to the heart of every golfer great and small is big hitting. So far as I know, the biggest hitter in the history of the game is George Bayer, the cinema-strips of whom have been adorning the pages of *Golf Illustrated*. They will have shown to readers who have not seen him that, whatever else he may be, he is certainly no common 'slasher'. The only criticism I have of these pictures is, if I may say so, that they do not reveal his very simple secret, namely his size. If they had only had Hogan, or even for that matter myself, standing beside him to act as a measuring scale, you would have seen at once what a colossus he is.

I have recently been writing, though in different connections, about two other big hitters—Viscount Cobham, who is to be Governor General of New Zealand, and Ted Dexter, the present Cambridge secretary, who was recently in the semi-final of the President's Putter. Cobham, with whom, as Charles Lyttelton, I used to play at Cambridge twenty-five years ago, I described as the longest hitter I had ever played with. At Mildenhall once in February he got a 'sucker' almost level with the third hole, which must have involved a mid-winter carry of upwards of 350 yards. I remember it so well because it was I, wandering incredulously on, who found the ball, and because I have so often in the intervening years pointed out the spot to equally incredulous undergraduates.

At Rye in a strong wind Dexter drove a measured 365 yards down wind and made 440 yards with a drive and a 3-iron dead against it. This is not, I think, quite on the Lyttelton scale but it is mighty hitting and few people at Rye that morning were talking about anything much else. Nevertheless let me add that Dexter is no 'slasher' either and I would be the last to contribute to any reputation he might be acquiring as merely a long hitter. He is a powerful but orthodox golfer of quite exceptional possibilities.

My comments on Lyttelton have drawn correspondents who (a) point out that in a book years ago I mentioned E. Nugent Head as the longest hitter I had ever played with and (b) ask 'what about Joe Carr and James Bruen'? Well, I confess that when I wrote about Head I had forgotten about Lyttelton and when I wrote about Lyttelton I had forgotten about Head. Now I do not know what to say. I do remember the classic occasion when Lister Hartley, myself and another scratch player were playing the 16th on the Old course at Addington and all failed to get anywhere near the green with a brassie. We then marched on for 50 or 60 yards to Head's drive and it became clear that he could not only reach the green but could do it with an iron. As it happened, this particular shot finished in a shower of earth, grass and small stones. When asked what he took, Head replied darkly, 'I stood in front of a 4'.

So far as I am concerned, I must leave it as a dead-heat between them—but if only we could have set them up side by side, as they were in those days, given them a dozen balls apiece, goaded them on with a little badinage, and let them let fly. That would have been one of the sights of the century!

Joe Carr, of course, is a mighty hitter with a real 'slashing' style, though I believe he has recently been trying to contain it somewhat, but my money, up to 1947 at any rate, would have been on Bruen, if only because of two shots which have been imprinted in my mind since the championship final that year. They were at the 14th at Birkdale—the long hole going away to the left of the clubhouse. Yardage is really no measure of long hitting—otherwise Craig Wood would be the longest hitter ever seen in Britain, which he palpably is not. After all, in the Open of 1933, he drove 425 yards, down wind and on ground like concrete, into the bunker set to catch your second shot at the 5th at St Andrews.

The 14th at Birkdale is, what?—540, 560 or even 580 yards. I do not know. It does not really matter. Suffice to say that Bobby Sweeny, after a drive and a brassie, had quite a substantial shot for his third. Thee was a slight breeze against, the hole is all slightly uphill, and the ground was soggy—a fact which I remember because I was standing just opposite Bruen's drive when it pitched. This shot bounced forward no more than a yard. From here he *pitched* on the green with a spoon.

Then, of course, there are Harry Weetman and the Frenchman, Ado, whom I bracket together because I once saw them lashing it out together in an individual long-driving match at Monte Carlo. With one ball to go Ado was just behind, whereupon he borrowed Weetman's driver and hit it ten yards past him. Then again during the German championship at Frankfurt some months ago there was a long-driving tournament from the elevated 18th tee, with the spectators waiting out of range along the fairway. Successive players managed to push the long-distance peg forward a few yards at a time. Finally the name Ado (it is pronounced 'Addo') was called through the megaphone from the tee. Down on the fairway we at once withdrew respectfully about forty yards—but it was not enough. Ado's first shot pitched among us, not less than 60 yards past the previous best. When he came down, it transpired that this time he had borrowed a ladies' driver!

Why, it is asked, do not these mighty bashers win the championships? The answer is that very often they do—when they are in the championship-winning class at all, which, with great respect, neither Lyttelton nor Head ever professed to be. Carr and Bruen have both been amateur champion and Weetman has been professional champion. Beyond a certain point, however, the dice are so heavily loaded against them that their length—rather unfairly they might claim—becomes a danger rather than an asset. As length increases, the angle of safety narrows, so that Bayer, for instance, has had to force himself to keep back with the normal long hitters if he is not for ever to be in the rough.

By a scrap-paper calculation based on our old friends the 'equal triangles', I estimate that, if the same accuracy were demanded of me as is demanded of Bayer at full stretch, I should have almost exactly half the fairway to aim at.

Still, it does not alter the fact that, when he does really let go, it is a sight for the gods.

13 November 1958

Drawing the Crowds

The first great golfer I ever travelled to see—and, of all those whom I have watched in the years since, he is the one whom I would genuinely love to see again—was Abe Mitchell. I cannot believe that it was only because he was the first that I still think that in some ways he was the greatest.

It must have been in the comparatively early twenties and the occasion was a fourball exhibition match at Letchworth. I can not only see Abe now, with his jacket and plus fours, but I can hear the sound that his club made on the ball. At the risk of being accused of romanticising I declare that, if I were blindfolded and could hear six great players driving off today, I could tell from the 'crack' which was Abe Mitchell.

Of course this may be only hero-worship in a boy of twelve, suddenly infatuated with golf. Yet I wonder. There must be many readers of *Golf Illustrated*, among them his professional contemporaries, who felt the same way about Mitchell. He reduced the golf swing to total simplicity.

Contemporary with Abe, of course, was George Duncan and I am not at all sure that he was not playing on that day. I wonder whether he remembers? George was the perfect complement to Abe. While Abe hammered the course into submission, George would snipe at it by suddenly flashing the ball out of a bunker with his spoon and holing a long putt, almost 'on the run' for a three.

It goes without saying that anyone who knew Hagen would probably go farther to see him play again in his prime than anyone else in the world. Yet the first time I saw him I had eyes only for another. It was during the 1929 Ryder Cup match at Moortown. Four of us from Cambridge got up at four in the morning in order to drive there, in a Riley Nine, to see the play. Our eye was caught by a tall, slim, boyish, handsome figure in a grey windcheater, as we would now call it, whose swing seemed to us to bring a new poetry of motion to golf, and we followed him devotedly for the whole of the day. His name was Horton Smith. Though 'down' most of the way, he beat Fred Robson by 2 and 1 and next year he swept the board in America.

Among amateurs, Bobby Jones, of course, stood and stands supreme. I think there can hardly be any doubt about this, even among the fine young golfers of today who were not even born when he retired, with all worlds conquered, at the age of twenty-eight in 1930. For the sheer rhythm of his swing and gentleness of his slow, 'wristy' touch on the greens Jones can hardly have been surpassed and beside him many of the 'bashers' of today and yesterday appear like cart-horses, powerful, but uncouth.

Among women golfers Joyce Wethered must stand equally supreme. The late Mrs Zaharias, of course, stands out, not only as a great golfer, but as presumably the greatest all-round woman athlete of all time. Yet I cannot see myself going out of my way to watch her. To see the rhythm, grace and balance of Miss Wethered's golf would be a relevation to many a male today.

When all is said and done, however, the man I would go farthest to see again hitting a golf ball in his prime is my own contemporary Henry Cotton. I am quite sure about this. I am not talking about who won how many Opens in how many years and how difficult was it at the time. I simply say that in my own adult experience nobody hit the golf ball with quite the directness and economy of movement that Cotton did.

He also, I think, hit it more straight than anyone I remember—by which I do not mean simply 'in play' but in a dead straight line. For hole after hole his second shots would be drilled on the flag and you could not see why, if you hit them that way, with your hands so clearly directing the rest of your body, they should ever be otherwise.

Perhaps I am doing Cotton an injustice in using the past tense even now, for at 51 he still finishes high in the tournaments and when I played a few holes with him the other day his shots were still as straight as though he were firing them from a rifle.

8 January 1959

Human or 'Unhuman'?

Are great golfers 'human'? Or, perhaps one should say, 'Can a man be a great golfer and remain "human" while actually performing on the golf course?' I take as examples four whom I look upon as the greatest of my own time: in the United States, Hagen, Jones and Hogan, and in Britain, Cotton. In three cases—the exception being obviously Hagen—I should say that their greatness depended largely in their ability to render themselves 'unhuman'—not to be confused with 'inhuman'—in the course of play.

The difference between greatness and being merely top-class is only a stroke or two per round—sometimes only a single stroke in four rounds. To achieve this final margin demands that a man be able to wrap himself in an impenetrable cocoon of concentration to protect him from physical diversions—like being held up on the tee for twenty minutes at a crucial moment or being addressed by some clot who wishes to remind him of the exhibition match in which he watched him play at Little Puddlecombe—and from the mental shocks inherent in the slings and arrows of golfing misfortune—like missing a short putt or finding his ball in a heel-mark in a bunker.

He cannot afford to look round him and admire the view, or to engage in any conversation except desultory exchanges which can be carried on without diverting the mind from its main train of thought.

Those whose work entails attending cocktail parties will know exactly what I am driving at!

He must be able, furthermore, to apply the whole of his mind to one shot at a time, forgetting, as though it had never happened, that he has either holed a long putt on the last green or missed a short one. Yet all the time some other department of his mind must remain aware that he needs three fours for a 69 and a total of 283 and that X is reputedly four under fours and looks like finishing in 284 unless he gets a three at the 17th, in which case. . . .

All this has to be transmitted from one part of the mind to another, if he is to make the correct decision as to whether to go for a three at the 15th and risk a five. Yet the receiving part of the mind, having accepted the signal, must immediately and completely eliminate it while it gets on with the business of playing the shot. How can a man do this for hours, weeks, years at a time and still remain 'human' while he is doing it?

One of the outstanding qualities of human-ness is imagination, and this, I suspect, has been a quality common to the greatest golfers—so long as they keep it out of their golf. Imagination, I believe, is what has driven these men on. Imagination of what life might hold for them, in the way either of money, travel, social advancement or simply good company, if they could jump several rungs in the ladder through excelling at golf.

It is one thing to dream of becoming a great golfer but quite another to survive the ten years' hard grind of physical and mental discipline which is probably the smallest price you will have to pay. And even if you get to the top, you have still got to go on paying the price if you want to stay there. I am sure that applied to Jones, Cotton and Hogan, though each survived to enjoy the luxury of 'free-wheeling' when the long, uphill grind was past. Jones's career, alas, was cruelly cut short by illness; Cotton's continues, and Hogan's has only just begun.

Hagen, on the other hand, having got to the top the hard way, seems to be the only one who thoroughly enjoyed himself while he *was* at the top—and yet contrived to stay there. His philosophy was summed up by the words quoted on the title page of his book: 'I never wanted to *be* a millionaire. I just wanted to live like one.'

Yet, when I come to think of it, I have had the pleasure of knowing all the great golfers of my own period fairly intimately and have without exception much enjoyed their personal company. Perhaps the answer, to paraphrase George Orwell, is 'All great golfers *are* human—but some are more human than others'.

5 March 1959

Golfers who Know Go to their Pro

Many golfers become proficient without ever having a lesson, reading a book, or giving any calculated thought to the business of the golf swing. I envy them. And yet in a way I don't, for they have missed a lot of innocent intellectual fun in studying the methods of the masters and trying to find out what makes the experts tick while they themselves never quite do so. These people are known as 'natural golfers'—but I often wonder whether any really great golfer has been natural.

Two that come to my mind are Walter Hagen and Harry Bradshaw. Both are tremendous 'swayers', which, of course, is all wrong—unless you care to judge by results. Hagen, who could have been a great baseball player and took to golf behind the caddie shed, never, I think, seriously tried to groove or mechanize his game. He relied on nature, nerve and touch.

The same I am sure can be said of Bradshaw. He must, of course, be in the correct hitting position at the moment of impact or he would not get such wonderful results but if there is really such a thing as correct style then most of Harry's is incorrect. He is in many ways my ideal golfer—more and more to be taken as a model by the young as the game becomes increasingly earnest. Successful but completely unspoiled, approachable on the course and affable and good-humoured off it, still managing to keep golf a game while making it his business. And he can size up a shot, choose his club, hit the ball on to the green and be walking after it, all in the time that it takes an American to test the direction of the wind.

The 'natural' golfer also misses an aspect of the game for which I myself have always been grateful, namely, lessons with the pro. It so happened that I became infected with the golf bug at the age of eleven and being an only child and living in the country far from the allegedly more beneficial influence of team games (I did once play goal for the village: we were beaten 11–2, but I still declare that only one of them was my fault), my three lessons a week with the pro were the highspots of my life. From these grew a lifelong respect for the golf club professional and friendships which I retain to this day.

It is true, I think, that early lessons from the pro do tend to make one grow up into a thinking golfer rather than a natural one, and, of course, you may tend to overdo it at times and forget that the main thing is to grasp the weapon in two hands and swipe the ball with it, but it is your own fault if you let yourself grow into a 'crank'.

Of one thing I have no doubt, that the growth of instruction as an art over the last thirty years has brought into being, I will not say a standardized method, but at least the basic essentials of what is agreed to be a correct method. Probably Harry Vardon used them all, but certainly the top class amateurs of, say, the early thirties did not. You could tell them by their individual styles a mile away.

For myself I think instruction is in danger of being a little over-done, and if I am deemed a reactionary for saying so, well I cannot help it. Attributing the very worthiest of motives to everyone con-cerned, I still cannot quite reconcile myself to the idea of golf unions offering to pay for lessons for an ex-amateur champion and the holder of the President's Putter. Yet I confess that my spirit did not when the R and A selectors appointed two 'coaches' for the Walker Cup possibles, which in a way is the same thing. Illogical maybe, but there you are.

Many people go through their golfing life without ever sampling the immense fun of hitting shots under the kindly eye of the pro. Club golfers on the whole are an unimaginative lot. Many will play in the same fourball at the same time on the same course for fifty Sundays in succession. The vast majority have never even played round with the pro. On the other hand, so far as teaching is con-cerned, professionals in England and Scotland are much handicap-ped by comparison with their brethren in, from the golfing point of view, 'newer' countries. When most of our courses were laid out, nobody thought in terms of a practice ground. Even at some of the best clubs a professional wishing to give lessons has to scurry like a poor relation from fairway to fairway.

All the same if the average 18-handicap player wants to take four shots off his game, he has only to book three half-hours with the local pro—at a fee rather less substantial than that demanded by a London cabbie. Why not try it? You've no idea what fun it is.

1 October 1959

Restrictive Practices

The life of a successful golf professional—and to be successful he need by no means fight his way into the top flight of tournament players—offers many rewards. In playing and teaching golf he is doing something which he enjoys, which is perhaps the most important single factor in one's job in life. He is mingling in his club with a variety of folk who are probably in their most congenial mood in the circumstance in which he meets them. His work takes him into the open air, and a sizeable proportion of his emoluments need never find their way into the pocket of the tax collector. What can a man want more?

With so rosy a prospect in view why do not more young amateurs cross the line? The answer, I think, lies almost wholly in the restrictive practices of the Professional Golfers' Association. Human nature is the same the world over and the desire not to 'overcrowd the boat' is a natural sentiment. Nor can I afford to take a 'holier than thou' attitude in the matter, for journalists do the same thing and put every possible impediment in the way of what they are pleased to call the 'player-writer', who may well know a great deal more about his subject than many of the regulars and thus from an editor's point of view be a good deal better bet.

It takes a good deal of nerve for a youngish successful amateur to turn pro. Outstanding cases are Eric Brown and Norman Drew. Brown won the Scottish Amateur championship at the age of twenty-one. He turned professional and was kept out of the PGA for five whole years. This always seemed to me to be a quite monstrous injustice to a young fellow of that age. It meant that for these five years he could play in none of the sponsored tournaments and for competitive experience he had to spend money on travelling round the continental championships. When he won the first tournament in which he was eligible to play, at Llandudno, I remember writing that I hoped he would win every other event that season!

Norman Drew turned pro soon after the Walker Cup match at Kittansett in 1953. For some years, so I gather, he had a pretty lean time and he has had to wait until the current season to make his mark in his chosen walk of life. In the meantime any Tom, Dick or Harry who is in possession of a union ticket in his own country could come and play in the British tournaments.

Personally I have always felt that a competitive affair like professional golf lends itself particularly ill to restrictive practices. Once a man has chosen his career he should be entitled to pursue it to the best of his ability.

Another good ground for making it easy to turn pro is that you thereby help to eliminate the questionable amateur. This has been very noticeable in women's golf in the United States. Since they formed a women's professional tournament circuit some years ago, in which the leading women golfers could respectably cash in on their skill, we have managed to hold our own in the Curtis Cup matches in which, with the odd exception, the Americans have fielded teams of complete amateurs.

Which amateurs in recent years would have made good professionals? I can think of two who in my opinion might have won the Open championship. The first is Ronnie White. In the late forties in England he stood alone. He was probably one of the straightest and most accurate amateurs of all time. He bisected the fairways for days on end and in the Walker Cup match of 1949 at Winged Foot his shots were so exactly similar that they christened him 'one height White'. In the end the English Golf Union altered the bogeys of nearly all the courses mainly to avoid making White plus four.

The other obvious selection who, with the extra 'edge' that comes from having to play for your bread and butter might have won the Open, is, of course, Joe Carr. Joe plays a great deal of golf, but there is a world of difference between this and playing for a living. Even so, he came as near as dammit to winning the Dunlop Masters tournament the other day at Portmarnock. A man who can break 70 on that mighty course three times in succession as an amateur might have conquered the world as a professional.

5 March 1960

The Appeal of Challenge Matches

The challenge match contravenes almost every modern tendency in golf. I am therefore wholly in favour of it. It is match rather than medal, personal rather than impersonal; and, when all is over, somebody has to admit that in fair combat, under conditions agreed upon beforehand by all concerned, he has been beaten by a better man. This, in my opinion, is the essence of golf. Everything else, except the Open championship, is a variation on a basic theme which today is almost forgotten.

The blaze of publicity which attends so-called sporting functions today has contrived, probably unintentinally, to make defeat synonymous with dishonour. No better example could be found than the current Test cricket in Australia. To read most of the reports you would think that the wretched Peter May and his men were involved in a battle to the death with the hostile tribes of Australia and had ingominiously run from the field of battle, leaving the honoured name of England trampled in the dust, etc., etc.

It does not seem to have occurred to anyone to lift their hat to what must be a wonderful team of young Australians and congratulate them on their victory in a series of games with bat and ball which count but do not matter.

In medal-play at golf there is one winner, but no losers. Ask the man who finished tenth how he got on and he will reply 'I finished tenth'. If you are not careful he will tell you how and why, but that is another matter. The point is that he will not reply 'I was beaten by Smith, Jones, Robinson, and so-and-so and so-and-so'. In match-play no such evasion is possible. He may go round and round the point and tell you about the condition of the course, the fact that his wife was ill and his lumbago no better, but in the end the truth will out. He was beaten personally, individually and irrevocably by Smith.

The game of golf always was, and should be again, 18 holes. Why do they now call 18 holes a 'sprint?' Because they are *afraid*. Afraid of being beaten; afraid that somebody who according to last year's book of form they should beat may now upset the accepted applecart and win. Let us go on and on until the 'right man' is up, and then we can stop: 144 holes if need be. Better still, let us play by score instead of match like the Americans do, and then neither need be beaten. One will be the winner. The other, most creditably, will finish second.

I am old enough, just, to remember those two great challenge matches, Hagen v Mitchell and Hagen v Compston. I have only to think of them to recapture the intense and partisan thrill with which they were followed all over the country. I don't know whether the players put up the £500 themselves. I presume they had backers—but, make no mistake about it, they wanted to win.

Nowadays when the public pay to watch the final of any of the few remaining match-play professional tournaments, they may not know it, but it is twenty to one that the contestants have agreed beforehand to split the prize money. One will go into the handbook as the winner. The other will be the loser. As to the moral of this, I make no comment.

What happens now? Mr Joe McGrath in Eire declares to the world that he has £500 which says that Bradshaw and O'Connor will beat 'any two of you, anywhere'. We have a lot of noise from Scotland about Brown and Panton.

The two of them, I am told, are to play an exhibition match with Bradshaw and O'Connor in Glasgow this summer. Exhibition match, my foot! Let us have a challenge match. Let some enterprising Scottish newspaper raise the stakes to £1000, with a guarantee that each player is risking not less than £100 of his own money, and farm the rest out to Scottish clubs, so that all the members can have a pound or a tenner or half-a-crown to back their men against the marauding Irish.

What a match that would be! Thirty-six holes in Glasgow, thirty-six in Dublin, and no quarter asked or given. It would not surprise me if the gate were double that of the last day of the Open championship.

We might even, I suspect, see again something on a par with the splendid scene at Musselburgh in 1855 when Willie Park and Tom Morris were playing the last of their six challenge matches and the spectators interfered with poor Tom's ball to such an extent that the referee stopped play and Tom and his manager retired to a neighbouring public house.

Park—to quote the handbook—waited for some time and then sent a message to say that if Morris and his manager did not come out to play to finish he would play the remaining holes and claim the stake. Morris and the manager stayed resolutely in the pub, Park finished the round, and was awarded the money.

Those were the days. If we cannot quite see either Bradshaw and O'Connor or Brown and Panton retiring to a public house in the middle of the game, we may be quite sure that the feelings in the hearts of the spectators will not have substantially changed.

26 May 1960

The Competitive Spirit

How long does the competitive spirit last? I suppose the simple answer is that it varies enormously from one individual to another. Some quite successful golfers scarcely had any at all, remaining 'names' for a long time, but never managing to break through, either to win a championship or a match in the Walker Cup. Others had a competitive spirit which raised them to heights which their technical abilities would not have attained alone. I remember well an example of both.

The first was a wonderful golfer, nationally known and popular, but on great occasions always a loser. I felt sure at the time that I knew why this was, and time has not altered my opinion. It was because, before he went out in a championship or Walker Cup match, his mind had dwelt on *what reason he would give if he lost*. The seed of doubt was sown, and it was always fatal. His reasons for losing were always excellent. The fact remained that he lost.

This friend of mine shall, of course, remain anonymous, but as an example of the other kind—the man whose competitive spirit exceeded, if I may say so, his technical ability—I cheerfully name another old friend, General Critchley. He held simultaneously the championships, I believe, of France, Belgium and Surrey, and would back himself to beat almost anybody in a man-to-man encounter where he could direct his personality and determination (not to be confused with any form of gamesmanship) directly upon an opponent. He beat many a man who, according to the book of form, might have given him three or four shots.

These sterling qualities served him well when in his middle sixties he suddenly and without warning lost the sight of both eyes. It is easy to be fulsome about things like this, but it is fair to say that he seemed to look on sudden blindness very much in the way he used to look on a golf opponent. Counter-attacking without hesitation he defeated this particular opponent by about 5 and 4, almost, as it were, without losing a hole.

It was the Americans who coined the expression about a man being a 'good competitor' as against merely a good golfer. Hogan at his peak was, I suppose, the supreme example of a good competitor. It means that one has the ability, when the pressure comes, to tighten the screw. When the spirit has left you, all that happens when you tighten the screw is that the thread goes.

I had a good example of this myself in my undergraduate days. I was at the time, within my own limitations, a fairly good competitor—more liable to get a four at the 18th than the 1st. Coming back from my first big tournament—it was the Midland Open championship at Luffenham Heath, I remember—I fell asleep while driving the car (having had only black coffee for dinner, I may say!) and it turned over three times, depositing me on the grass verge, where I was later discovered by a passing commercial traveller. I felt perfectly all right, but it was later diagnosed that I had 'delayed concussion'. From that moment any talent I may have had as a good competitor departed and it took the best part of two years to get it back. Now, of course, it is gone for ever.

I found, when in what I am pleased to call my prime, that towards the end of the round one could nearly always hole one vital putt of anything up to four or five yards, provided one recognised at the time that this was the one that was going to matter. If it happened on the 17th, it was no good asking for another on the 18th. The battery, as it were, was completely exhausted by putting everything into the one at the 17th.

This brings me to a point which my colleague, Henry Cotton, has often mentioned and with which, though it is apparently inexplicable, I entirely agree. He remembers, and in my humble way so do I, that in order to hole a doubtful putt you had not only to hit it in but also to 'will' it in. It is these constant and concentrated efforts of willpower that make competitive golf such an exhausting game and leave a man feeling at the end that he has walked not five miles but twenty-five. You have in fact given till there is nothing more to give.

No man to my mind can be classed a really great competitor, as distinct from great golfer, unless he is prepared to expose himself to knock-out match-play, where one man is going to win and the other is going to pack his bag. When you hear anyone saying that 18-hole match-play is a matter of luck, no real test, etc., you may be certain that secretly he himself lacks the guts for it. Who, by this definition, are the best competitors today? Among the amateurs I think I should pick Guy Wolstenholme; among the professionals, without any doubt, Eric Brown.

21 July 1960

Lean Times for the Professionals

The performance of the amateurs at St Andrews was unprecedented, at any rate in my own memory, and a very heartening affair it was. One could not help recalling the remark of a youngish professional, when everyone was waiting to see what the qualifying score would be, to the effect that he assumed that the amateurs did not actually *count*. In other words he thought it was just another PGA competition! At any rate, count they certainly did, to the tune of 13 out of 74 qualifiers for the championship and 9 out of 47 for the final day.

I have not myself the slightest doubt that this extraordinary achievement by the amateurs is an indirect result of the appointment of Raymond Oppenheimer and his body of British selectors some five years ago. Not all the amateurs came under the direct eye of that body, but the encouragement they gave to amateurs, of whatever age, background or nationality, contrived substantially to raise the level of what would do to 'get by'. The best man of his day is, roughly speaking, as good as he has to be. Raise the standard of what it requires to win and you find a whole tribe of players chasing the top man, each of them now good enough to have beaten the top man some years before. I suppose the most obvious example of this is the four-minute mile.

The two pace-setters in the Open were the big fellows, Guy Wolstenholme and Joe Carr. It was hard on Joe that he should have started 3, 4 when the rain came down and washed out Friday afternoon, and have started 4, 6 the next day, but that is how life goes. Both beat every British professional except Bernard Hunt and, if Wolstenholme's final putt had not hit a little bump a yard from the hole, it would have gone right in the middle instead of stopping an inch short. Then he would have had the honour not only of doing the lowest 72 holes ever recorded by an amateur in the Open (which he did) but also of being led by no British professional at all and being beaten only by the winner and runner-up.

There is no doubt that so far as international competition is concerned the British professionals are going through a very lean time indeed and some very hard words were written about them. It was even suggested that they ought to set up, or someone ought to set up, a sort of 'school' for them, but it was not made quite clear who was going to teach them. Perhaps I might offer my own services? I should like to see the faces of Weetman, Hunt, Alliss, Brown and Rees when they turned up for their first lesson!

Since my earliest boyhood I have lived among golf professionals, and number, I like to think, many, many friends among them, so I am not being beastly about them when I say that perhaps over the last ten years they have had things a little too much their own way and have grown to a public status which perhaps they have not earned the hard way. Sponsors put up thousands of pounds for them to play for (and the best of luck to them!), but what is good enough to win at home when Australia, South Africa, the Argentine and the United States are not around is not good enough to win when they are.

I do not quite know the answer to this. It may be that David Thomas has it. He is big and strong and fit and young, and just before the Open he announced his intention of making his living from the playing of golf and give up his club job at Sudbury to take his chance in the wide world wherever golf was being played. This was a courageous decision in which all wish him well and it was one of those typical kicks of fate that he should fail to qualify at St Andrews immediately afterwards. Never mind. Let it spur him to even greater efforts.

Now I come to a more controversial point. I ask, with perfect sincerity, 'Does it really *matter* whether British professionals can hold their own in competition with others from all over the world who are purely golf players?' If a man spent the winter playing 72-hole tournaments in the sunshine, against savage competition, all the way across America, is it not humanly certain that he would emerge a better tournament player than if he had spent the winter at, say, Selsdon Park, South Herts, Hartsbourne or Buchanan Castle? It would be remarkable if he did not.

So we come to the question, what is the function of the professional in golf? I have never wavered in my own belief that his place is primarily in the pro's shop and only secondarily on a circuit of sponsored tournaments. Just as the handicap amateur is the backbone of the club, so the club professional is the backbone of professional golf. The members like to see their best amateur distinguish himself in the Open championship, but are by no means brokenhearted if they have no amateur good enough to enter at all. So, again, they like to see their professional do well in tournaments if he can, but the place they really want to see him is in the club.

One final point. The professionals have now shown that they are simply not good enough to warrant any longer keeping out young players by what is virtually a trade union closed shop. Let us suppose for a moment that six or eight years ago it had entered Wolstenholme's head to turn pro (and may I emphasise that I have not the slightest grounds for supposing that it did). The rules of the PGA would have proved a complete deterrent. Yet with eight years of professional play behind him it is likely that Wolstenholme would be dominating and inspiring professional golf at this time just as Henry Cotton dominated and inspired it before the war. And we might well have had a British Centenary Open champion.

29 March 1962

An 'ex-Ryder Cup Player'?

Whether my old friend, Jack McLean, ever made £10,000 a year, I do not know. If he did, then it was due largely to his own efforts and it would certainly not be true to say that the appointment as professional at Gleneagles automatically carries with it a five-figure income. In any case income these days is not what you receive but what you keep. The newspapers, for instance, keep referring to Dr Beeching's £24,000 a year. What they might more accurately refer to is the £17,000 a year that British Railways, which is us, have to pay the Government in tax for the privilege of employing the doctor for the remaining £7000.

Nevertheless, had I known at the age of, say, twenty how much a successful professional might be making by the time I had turned fifty, I should have been sorely tempted to join the ranks—though not, of course, if I had known that a mere three years later I was to fall into my present pleasurable way of life and live happily ever after.

I should not, I think, as my friends will doubtless concur, have won the Open, but I think I should have won the odd tournament here and there and might well have played once in the Ryder Cup team—largely, like Jerry Barber and Paul Runyan, who are smaller than I, on account of an extremely crafty short game. I should certainly have worked very hard for this, in order to carry with me for life the valuable appendage, 'the ex-Ryder Cup player'.

This would be expecially valuable when, at a comparatively early stage in my career, I set myself up as a possible teacher. This is a role in which, frankly, I rather fancy myself even today. The words 'Physician heal thyself' may enter the minds of our less charitable readers, but the fact is that you do not have to be a great player to be a great teacher. When I watch longish handicap players driving off the first tee—I cannot see myself thank goodness—I think to myself: 'I know I could bring that fellow's handicap down three shots in three hours', and I still have a frustrated urge to do so.

As a professional, I should be inclined to say to new pupils: 'How much is it worth to you to get your handicap down?' and to charge accordingly. Ten pounds a stroke would seem a reasonable minimum. 'Rush' jobs might be as much as £25. The truth is, of course, that you could reduce most 12-and-over handicaps by a couple of strokes without ever taking the sufferer on to the course at all. I often think that, if most people applied as much common sense to their business as they do to their golf, they would be bankrupt within the year, and that an hour's discussion on the elementary art of not wasting shots by sheer lack of thought would in itself cut two strokes a round from almost every long-handicap player's game. (Incidentally a rather good book on this subject was produced a year or two ago by the American professional, Doug Ford, called *The Brainy Way to Better Golf*.)

As a fashionable teacher one would be laying the basis of an income which would last when one's playing days were over—not only as a teacher but as an 'authority' on golf, from which would come newspaper articles, endorsements of products, and such like. This is what Bill Cox and John Jacobs have done with such success. I will not risk letting *Golf Illustrated* in for a libel suit by suggesting that their playing days are over—but they will know what I mean.

And now I come to a point which makes me envious even as I write of it. The essence of income, as I have said, is not what you earn but what you keep. Successive governments in their wisdom have decreed that the harder you work the more you earn by your industry and skill, the greater proportion of it is confiscated in order to pay the rent for people who already own a Jaguar and a telly. What you make by gambling, however, is tax free.

Now, if there is one game in which 'form' really runs true, it is that of the good, steady-nerved professional golfer playing on his own course. He can look at the weather, the condition of the course and the position of the tees, and know for a certainty his maximum score. He knows he will not take more than, say, 70. He might take 66.

This is an impregnable position from which, year in and year out, to bet. I know because I was for many years a very steady, pedestrian type of scratch handicap player (when scratch was no better than about two today, but that does not alter the point), and I remember how deeply affronted I felt—almost 'robbed'—when very occasionally I was beaten by a handicap player when I was really trying!

The scratch player—and how much more this applies to the professional—has two advantages which load the scale impossibly against his victims. Firstly, he is 'one up' from the word 'go' by virtue of his evident supremacy, and it takes a very level-headed handicap player to ignore his opponent's shots and concentrate on his own. Secondly, the wretched opponent as though this were not enough, only gets three-quarters of the difference in their handicaps. Heaven knows why, but there it is.

Given all this, and a nice rich club with a gambling element somewhere south of London, and I could see averaging about £3000 a year, 'free of' for the best part of thirty years. If only I were twenty again!

8 November 1962

Importing Attractions

Several tournament sponsors last year decided to invest money in bringing players over from the United States. Carreras secured Jack Nicklaus for their Piccadilly tournament at Hillside, Southport; Martini brought Bob Rosburg and Tom Nieporte to St Andrews; and Carlings brought Gay Brewer to St Annes.

The Open championship is, of course, different, but we may note in passing that various equipment firms in the States sent Sam Snead (doubtless after a good deal of resistance on his part), Gene Littler and Phil Rodger, and we may only hope that this may become common practice. The more that the younger Americans can be enabled to see Europe the less insular they will become.

Those who were brought over by sponsors in this country failed to make the slightest impact in the tournaments in which they played, but this was due mainly to the fact that they allowed themselves little or no time to acclimatize. Golf in Britain is more different from golf in America than American golf is from British—if you see what I mean!—and you simply cannot fly the Atlantic one day, have a round the next, and then expect to do yourself, or your sponsors, justice. Nieporte, delayed on the way, had four holes practice on the Old Course at St Andrews, which is probably the most difficult to 'learn' in the world.

Nicklaus also took on the added responsibility of contracting to play—and again in the Open—with British clubs, which I understand he had never seen before. I have seen these clubs being made and am convinced that they rank with the very best in the world. Nevertheless, I do not think you can travel to any country, pick up a strange set of clubs, and be at no disadvantage whatever. Quite apart from that, however, Nicklaus came straight from a temperature of 85 degrees to the very best of our English summer as exemplified at Southport. He played in three sweaters, waterproof trousers and a woollen hat and, when I had a talk with him later in the evening, he was sitting huddled over his sitting room fire in the hotel and his hands were still perished with cold.

It is significant, perhaps, that after only just qualifying for the final day at Southport he went straight back and won the US Open, so that no one could say that the sponsors were not backing a talented horse.

Whether in this, or other cases, they got their money's worth, it is for them, not an observer like myself, to assess. Firms who sponsor golf tournaments do so solely, and quite properly, for the publicity it brings them and for the chance it offers them of entertaining their friends and customers—though a small voice adds that, with the present penal tax, if they had not spent X thousand pounds on doing so, the Government would have taken 52½ per cent of it anyway, so what the hell!

The very announcement that Nicklaus was coming produced a tremendous amount of publicity for the Piccadilly tournament and whatever they paid him—and I have no idea—it was probably worth it. With the other Americans who flew in and flew out, I doubt whether it was. On the other hand the presence of a 'known' American professional who is prepared to come in time and give the appearance of trying, really hard, would undoubtedly be an asset to any tournament.

We then come up against the difficulty of time and money. Rosburg and Nieporte, for instance, were able to come because the Martini tournament coincides with the so-called 'Tournament of Champions', for which, though first-class performers in America, they did not happen to be eligible. It would require a very great deal of money to persuade a top-ranking player to take, say, two weeks off from the lucrative American circuit in order to practise for, and play in, one tournament here—even if he were not breaking an obligation to play in the two tournaments he would have to miss at home.

(Branching off at a tangent, this is one reason, though a minor one, for holding the Open in September, namely that American professionals would be more free of domestic responsibilities, if they thought it worthwhile to compete.)

Whether it is worthwhile for sponsors in Britain to combine forces and funds to bring celebrated players over from America is an interesting question, but it would undoubtedly lead to complications; such players would require not only their fare and expenses but also a guarantee—in other words 'appearance money'—for which no one could blame them, but if they get 'appearance money', why should not Thomson and Nagle and O'Connor and Alliss and the rest of them get 'appearance money' too?

One thing I do know. If I combined with another sponsor to bring a celebrated American over here, I should want him to play in the other man's tournament first and mine second!

29 December 1966

A Good 'Birdie Putter'

I have a strong impression that there are a great many more very good young golf players about the place today than when I myself was at their enviable time of life. With nearly 60 million people on our island and with many more people having much more money and with the improvement in golf shafts it would be surprising if this were not so. Also it is my impression that on the whole those in the age group of seventeen-plus are substantially bigger than my own contemporaries were at the same age. Finally, it does seem to me that much has been learnt since the war on the best, and safest, way of hitting the ball and it would be surprising, again, if this were not so, if only on account of the gigantic rewards now hanging like carrots in front of young golfers.

Thus, if I were looking for a young 'hope' of real promise, I should expect to find quite a host of them capable of hitting really fine golf shots. Some would be doing it naturally, like Peter Alliss, who says with a perfectly modest sense of realism that the mere action of hitting the ball has never presented him with any serious problem, right from his youngest days. Others would be 'made' players, like perhaps Nicklaus and Gary Player. There would be plenty of both.

The man who caught my eye would not necessarily have to be very big. Apart from Ralph Guldahl in the thirties Open champions have never been noticeably big, and sometimes mere size seems almost a handicap. George Bayer could handle a 2-iron just as though it were a toothpick, yet in the end he proved too big for most courses to contain him and his vast length had to be cut down to size. On the other hand our man would have to be strong and wiry and if he started on the small side then he would have to build himself up the hard way, as Gary Player did. I do not think you have to be bulging with muscles and bursting with fitness to reach the top, but no unfit man can do so. As I write, they are still searching for a man on the run from Dartmoor, a man who it is said can lift a warder up in each hand and do fifty 'pull-ups' with one arm. Yet for all his strength I doubt whether he would make a top-class golfer.

In the end it is the more indefinable mental qualities which separate those at the top. I think it vastly important not to be a self-excuser or 'alibi merchant'. Those prone to cry 'we was robbed' seem, ironically enough, those most likely to be robbed. Then they get round to thinking they have been robbed when in fact they haven't, and then they are done. I can think of three very high in the professional ranks and two in the amateur (and probably more if I tried) who failed to make the grade because in the end they began to have excuses ready in advance.

Some people get the breaks and some don't. It is said that the luck evens out in the end and broadly speaking this is true. All the same, over the long period as well as the short some people do tend to be luckier than others and they tend also to be the sort who accept their luck cheerfully and make use of it. It is rather allied with the question of being a good 'birdie putter', as it is sometimes called. It would be essential for our man to be a good 'birdie putter'. I personally was always a bad one—but then I did not have all that number of putts for a birdie! Even so, if I had a ten-footer on a par four hole, I was always more likely to squeeze it in to save the par four than to make a birdie three. When you get good enough to have a great many putts for birdies, you simply must not be frightened of how many you hole. Most of us, when we happen to hole two good putts running and are left with a third, are liable to feel that the law of averages is against us.

One of the most important things is to be able to take the emotion out of putting, which I am sure that Locke did, largely through adhering so strictly to his 'drill', the automatic set of movements which never varied between one putt and another of any length in any part of the world. It was a sort of shield against the torrent of emotions which would pour through you and me in the unlikely event of our having a four-footer, as Locke did at Sandwich, with 'This to tie for the Open'. He set the machinery in motion and it became just another four-foot putt—so he holed it. The thought of what I might have done to it in similar circumstances is enough to make one wake screaming in the night.

Nevertheless, I agree basically with Henry Cotton's belief that although putting is a matter of mechanics—in other words, if you hit the ball in one way it is certain to go in and if you hit it in another way it is certain not to—when the crisis comes there are reserves of pure willpower which can be brought into play to squeeze just this one, somehow, into the hole. There is of course no logic behind this belief but I know exactly what he means and I believe it too. Indeed, I remember it, perfectly well.

I think Palmer is right when he says that on the whole our best players are defensive, and that Cotton is right when he replies 'and so would you be, if you played on our courses'. To be aggressive, you must be reasonably sure that, if you take a risk and it does not come off, you are not going to be met with total disaster. Big watered greens, little rough, beautifully tended sand bunkers—these are what make for aggressive golf. I should want our man to be capable of aggressiveness and I should try to enable him to play in the sunshine on this sort of course, whether in the Far East, America, or wherever, for at least eight months in the year. Needless to say, I should find it necessary to accompany him as manager.

9 March 1967

No 'Spoilt Darlings' in Golf

The 'spoilt darlings' of our age are beyond question the long-haired, unwashed pop singers and the skinny, illiterate little mannequins by whose skilful promotion the boys in the back room make such enviable fortunes. Professional sportsmen to my mind come far behind, unless perhaps the equally illiterate negro prizefighters count in that category, though 'sportsmen' would perhaps be stretching the use of English a little too far. If some professional games players seem to be doing pretty well these days, it is only because the pendulum has swung in their direction.

Perhaps it was the soccer players that started it. So far as I remember, the maximum wage was £12 a week, and a lot did not even get that. Even, if, like Alex James, you were largely responsible for filling an enormous football ground Saturday after Saturday and for the merry clatter of thousands of pounds at the turnstiles, you were still meant to get only £12 a week. Otherwise, it was thought, some clubs would offer you more than the others could afford and the wealthy clubs would have all the best players. It was only after extreme efforts by the players themselves that the principle of the labourer being worthy of his hire was accepted in football and a man who draws the crowds can earn £100 a week in a free market and plenty of 'perks' to go with it. One wonders whether we should have won the World Cup and whether football would have seen the revival it is enjoying today if the Charltons and Laws of this world had still been on £12 a week?

I think that perhaps 'free market' is the key. A man wants to do as well for himself as he can. On the other hand in a free market nobody is compelled to pay him more than he thinks he is worth. In this respect I think that the Professional Golfers Association a year or so ago went slightly off the rails—though fortunately without damage to the engine, so to speak. Professional golfers, though belonging to an association or union, are in fact essentially individuals, making individual contracts with clubs, equipment makers, and the like. Some become millionaires; many eke out a very modest living at small clubs with a good deal less income than they could earn in a neighbouring factory. It was on behalf of these that the PGA suggested that there should be a minimum wage (I think it was £10 a week, but the actual figure does not really matter) below which clubs should not be allowed to retain professionals, or below which members of the PGA should not be allowed to accept employment—I forget how it was worded.

This was well meant, but I thought it inadvisable at the time, and still do, because much as one might sympathize with the borderline professionals who preferred life as it was to life in a factory, they were still in a free market, in which there was no possible way of making small clubs pay a sum which they did not wish to, or could not, afford. As a matter of fact I believe there are a great many of these 'marginal' clubs and that they are comparable, if I may be forgiven for putting it in that way, with our ancient village churches, where it is so often found that a church can no longer support or justify a parson all to itself. Nowadays a single incumbent will serve two or even three parish churches, from a modern vicarage built from the proceeds of selling a couple of old and unplayable ones for conversion into flats or council houses.

Golf is a more popular but less 'rich' game than it used to be and I foresee the time when one man may become professional to two or three neighbouring clubs at a time, having his regular 'days' at each and probably fully booked with lessons for the whole of the week. On other days he would probably have to share a certain amount of business, like sale of balls and hire of trolleys, with the steward, who would be permanently on the spot, but I should envisage the professional having a showcase in the club for sweaters, shoes, clubs, and so forth.

As for the sale of clubs I foresee more and more newcomers to the game buying the 'short sets' that are now being advertised and in the marginal clubs fewer and fewer people prepared to buy complete new sets at the full retail price. Nearly everyone who has that sort of money knows someone through whom he can get them at a discount under the 'old pals act' and I fancy that the professional must be prepared to cut his prices, like the small grocer in face of the supermarket, if he is to remain in the business of selling clubs.

At the top end of the scale it is probable that some of the professional golf players who seem to spend as much time in the air flying from one continent to another as they do in amassing their millions on the ground are the wealthiest men produced by any sport at any time, not merely for the money they make, but for the prudent way in which it is handled on their behalf. Thus they do not end as that great gentleman of the ring, Joe Louis, was allowed to end, namely owing so much in income tax that, however much he earned for the rest of his life, the taxed income from it would not be enough to pay the interest on the tax he already owed. Work that one out. It is almost the only way in which you can finally beat the gatherers of taxes!

As for our golfing millionaires being 'spoilt darlings', I have the pleasure of knowing most of them quite well and I must say that they are without exception among the most modest of men.

22 February 1968

Natural or Made?

In answer to the questions—Was Vardon better than Jones? Was Hogan better than Palmer?—it is impossible to give the wrong answer since there is no right one.

Nor is it possible, I find after a good deal of thought, to define a natural player, though it is comparatively easy to pick out 'made' ones. At first it occurred to me that it might lie partly between those who spent hour after hour on the practice ground and those who didn't and indeed there may be a little something in that, though not of course the whole story. Bobby Jones, surely the greatest of them all, would seem by that definition to come half way between the two. He won the Georgia State championship, I think I am right in saying, at the age of fourteen and clearly golf was pretty well his whole life at that age.

On the other hand in the days of his greatness he spent months on end playing nothing more serious than fourballs with his father and other cronies at East Lake. There were few tournaments and it always interests me to reflect that when he went to play in the Amateur at Pebble Beach, on the coast of California, it took him four days in the train each way—and he was beaten in the first round! Of practising, however, he says firmly that the only point in it is to correct a specific fault and that when this is done there is no point in going on, since all you can do is to contract another. This seems to me essentially a 'natural' attitude.

The most completely 'made' player according to most people's book would surely be Gary Player. He built up his somewhat frail physique into that of a very strong and wiry man and there is the same deliberateness about his method, too. You can see him 'thinking' with each shot, consciously getting his feet into place and setting the club behind the ball.

He was advised to build himself up in this way by one who to my generation would come automatically to mind as a 'made' player, namely Henry Cotton. He, too, had to build himself up—though that really is not part of the question—but he worked on his game, experimenting in all manner of ways, thinking and thinking, till almost by a process of elimination he had got rid of all the frilly bits and was left with the absolute bare essentials of the golf swing.

Perhaps the greatest of all the 'made' players in the end must be Hogan, the machine-made product after hour after hour after hour on the practice ground, firing off hundreds of balls in a single day, and day after day at that. The fact that in the end it became almost second nature does not make him a natural player. In the end his game became almost like firing a rifle. If you could imagine a competition with every competitor hitting fifty balls with every club from a driver to a 7-iron, the winner to be the one whose caddie had to take the fewest paces in order to field them, Hogan would have won by the length of a street and indeed might still do so, for his long game seems as good as ever and it is only the dreaded twitch on the greens that lets him down.

For the totally natural players I should turn first to Ireland, in the persons of Bradshaw and O'Connor, who after all were good enough to win the Canada Cup, together with those two great amateurs, Joe Carr and James Bruen; and here perhaps I begin to come near to being able to define a natural player, namely one who relies on his eye and the feeling in his hands rather than an artificial 'repeating' swing. Bradshaw was always, of course, a law completely unto himself, swaying at least a foot to and fro in the course of the swing and holding a number of fingers of his right hand hanging down off the club like bananas. Yet, at a height of 7500 ft and carrying a good deal of weight, he managed at Mexico City to tie for the individual prize in the Canada Cup, a truly remarkable achievement when you come to think of it. O'Connor has what used in my earlier days to be called the perfect 'caddie swing'.

Let Irish readers not be insulted, however, for this was something of a compliment. It meant that a person was swinging the club by the pure light of nature, as caddies were wont to do. O'Connor's swing reminds me of the time when 'style' was reckoned very highly and to say that so-and-so had a 'beautiful style' was reckoned praise indeed. Nowadays it is only effect which counts, in other words 'not how but how many'—a saying which in the Latin version of *Non quomodo sed quoties* the Home Park club took as their motto—and with millions of dollars at stake the players of today can hardly be blamed if that is their motto too.

I should not call Carr and Bruen 'stylists', much as I have enjoyed watching both hit the ball, especially off the tee, but I do think both were 'natural' in the sense that they had not an automatic action to fall back on if their eye was not in that day. Try pointing the club directly over the teebox at the top of the swing, as Bruen did, and you will see what I mean.

I leave till last perhaps the greatest 'natural' of them all, namely Walter Hagen, who was also a 'natural' in the sense in which boxing promoters use the word. He was certainly no great stylist and swayed forward considerably as he came on to the ball, this probably being the cause of his hitting, and expecting to hit, a number of downright bad shots every round.

He was flamboyant, of course, and appeared on the surface to take golf, and life, very easily, but when someone asked him the inevitable question, to what did he attribute his success?, he looked the man in the eye and slowly replied 'Waal, I do try, you know'. All the same I still cannot resist thinking of him as the supreme 'natural' of all time.

Index